LOCKE AND
THE COMPASS OF HUMAN
UNDERSTANDING

LOCKE AND
THE COMPASS OF HUMAN
UNDERSTANDING

A SELECTIVE COMMENTARY
ON THE 'ESSAY'

JOHN W. YOLTON

Professor of Philosophy
York University, Toronto

CAMBRIDGE
AT THE UNIVERSITY PRESS
1970

Published by the Syndics of the Cambridge University Press
Bentley House, 200 Euston Road, London N.W.1
American Branch: 32 East 57th Street, New York, N.Y.10022

Library of Congress Catalogue Card Number: 76-112477

Standard Book Number: 521 07838 5

Printed in Great Britain
at the University Printing House, Cambridge
(Brooke Crutchley, University Printer)

For Jean

CONTENTS

PREFACE

The topics discussed in this study have occupied my attention for some years, when I have taught students about Locke and when I have thought about the issues his *Essay* raises. An uneasiness with the analysis usually accorded to Locke drove me to try various devices for approaching his work in fresh ways. At one time, in a graduate seminar at Princeton, we read the *Essay*, taking Book 4 first. That device was useful for remedying the tendency to see Book 4 as inconsistent with Book 2, to find the 'rationalism' of the definition of knowledge incompatible with the 'empiricism' of the programme for the derivation of ideas. But having discovered that the definition of knowledge explicitly includes contingent as well as necessary relations, thereby linking the account of coexisting qualities of Books 2 and 3 with the formal account of knowledge of Book 4, it was still necessary to find the wider context within which the whole of the *Essay* was placed. That context is of course found in the very last chapter of that work, in the threefold classification of sciences.

In two graduate seminars which I offered at the University of Toronto in 1964-5 and 1965-6, and also in a similar seminar given at my own University, York in Toronto, I began to explore the topics in the *Essay* which seemed to me to bear upon that classification and also some concepts which I found were still obscure in our usual understanding of Locke. From those seminars, and from the reactions I received from the members, the pieces quickly took shape. A sabbatical leave from York University during the academic year 1968-9, aided by a Leave Fellowship from the Canada Council, gave me the leisure necessary for bringing the research and writing for this study to completion. That leave also enabled me to return to England, to Oxford in particular, where source materials are plentiful. Consultation with philosophers and historians in England during that leave was very helpful in the development of this study. During that year I read various sections of this study at a number of universities. Almost all of the first six chapters were, at different times, given trial runs in this way. I would like to record my thanks to those who listened and reacted to those papers at the Universities of Edinburgh, Glasgow, Leeds, Aberystwyth, Sussex and Durham.

In addition, I have benefited greatly from discussions with M. R. Ayers of Wadham College, Oxford. His willingness to read a large portion of an early draft of this study, as well as the opportunity he gave me of participating in a class with him on seventeenth- and eighteenth-century philosophy has been most useful.

Other philosophers and historians of science have also taken time from their busy programmes to read and give comments on various parts of this study: J. E. McGuire of Leeds; R. Harré of Linacre College, Oxford; A. C. Crombie of All Souls College, Oxford; P. Laslett of Trinity College, Cambridge; Roger Woolhouse of the University of York, England. Discussions and correspondence with Laurens Laudan of University College, London (now of the University of Pittsburgh) have also helped to correct some earlier excesses. The comments of David Bell of Glasgow and the detailed correspondence and discussions with W. von Leyden of Durham have helped to smooth out the analysis of action in chapter 6. The bibliographical skills of my wife, as well as her eye for style, have been invaluable aids throughout.

An early version of chapter 2 was read at a conference on The Thought of John Locke, held at York University, Toronto, in December 1966. The comments of Gerd Buchdahl of the Whipple Science Museum, University of Cambridge, on that paper at the conference were instrumental in producing the printed version in the collection of essays in *John Locke: Problems and Perspectives* (1969). Some sections of 'Locke on the Law of Nature', *The Philosophical Review* (1958), reappear in chapter 7. Portions of chapters 4 and 5 were read to a meeting of the Jowett Society at Oxford in May 1969 and will be published in a volume of their proceedings.

References to the text of Locke's *Essay Concerning Human Understanding* are given in arabic numbers in the order: book, chapter, section, as in 2.21.4. In a continuous discussion of some book and chapter, where the fact is obvious that I am discussing the same chapter, I give only the section numbers, as in 4, or 4, 7, 10, 12. References are to the fifth edition as reprinted in the two-volume Everyman edition.

J. W. Y.

INTRODUCTION

The final chapter of Locke's *Essay concerning Human Understanding* sketches a threefold division of the sciences which is meant to include 'All that can fall within the compass of human understanding' (4. 21. 1). The list of possible objects of the understanding is given as

> *first*, the nature of things, as they are in themselves, their relations, and their manner of operation; or, *secondly*, that which man himself ought to do, as a rational and voluntary agent, for the attainment of any end, especially happiness; or, *thirdly*, the ways and means whereby the knowledge of both the one and the other of these is attained and communicated.

Natural philosophy or the science of nature, *ethics*, and *logic* or *semiotics* are the names of the sciences which deal with these different matters. Divisions of science, maps of knowledge, were common in the early part of the century;[1] it was a time for surveying the fields of knowledge and for finding ways of improving the methods for extending human knowledge. The euphoria caused by developments in science as well as by the gradual realisation that scholastic methods and concepts were useless for advancing knowledge, led to an optimism which saw human knowledge expanding indefinitely. It was discovered that the ancients could be discarded, that knowledge could be extended by reliance upon human reason and experience; this is evident, as R. F. Jones has shown, in the tracts and pamphlets of some of the Elizabethan writers.[2] Bacon crystallised the growing faith and sketched a long-term programme. Other writers began to see the need to turn inwards, to examine the human understanding in order to discover how it works, what it might accomplish. There were various anticipators of this aspect of Locke's *Essay* in England. Read

---

[1] Of particular interest for a study of Locke is the brief division given by P. Nicole in essays which Locke translated: 'Knowledge is either of words, or of things, or of actions' (*Discourses, Translated from Nicole's Essays* by John Locke, edited by Thomas Hancock, 1828).

[2] *Ancients and Moderns; A Study of the Rise of the Scientific Movement in Seventeenth-Century England*, 2nd edition (1961).

from the beginning onwards—as one normally reads books—it is not always easy to discern any general pattern or programme at work in or behind his *Essay*. Even the last chapter appears tacked on, seems not to differ from any number of other chapters throughout that prolix work. Locke appears to wander somewhat aimlessly from topic to topic, dropping one theme here, picking it up later, mixing several questions together, adding bits and pieces as he thought of them. To be sure, the general epistemic claim is clear enough: no innate ideas or principles, all ideas to be derived from experience, knowledge to be a perception of the relation of those ideas. That final chapter of the *Essay*, however, enables us to place this epistemic programme in the wider, more general and more typical seventeenth-century concern with the classification of types of knowledge, kinds of subject-matter. The prolixity and disorganisation is still there, but with the aid of that simple classification we can begin to see a more ambitious plan working in Locke's mind. The totality of Locke's writings might be placed within this division, though he was not so systematic as to allocate different books to each of the sciences. Not much would be gained by classifying the Locke corpus in this way, but an understanding of his work can greatly profit from an examination of what Locke has said about or under this threefold division. In particular, his relations with the physical science of his day can be clearly seen.

Locke's treatment of the three sciences is not uniform. Natural philosophy consumes most of his attention in the *Essay*. What he says under that head, together with most of what he says about signs, constitutes a philosophy or epistemology of physical science. There is precious little anywhere in Locke's works of ethics, though when he discusses how to teach virtue to children in the *Education* and when he writes in a normative way in *Two Treatises* and occasionally in *The Reasonableness of Christianity*, we can reconstruct something of the ethical doctrine he accepted and shared with his contemporaries. The bulk of his remarks on ethics in the *Essay* is what would be termed 'meta-ethical' today: remarks about the role of moral concepts and principles in action, the motives that move a man to act, what an action is and how actions are possible, agency and the person. A careful look at these meta-ethical concepts in Locke is rewarding, primarily for an appreciation of his theory of action, which anticipates a number of points made by recent writers on action. I do extract some of the principles of action to which Locke appeals, but my main concern under the science of ethics is with his meta-ethical remarks.

One of the more interesting features of Locke on action is his notion that action-concepts are not primarily factual. They are what he calls 'mixed modes', they define and constitute what can be done. Natural philosophy or the science of nature is restricted almost entirely to factual or observational matters. Theory of action exposes general and conceptual connexions, science of nature uncovers contingent and particular truths. Demonstration is possible in the former, experiment and observation relevant in the latter. Locke's remarks on demonstration contain an attack on the logical formalism of his day (maxims and the syllogism) and a recommendation for an informal logic of concepts and a lay-out of argument similar in theme and attitude to that suggested by Stephen Toulmin in *Uses of Argument*. Appreciating the exact nature of the logic Locke was recommending helps to dissipate the misunderstanding of Locke's suggestion about a demonstrative morality: it was demonstrative without being deductive. Once the meta-ethical concepts have been clarified, disputes in ethics or politics have primarily to do with questions of conceptual connexions. Locke's discussion of property is an interesting example of conceptual clarification.

It is more difficult to fit Locke into a context on the theory of action than it is on the other two divisions of science. There were, of course, disputes over free will (Hobbes, Bramhall); Hobbes at least had a concept of the person. Sir Matthew Hale anticipates some of the points about action made by Locke. Moral principles were cited frequently in support of political and religious doctrines. But while the terminology and method of the way of ideas was used by many predecessors and contemporaries of Locke, and while his moral philosophy is quite traditional in content, it is not readily apparent that his analysis of action and agency was a consolidation of concepts already in use. It may be that Locke was at his most original in the science of action.

In explicating Locke's remarks on the science of nature, it is useful and necessary to place the *Essay* in the historical setting of the Royal Society and its general programme. The aims of that group were varied, both in general philosophy and in methods, but one predominant aim was to enlarge the observational knowledge of nature by compiling natural histories of phenomena. Not less important, even perhaps of greater importance for some (e.g. Boyle), was the desire to show that their method and their discoveries were not antithetical to religion. Boyle's *Some Considerations Touching the Usefulness of Experimental Natural Philosophy* (1663) is mainly concerned to vindicate science from this charge. The Royal Society ran into difficulties from the start of its incorporation on this score. The fact that Locke was a member of that society and was clearly associated with the new way of doing science undoubtedly contributed to the quick reaction to the *Essay* by the defenders of traditional religion. As I have shown in *John Locke and the Way of Ideas*, the doctrines of that work provided sufficient grounds for concern by Locke's contemporaries for the fate of a number of traditional theological and moral doctrines. I think it is also clear that his association with the Royal Society made it easy for his name and his doctrines to become caught up in the suspicion many people had towards that society.

Put in this context, we are able to see Locke's first division of the sciences as his account of the epistemology of the physical sciences. Thomas Sprat's *History of the Royal Society* (1667) attempted to defend and to explain the aim and methods of that group. Glanvill's *Plus Ultra* (1668) and *Scepsis Scientifica* (1665), like his earlier *The Vanity of Dogmatizing* (1661), were written also in defence of the Royal Society. There were other praises and justifications of the aims of the society, some brief, others longer. The Preface of Robert Hooke's *Micrographia* (1665) is especially important (as is the body of that work). Henry Power's *Experimental Philosophy* (1664) also contains accounts of the experimental method and the long-range goals and hopes of the society. Locke did not need to justify that method, but he did explicitly address himself to the task of explicating that method in philosophic terms. He wanted to show how the way of ideas could formulate and provide for the kind of observational knowledge of nature that his experimental friends were compiling. The plain, historical method of the *Essay* is a clear reference to the natural histories of phenomena made by Boyle, Power, Hooke, Sydenham; it was also a method which Locke attempted to apply in his study of the development of knowledge and awareness, a natural history of the understanding. The '*Origin and Variety of Forms*' in nature had been, Dr Basil Kennet wrote in 1705, '*well trac'd and pursu'd through all its intricate Mazes, by the Excellent* Mr. Boyle, *and other Experimenters, as Naturalists, and by* Mr. Lock *as a metaphysician*'.[1]

My examination of Locke's science of nature is not meant to be an historical study. I want to give a careful and precise exposition of some of Locke's doctrines, staying as close to the text as possible. Some indication of his many similarities with Boyle on the nature of body, with Hooke on the nature and improvement of the understanding, some references to statements of the method of the Royal Society by its members, help to shed light on what Locke was saying about the science of nature. I have tried not to let these references interfere with the forward progress of the exposition. Neither have I wanted to enter into polemics, since what we need is a much more detailed presentation of Locke's doctrines than is usually to be found. Occasionally, however, criticism or comment is necessary of some writing which is particularly important or misleading.

One recent book about which I must comment, here and in later chapters, is M. Mandelbaum's *Philosophy, Science, and Sense Perception* (1964). His chapter on Locke is an important study of Locke and science, being one of the very few such discussions, the only sustained and detailed one.[2] The importance of Mandel-

---

[1] In the 'Preface of the Publisher' in *The Whole Critical Works of Monsieur Rapin* (London, 1706). The Preface is dated 1705 but unsigned, though Kennet is said by all sources to be the editor and translator. This remark was quoted in 1718 in John Pointer's *Miscellanea* and again in 1750 in *Parentialia or Memoirs of the Family of the Wrens*.

[2] Fulton H. Anderson's 'The Influence of Contemporary Science on Locke's Methods and Results' is much too schematic to be useful, though it was a much earlier recognition of some of the points Mandelbaum makes in his chapter. One suspects that Anderson had much more detailed material among his papers when he died in 1968. James Axtell has also put Locke in the scientific context: see his *The Educational Writings of John Locke* (1968), chapter 4 and 'Locke, Newton, and the Two Cultures', in *John Locke: Problems and Perspectives* (1969). R. Harré's *Matter and Method* (1964) is also an important study of the corpuscular theory of matter in the seventeenth century. His analysis of Locke's use of this theory and his understanding of the primary and secondary quality distinction in Locke are

baum's chapter lies in its placing Locke within the scientific tradition, his clear recognition that Locke was defending much of Boyle's general account of body and 'the method of work of the virtuosi of the Royal Society' (p. 49; cf. 50, 51, 58). Locke's theory of knowledge must be examined in the context of the new science, at least initially, not in that of the philosophical debates that arose later. But Mandelbaum's account undervalues the importance and the influence on Locke of the method of making natural histories. His account of Locke and science is mainly concerned with the corpuscular hypothesis. I think Mandelbaum over-estimates the role and use of that hypothesis among seventeenth-century scientists, though I do not suppose any of them would have rejected that hypothesis. What is the case is that much of the work conducted by the members of the Royal Society (certainly in its early years) was not concerned to support or even to employ that hypothesis. That Locke accepted it and used it is beyond doubt. It was, however, the emphasis upon compiling natural histories of bodies, which was the chief aspect of the Royal Society's programme that attracted Locke, and from which we need to understand his science of nature.

In the minds of seventeenth-century writers on science, there was a distinction between the mechanical and the experimental philosophies. The latter was the method for getting data, compiling histories of phenomena. Historians of science, certainly philosophers of science who look at this period, tend to seize upon the corpuscular philosophy as the main ingredient in physical science at this time. It is of course dangerous to generalise about the aims and methods of the scientists of the seventeenth century, since they were not a homogeneous group, not even as members of the Royal Society. Moreover, the actual practices of scientists do not always coincide with their own statements of their methods. Nevertheless, there is a vast literature in the seventeenth century

accurate. But like Mandelbaum, Harré does not mention the natural history side to the science of that period, nor does he show Locke's interest in that method. It is an over-estimation to say 'Locke set himself the task of developing in a coherent, systematic and rational way what he took to be the fundamental tenets of the corpuscularian philosophy' (p. 93). R. M. Yost's 'Locke's Rejection of Hypotheses about Sub-Microscopic Events' (*Journal of the History of Ideas*, XII, 1951) is also a useful discussion, especially in showing how Locke accepted the corpuscular hypothesis but took the making of natural histories as the method to science.

about science, written by medical men, chemists, microscopists, and learned laymen. There is in this material (large in bulk, published from early in the century right through the period when Locke was writing his *Essay*) a consistent and oft-repeated attitude towards science; there are also firm statements about the aims and methods of the sciences. Judged in terms of the statements made by these writers, the corpuscular hypothesis was not the main feature of scientific thought and practice. Anyone who wants to see the documentation for this claim need only read R. F. Jones's excellent study.[1] The longer way to an appreciation of the Bacon-inspired stress upon experiment, observation and natural histories is to read the pamphlets mentioned and discussed by Jones. Those quickly and easily confirm Jones's account.

In seventeenth-century opinion the one factor more responsible than anything else for fallacious reasoning was the lack of sufficient data. Thus the need of heaping up experiments and observations, stressed by Bacon years before, was declared again and again. Experimental philosophy remains a thing distinct from the mechanical, and Bacon, who was the chief sponsor of the former, far outweighs in importance Descartes, who lent his great influence to the latter (Jones, p. 169).[2]

The more fundamental philosophy—mechanical or experimental —was without a doubt the experimental. 'The mechanical philosophy was considered by the scientists a *hypothesis*, the truth of which was gradually being revealed to their eyes through experimental verification, but experiment and observation as the proper method for the discovery of natural truths represented a faith,

[1] R. F. Jones, *op. cit.*
[2] R. M. Blake has shown that even in Descartes there is recognition of and stress upon the need for histories of phenomena. See his 'The Role of Experience in Descartes' Theory of Method', in W. H. Madden's *Theories of Scientific Method* (1960), pp. 75–104. Cf. A. C. Crombie, 'Some Aspects of Descartes's Attitude to Hypotheses and Experiments', *Collection des Travaux de l'Académie Internationale d'Histoire des Sciences*, XI (1960), 192–201. Jones's study was generally well received by historians of science, though some feel that he has made too sharp a distinction between the use of hypotheses and the gathering of data, too much difference between Bacon and Descartes and the influence each had in the century. Others quite rightly point out that Bacon's programme did not just call for the making of natural histories: hypotheses were important too. The attempt to characterise the attitudes to science and the programme of scientific investigation at this time is perilous but necessary if we are to understand Locke's analysis of the science of nature. By the end of chapter 3 I hope to have balanced any excesses that may appear in these introductory statements.

to doubt which was heresy, and which was common ground for all members of the Royal Society' (Jones, p. 185). To reject the mechanical hypothesis was possible. It was unthinkable that one could reject the experimental method. To reject the latter would mean going back to the older methods of quoting authority, book learning, deducing from axioms. We need not go over the ground on this matter so ably covered by Jones, but it is useful for the purposes of this study of Locke (Jones does not fit Locke into his survey) to sample here some of the writers on science and its philosophy whom Locke either knew personally or whose books were in his library. Others are referred to in the chapters that follow.

Robert Hooke is of particular interest, since he was both a scientist at the centre of the Royal Society activity and an acquaintance of Locke. Hooke's *Micrographia* has, as I point out in chapter 2, a number of attitudes and phrases similar to those Locke employs. Another work of Hooke's, probably written around 1666, is of even greater significance in its anticipation of Locke's general approach to the human understanding.[1] The aim of science is, Hooke says, to 'find out the true Nature and Properties of Bodies; what the inward Texture and Constitution of them is, and what the Internal Motion, Powers, and Energies are' (p. 3). The ancients did not make 'subtile Examination of Natural Bodies by Direction, Experiments, or Mechanical Tryals'; they made the evidence fit their hypotheses and theories, rather than the other way about (pp. 3, 4). Hooke's ultimate aim in this tract was to build as complete a history of all phenomena, natural and artificial, as was possible, so that eventually we might extract from those histories (by a 'philosophical algebra') general principles. But the application of the algebra was a long way off. The first step for improving our knowledge of phenomena was 'an Examination of the Constitution and Powers of the Soul, or an attempt of Disclosing the Soul to its self, being an Endeavour of Discovering the Perfections and Imperfections of Humane Nature, and finding out ways and means for the attaining of the one, and of

---

[1] 'The Present State of Natural Philosophy', in *Posthumous Works* (1705). For a discussion of this work and of the programme for a 'philosophical algebra', suggested but not developed by Hooke, see Mary B. Hesse, 'Hooke's Philosophical Algebra', *Isis*, LVII (1966), 67–83.

helping the other' (p. 7). The next step is to find a way to use the 'Means and Assistance of Humane Nature for collecting the Phenomena of Nature, and for compiling of a Philosophical History, Consisting of an exact Description of all sorts of Natural and Artificial Operations' (pp. 7–8). The third step is to find a 'Method of describing, registring, and ranging these particulars so collected, as that they may become the most adopted Materials for the raising of axioms and the Perfecting of Natural Philosophy' (p. 8). The order in these steps for improving our knowledge is important.

Medical doctors were also praising the method of experiment and observation as a way of breaking out of the older methods: it would, W. Simpson said,[1] 'worm out the *Galenical* Method' (preface). All former opinions are now being put to the test of 'matter of Fact, in *Experiments*; and what is found consonant to *Truth*, made forth by collateral *Observations*, is approved, the rest...is rejected'. Simpson gives expression to the general philosophy of physical science, what he calls 'an *Hypothesis* of experimental Philosophy' (p. 214). We must, he says, lay aside our books in order 'to lay a groundwork for a more facile, unprejudiced understanding of things'. Simpson recommends making up a book of experiments, taken from other books— a *Clavis Philosophica*—and then establishing a laboratory so that these experiments can be repeated and new ones undertaken. Jonathan Goddard also urged the chemist and physician to use only the method of experiment and observation.[2] Maynwaring generalised the method: 'Solid knowledge in Natural Philosophy, is the most necessary qualification, preparatory to make a good *Physician*: now this *Philosophy* must be experimental, solid, and certain: the *notional Theorems* in philosophy, the world hath too long insisted on, and spent much time to little purpose, in vain *ratiocination, speculative conjectures,* and *verbal probation.*'[3]

Sir Matthew Hale (in a book not in Locke's library) spoke of the 'want of a clear, and sensible, and experimented Observation' of things, and says that because of this 'our positions and con-

[1] *Hydrologia Chymica* (1669).
[2] A *Discourse Setting Forth the Unhappy Conditions of the Practice of Physick* (1670).
[3] *Praxis Medicorum Antiqua et Nova* (1671).

clusions touching their Causes, Effects, Order and Methods of their procedure are but fictions and imaginations, accomodated to our Inventions rather than to the things themselves'.[1] These stresses upon experiment and observation were of course not confined to England. The Italian Accademia del Cimento presented to the Royal Society in 1667 some of its experimental findings. This report was translated and published in 1684. The report says that it is not a perfect experimental history, but only a beginning. The authors comment that, if a few speculations are present here and there, they belong to individual members and do not represent the society. Their '*sole Design is to make* Experiments, *and Relate them*'.[2] The faith in experience, trial and observation is expressed throughout. Similarly, the French translation of Swammerdam's work, *Histoire Générale des Insectes,* 1682 (also in Locke's library), repeatedly emphasised experience and careful observation and description, in contrast to the older methods of authority, the truth of experience instead of 'sa raison trompeuse' (p. 45). We should attach ourselves to convincing experiences rather than following the proud reasoning of our minds and the prejudices of our imaginations (pp. 19, 27–8, 30–1, 33–40, 138, 169).

These are only a sample of the attitudes that can be found over and over in the scientific literature at the time Locke was writing his *Essay*. These attitudes are found in scientists of all sorts (not just in medical writings), as well as in writings about knowledge in general. If we shift our attention from the background assumption of corpuscularianism to the interest in the production of natural histories of phenomena (viewed with ordinary eyes and with instruments), we shall see the relation between Locke's epistemology and his account of the science of nature. His epistemology, the main facet of the science of signs, may have been handcuffed by the concept of certainty; it was not controlled by a notion that all knowledge is deductive. The idea-signs in terms of which our knowledge of body is couched are derived from the things themselves, from the objects of observation. Mandelbaum finds a continuity between Locke's account of

---

1 *The Primitive Origination of Mankind* (1677), p. 8.
2 *Essayes of Natural Experiments Made in the Accademia del Cimento* (1684). Locke had in his library a copy of the original Italian edition, published in 1667.

ordinary and scientific knowledge, but he wrongly identifies scientific knowledge for Locke with knowledge of insensible particles. There were arguments advanced, almost entirely by Boyle (as Mandelbaum establishes) which sought to justify the corpuscular hypothesis, arguments which lean heavily on analogy. At one point in the *Essay* Locke repeats several of those arguments. He took the corpuscular hypothesis as true, though he sometimes characterises it as the most intelligible account. But the science of nature for Locke was not primarily concerned to establish or even to use that hypothesis. The natural histories recorded data of what was observed by the senses, of ordinary objects as well as what was observed through microscopes and telescopes. Locke's realism, which Mandelbaum rightly stresses, includes a realism of particles, but it was more properly concerned with a realism of ordinary gross objects. That was also, incidentally, where Newton insisted science began.

Once one has located scientific knowledge with the insensible particles, the question inevitably arises how science can justify the assertion that there *are* particles which cannot be, or are not, observed. Even more difficult is the description of those particles. A major task then becomes that of explicating and justifying 'transdiction', inferences from observed to unobserved. For Mandelbaum, this task is of major importance for the philosophy of science. His discussion of Boyle's efforts to justify and support such inferences and of Newton's recognition of the problem is well documented and convincing. Locke, too, was aware of the problem, but the corpuscular hypothesis was not an hypothesis he sought to justify: he accepted it and appealed to it in his account of the causation of perception and in his account of the nature of matter. It was one of a number of ingredients in Locke's metaphysic of nature. The usual justificatory questions philosophers put to existential claims are, for the most part, irrelevant to Locke. The most common such question is how can Locke, in terms of his own theory of knowledge, claim that there are insensible particles, even (since knowledge is limited to the perception of relation of ideas) ordinary objects? If the immediate objects of awareness are our own ideas, how can Locke talk of tables, chairs, and gold, to say nothing of insensible particles? On what grounds can the distinction between primary and secondary qualities be drawn? How can dreams and illusions be distinguished from reality and veridical perception?

The fact that Locke raised those sceptical questions in 4.4 of the *Essay* suggests that he saw the justificatory questions as legitimate and important. Moreover, he does produce what look like *arguments* for the reality of sensory knowledge as well as what appear to be standard arguments for the primary–secondary quality distinction, e.g. the hot and cold water argument, the colour of porphyry, the pounding of an almond examples. These arguments are only briefly referred to, the conclusion is usually put as an appeal: 'Can anyone think any real alterations are made in porphyry by the presence or absence of light' (2.8.19), 'What real alteration can the beating of the pestle make in any body' (2.8.20). Four arguments are sketched in 4.11.4–8 for establishing the reality of sensitive knowledge, standard arguments in the history of the problem of real knowledge. Locke would seem, then, to have at least indicated the grounds and support for the distinction between primary and secondary qualities and for the claim of the reality of the external world. I do not see how it could be said, however, that Locke devoted care and attention to justifying these claims. He was much more interested in asserting the claims as a way of getting on with the task of showing the origin, extent, and nature of knowledge. None of the arguments to which he refers is definitive, none can survive the attacks of the sceptic. (What arguments can?) Locke's attitude towards the sceptic is not sympathetic. He treats him in a cavalier fashion.

But yet, if after all this anyone will be so sceptical as to distrust his senses and to affirm that all we see and hear, feel and taste, think and do during our whole being is but the series and deluding appearances of a long dream, whereof there is no reality, and therefor will question the existence of all things or our knowledge of anything: I must desire him to consider that, if all be a dream, then he doth but dream that he makes the question, and so it is not much matter that a waking man should answer him. But if he pleases, he may dream that I make him this answer... (4.11.8)

In general we overwork the justificatory demands in philosophy. To restrict what can be said to what our logic or epistemology

sanctions is to rule out of philosophy many of the most interesting and fruitful claims about man and the world. With Locke in
particular, the result of insisting that no sentence be allowed to
appear in the *Essay* which is not conformable with the definition
of knowledge in Book 4, or consistent with the account of idea-
genesis in Book 2, is that Locke is inconsistent in a number of
claims (or unable to advance those claims) which are fundamental
to his metaphysic of nature. For a proper understanding of Locke,
we must view his accounts of the sciences of nature, action, and
signs in the context of the general world view he accepted. I
have tried to sketch in that view in chapter 1. A. C. Crombie has
remarked about science that 'there has never been natural science
with no preconception at all of theoretical objectives of a philosophical kind'.[1] We are used to this notion, to seeing the relevance
of philosophical presuppositions and preconceptions to science,
to understanding that we should not apply the same criteria to the
preconceptions as to the scientific conclusions. Not all philosophers
are prepared to give to philosophy itself the same recognition of
background attitudes in terms of which the philosophy is to be
understood. What Crombie says about science is just as true for
philosophy:

But the form the questions take, the direction and extent to which
they are pressed in the search for an explanation, will inevitably be
strongly influenced by the investigator's philosophy or conception of
nature, his metaphysical presuppositions or 'regulative beliefs', for it
is these that will determine his conception of the real subject of his
inquiry, of the direction in which the truth hidden in the appearances
will be found. It is these that will often determine what a scientist
regards as significant in a problem...[2]

Many of Locke's regulative beliefs can be found in his metaphysic
of nature, but those beliefs cannot themselves be derived in the
way which Book 2 of the *Essay* specifies. This is not a fault in
his philosophy, it is a fact (inescapable for any philosophy) which
must be accepted.

But surely, it will be said, if a man makes and emphasises the
claim that all our ideas come from experience, it is legitimate to

---

[1] *Augustine to Galileo*, II, 291. [2] *Ibid.*

ask him to account for the idea of insensible particles. And if a man says that we know things only by means of ideas, it behoves him to explain how we can claim or know there are things other than ideas. It may turn out—as I argue in a later chapter—that the way of ideas is misread as a representative theory of perception, or that the usual understanding of representative theories fails to fit Locke. That point aside, however, I would insist that Locke did not address himself to justificatory questions, nor do I see why he must make his metaphysic of nature conform to his science of signs. His inquiry into the original, certainty and extent of knowledge is descriptive, not justificatory. In his detailing the aims and purposes of his *Essay* (1.1.2-5), Locke does not cite questions of the justification of knowledge. He in fact accepts from the beginning that there *are* objects about which we acquire ideas and knowledge. He also insists from the start that human knowledge is limited, that belief and probability in many matters must be accepted in lieu of knowledge and certainty. We might attempt to save Locke from the embarrassment of asserting more than his definition of knowledge allows, by invoking his distinction between knowledge and belief, crediting to belief the claims not sanctioned by his theory of knowledge and the way of ideas. But such a gesture would be both too generous and inadequate, too generous because the distinction between knowledge and belief is made within the conceptual framework which raised the problem of justification, inadequate because there is no satisfactory account of the origin of those ideas constituting the metaphysic of nature employed by Locke.

Whether we think Locke can be made consistent or not, my suggestion is that more value can be derived (and more understanding of Locke and of his century) by asking ourselves what it is that Locke says about the various concepts and issues raised in the *Essay*, rather than struggling to find a justification for what he says. Locke had definite views about each of the three sciences he distinguishes. Our reading of Locke in the past has been hampered too much by asking the justificatory questions. Another hampering factor has been the habit of labelling the doctrines of the *Essay* 'realist', 'nominalist', 'representationist', and then interpreting what Locke says in the light of those labels. Taking my cue from the division of the sciences which Locke gives, I have tried to uncover what he says by a patient attention to the text, by asking of the text the questions which Locke very probably put to himself. Until we know more precisely than I think we now do just what his understanding was of the sciences of nature, action, and signs, we are in no position to claim that we know or understand the doctrines of the *Essay*.

I

THE NATURE OF THINGS
THEMSELVES

The nature of things 'as they are in themselves, their relations, and their manner of operations' is one of three areas that, according to Locke, come within man's understanding (4.21.1). The constitution, properties, natures, and operations of body and spirit are the subject-matter of natural philosophy.[1] Speculative truth is the goal of natural philosophy, truth which man must fetch from diverse sources: 'God himself, angels, spirits, bodies' (2). Contemplation is suggested as the means for attaining this sort of truth. Locke was not concerned in the *Essay* to extend speculative truth. Rather he was interested in 'things as they are in themselves knowable'; this third and last formulation of the first division of the sciences (5) reveals Locke's main objective, not to extend our knowledge of things but to show us some of the ways of doing so, even to explain how Boyle, Newton, Sydenham were extending human knowledge. The scope of things knowable is far less than that of things speculated about. Locke's account of the former goes on in the context of the latter, he has a metaphysical theory of nature which falls outside his own account of knowledge but which in many respects provides the causal and explanatory basis for human cognition and for what knowledge of nature is possible. Locke did not try to provide a theory of knowledge which would justify all the beliefs and claims he made about the world. Working within a fixed conceptual context, Locke sought to elaborate an account of human understanding which would make sense of the new science of nature. The body of speculative truths about the world found in the *Essay* reflects some of the common notions of the day and some of the scientific hypotheses of his contemporaries.

[1] Cf. *Some Thoughts concerning Education*, sect. 190: '*Natural Philosophy* being the knowledge of the Principles, Properties, and Operations of Things, as they are in themselves.'

Locke worked with the firm belief in a purposive universe: 'Nature never makes excellent things for mean or no uses' (2.1.15). Nor has nature any chasms or gaps (3.6.12), the chain of being goes on above and below us in 'easy steps and a continued series of things'.[1] These steps are exemplified by fishes that have wings, birds that live in the water and have cold blood, amphibious animals, even by 'what is confidently reported of mermaids or sea men'. The ascending scale is guaranteed us by the 'magnificent harmony of the universe and the great designs and infinite goodness of the architect'; the descent from God's perfection is matched by an ascent towards that perfection. The number of spirits above us may be infinite (4.3.27), more orders of them than

[1] Statements of the great chain of being were, of course, common in the seventeenth century. A few examples from books Locke had in his library are of interest. Thomas Browne, *Religio Medici*: '...for there is in this Universe a Staire, or manifest Scale of creatures, rising not disorderly, or in confusion, but with a comely method and proportion: betweene creatures of meere existence and things of life, there is a large disproportion of nature; betweene plants and animals or creatures of sense, a wider difference; betweene them and man, a farre greater: and if the proportions hold one, between Man and Angels there should be yet a greater' (p. 69, 4th ed. 1656). N. Fairfax, *A Treatise of the Bulk and Selvedge of the World* (1674): 'Such is that wonderful and most comely Chain of Being, which winds up into the World, that if the small and lowermost things therein make shift to show themselves, 'tis always by the leave, or with the help of the Bigger and the Higher' (Epistle Dedicatory). William Petty (a contemporary whose books were in Locke's library) left in MS several drafts of a paper on the scale of creatures: 'That between God and man, there are holy Angells, Created Intelligences and subtil material beings; as there are between man and the lowest animall a multitude of intermediate natures...' (p. 21; cf. 25–6, *The Petty Papers*. The editor dates these papers as 1677). Sir Matthew Hale also expressed this common notion, though Locke did not have this particular book of Hale's in his library: he speaks of the system, order, and excellence of all created Beings and says most are imperceptible to man, e.g. spiritual Beings and the refined parts of material existences. Then Hale says 'we cannot but suppose that there are diverse Ranks of created Beings intermediate between the glorious God and Man, which far surpas man in perfection of Nature and Operations.' Hale cites Angels and possible material beings of a more refined substance and more advanced forms than man. 'We see a multitude of Creatures between us and the lowest rank of Animals specifically and gradually one below another; and doubtless there are, or may be, many ranks of Beings intermediate between the glorious God and Mankind, that have specifical gradations one above another' (p. 15, *The Primitive Origination of Mankind*, 1677). For another near-contemporary statement, see *The Natural History of Insects, Compiled from Swammerdam, Brookes, Goldsmith, etc.* (Perth, 1792): 'It is thus that Nature chuses to mix the kinds of being by imperceptible gradations, so that it becomes hard to determine where animals end, or vegetables begin. In this there are evident marks of her wisdom in filling up every chasm in the great scale of being...' (p. 5. Cf. Bishop Wilkins, *Of the Principles and Duties of Natural Religion*, 1675, p. 17).

of bodies. In *The Reasonableness of Christianity*, Locke says there are 'infinite numbers and degrees of spirits out of the reach of our ken or guess' (*Works*, VII, 134); the *Essay* says there are at least 'several degrees of angels' (2.10.9).[1] The rule of analogy, if nothing else, makes the ascending scale probable (4.16.12). The descending scale includes insensible particles of matter, 'it being manifest that there are bodies and good store of bodies, each whereof are so small that we cannot by any of our senses, discover either their bulk, figure, or motion' (2.8.13).

The close interlocking of objects in nature, the lack of chasms or gaps, affects not only the total scale of nature: it affects as well the nature of each object in that scale, certainly each material object. Ordinarily, we consider each material object 'as an entire thing by itself, having all its qualities in itself and independent of other things' (4.6.11). This ordinary way of thinking about objects overlooks the many relations bodies have to other bodies. The life and motion of animals is dependent on 'extrinsical causes and qualities of other bodies'. We can discover some of these extrinsical causes, such as air for life, but the extrinsical dependencies very likely extend much further than we suspect. Think of the way our whole life depends upon the sun and the movement of the planets. The

great parts and wheels, as I may so say, of this stupendous structure of the universe, may, for aught we know, have such a connexion and dependence in their influences and operations one upon another, that perhaps things in this our mansion would put on quite another face and cease to be what they are if some one of the stars or great bodies incomprehensibly remote from us would cease to be or move as it does (*ibid.*).

---

[1] Locke says that there is some reason to suppose that spirits (he means angels) 'can assume to themselves bodies of different bulk, figure, and conformation of parts' (2.23.13). This supposition seems to have been based upon 'the report of things that our philosophy cannot account for', though what reports Locke had in mind is not clear. Locke was always fascinated by reports of monstrous births and other strange phenomena. However, this supposition, 'that angels do sometimes assume bodies, need not startle us, since some of the most ancient and most learned fathers of the Church seemed to believe that they had bodies'. Separate spirits, as he sometimes calls angels (separate from body) do not always assume bodily form. Moreover, as separate, they have the power of communicating their thoughts immediately, without reliance upon 'corporeal signs and particular sounds' (36).

It is the observed features and qualities of bodies about which
Locke speculates here, the qualities that appear to us. If we could
put a piece of gold by itself, 'separate from the reach and influence
of all other bodies', it would immediately 'lose all its colour and
weight, and perhaps malleableness too'. Similarly, left to itself,
water would cease to be fluid. The extrinsical dependence of
animals includes their 'life, motion, and the most considerable
qualities to be observed in them' (4.6.11). Locke gives many
other examples of the dependencies and relations of bodies upon
bodies for the qualities 'by which we know and distinguish
them'. In general, bodies 'would not be what they appear to us
were those bodies that environ them removed'. Things may seem
to be entire by themselves but they are 'but retainers to other
parts of nature for that which they are most taken notice of by
us'.

We find similar notions in Boyle: 'For we must consider
each body, not barely, as it is itself, an entire and distinct portion of
matter, but as it is a part of the universe, and consequently placed
among a great number and variety of other bodies upon which
it may act, and by which it may be acted on, in many ways'.[1]
In the *History of Particular Qualities* (1669), Boyle repeats this
point:

And every distinct portion of Matter, whether it be a Corpuscle or a
Primary Concretion, or a Body of the first or of any other order of
Mixts, is to be considered not as if it were placed *in vacuo*, nor as if it
have Relations only to the neighbouring Bodies, but as being *placed
in the Universe, constituted as it is*, amongst an Innumerable company of
other Bodies, whereof some are near it, and others very remote (p. 21;
cf. pp. 14–15, 35).

The qualities of body resulting from the influence of the system
of the world are what Boyle calls *Cosmicall*.[2] Thus, the doctrine
Locke was referring to, in saying bodies are retainers to other

---

[1] *The Origine of Formes and Qualities*, 2nd ed. pp. 18–19.
[2] 'The Systematicall or Cosmicall Qualities of Things' (1669. In *Tracts*). Cf. Hooke:
'We ought to conceive of things as they are part of, and Actors or Patients in the
Universe, and not only as they have this or that peculiar Relation or Influence on
our own Senses or Selves.' 'The Present State of Natural Philosophy', p. 9, in
Posthumous Works.

2-2

parts of the universe, was clearly taken from Boyle.[1] The distinction between absolute and relative properties of body was so important to Boyle that he has a special section in the *Origine* on the relational properties. Boyle was concerned that we do not treat as real entities or as inherent properties, qualities which bodies have only because they stand in relation to other bodies or to perceivers.

And...I do not see, why we may not conceive, that as to those Qualities (for instance) which we call Sensible, though by virtue of a certain Congruity or Incongruity in point of Figure or Texture, (or other Mechanical Attributes,) to our Sensories the Portions of Matter they Modifie are enabled to produce various Effects, upon whose accounts we make Bodies to be endow'd with Qualities.... (*Origine*, p. 13.)

The ability of gold to dissolve in *aqua regia* is not in the gold 'any thing distinct from its peculiar texture' (p. 4). The ability of powdered glass to poison is similarly not a new, superadded quality, is *nothing but* the glass itself (p. 6). These relational properties are ones 'whereby we distinguish' one object from another.

The 'observable qualities, actions and powers' of bodies are, Locke insisted, a function of the environment of bodies. Bodies interact with one another as well, that interaction is a result of the causal effects of one body upon another. Material causation is by impulse,[2] motion being one of the primary and fundamental properties of body. There are other primary properties of body, properties which bodies have in themselves which are not retainers to the rest of nature, which are the bases on which the observable properties depend. These primary properties of body can be discovered through physical analysis or through conceptual analysis, they are the qualities which 'sense constantly finds in every particle of matter which has bulk enough to be perceived' and which 'the mind finds inseparable from every particle of

---

[1] Dr von Leyden says that Locke's source for this notion 'was most probably Pascal' (*Seventeenth Century Methaphysics*, 1968, p. 159). Reading Locke alongside Boyle shows, I think, that we need not look abroad for the source of these passages though Locke very likely knew the Continental form of this doctrine. Pascal's *Pensées* were in his library.

[2] Locke modified this claim later in recognition of Newton's hypothesis on gravitation. See below, p. 24 n. 1. Nevertheless, bodies do act by impulse upon other bodies; that is one of the ways, the most ordinary way, in which gross objects act.

matter' (2.8.9).[1] These qualities, e.g. solidity, extension, figure, mobility (the list expands and contracts in Locke's discussion), are the *original* ones of matter.[2] The term 'original' for Locke means 'first', those qualities which body first had because they are essential to body, as well as 'non-relational' qualities body really has 'whether anyone's senses perceive them or no' (2.8.17,23).[3] They are the qualities body has when 'considered barely in itself' (2.23.37). As Boyle said, if we 'should conceive, that all the rest of the Universe were annihilated, except any of these entire and undivided Corpuscles...it is hard to say what could be attributed to it, besides Matter, Motion, (or Rest,) Bulk, and Shape' (*Origine*, p. 25). Boyle adds, as a way of underlining the non-relative or non-comparative nature of these basic qualities, that bulk 'though usually taken in a comparative sense, is in our sense an absolute thing, since a Body would have it, though there were no other in the world'. In a latter passage, Boyle comments that bulk, figure, and motion or rest 'belong to a Body, as it is consider'd in it self, without relation to *sensitive* Beings or to other Natural bodies' (p. 65). There is, Locke suggests, even some kind of relation in these non-relational qualities. Even 'considered in the things themselves, do they not depend on the bulk, figure, texture, and motion of the parts?' (2.21.3). It is the behaviour of the insensible corpuscles which determines the specific extension, figure, etc. of the object. This is not an extrinsic relation, however: it is rather intrinsic to the object itself. When we have ideas of these original qualities, we do so because imperceptible bodies come from the object, communicate motion to our nerves or

---

[1] Boyle considered motion to be more important and fundamental than bulk, figure, rest, situation, and texture, but all of these were inseparable from matter. See *Origine*, pp. 2–8; cf. Power, *Experimental Philosophy*, p. 102: 'the very nature of a Body consists onely in extension, which is the essential and unseparable property of all Bodies whatsoever'. But see below, p. 26 n. 1.

[2] Boyle's list varies also, e.g. 'local motion, rest, figure, shape, order, situation, and contexture', 'figure, size, posture, rest, order, or texture', in *The Excellency and Grounds of the Corpuscular or Mechanical Philosophy* (1674), reprinted in M. B. Hall, *Robert Boyle on Natural Philosophy* (1965), pp. 190, 192; cf. 208.

[3] Since the original qualities are first, their relation to other qualities is causal. Boyle used 'original' in this sense in his *Origine*. Another contemporary chemist speaks of principles from which 'all vegetables draw their origins, viz., from Water, Salt, and Sulphur'; every herb 'hath its original from a certain sulphurous salt' (Glauber, quoted in Marie Boas, *Boyle and Seventeenth Century Chemistry*, pp. 88, 87).

animal spirits which carry the motion to the brain, 'the seat of sensation' (12. The brain is called 'the mind's presence room' in 2.3.1). It is the motion in the brain that produces our ideas.

The action of the insensible particles of bodies is threefold. It produces ideas in perceivers, (*a*) some of which ideas resemble the qualities of bodies (the original qualities), (*b*) others of which resemble nothing in the bodies. The action of the insensible particles also (*c*) effects changes on other bodies, more properly in the original properties of other bodies. Locke was not very explicit as to the difference in the action of the insensible particles which bring about three such different effects. It was sufficient for his purposes to credit those actions to particular configurations of particles. Besides the original properties, the insensible particles have dispositional or relational properties, causal properties Locke calls 'powers'.[1] These qualities 'are nothing in the objects themselves but powers' (2.8.19), the ideas correlated with these qualities (e.g. colour, sound, taste) have no resemblance to anything in bodies, there is nothing *like* those ideas existing 'in the bodies themselves' (15). What is 'sweet, blue, or warm in *idea* is but the certain bulk, figure, and motion of the insensible parts in the bodies themselves'. If we take away the sensations of a perceiver, these qualities or ideas 'vanish and cease, and are reduced to their causes' (17).[2]

[1] Cf. Boyle, *Origine*: 'if there were no Sensitive Beings, those Bodies that are now the objects of our Senses, would be but *dispositively*, if I may so speak, endow'd with Colours, Tastes, and the like' (p. 31). Boyle even suggests that 'Bodies may be said, in a very favourable sense, to have those Qualities we call sensible, though there were no animals in the World, for a Body in that case may differ from those Bodies, which now are quite devoid of Qualities, in its having such a disposition of its Constituent Corpuscles, that in case it were duly apply'd to the Sensory of an Animal, it would produce such a sensible Quality, which a Body of another Texture would not' (pp. 31-2).

[2] These sensible qualities are, Boyle said, 'nothing of real and Physical [in the body] but the Size, Shape and Motion or Rest of its component Particles, together with that Texture of the whole' (*Origine*, p. 27). Bodies by themselves can only affect each other via motion by changing the situation or texture of bodies. These bodies being put in 'a World constituted as ours now is, and being brought to act upon the most curiously contriv'd Sensories of Animals, may upon both these accounts exhibit many different sensible Phaenomena; which however we look upon them as distinct Qualities are consequently but the Effects of the often mention'd Catholick Affections of Matter and deducible from the Size, Shape, Motion (or Rest,) posture, order, and the resulting Texture of the insensible parts of bodies' (*Origine*, pp. 37-8).

Ordinarily, we make no distinction in our talk about bodies, saying indiscriminately that this desk is brown and that this desk is rectangular and hard. Locke was concerned to argue that this common way of thinking and talking about bodies does not match the nature of things themselves. Two analyses of body are possible, we can find both in the history of philosophy. (1) Under the first sort of analysis, objects (e.g. desks, chairs) are said to be a collection of powers and dispositions. In terms of chapter 8 of Book 2 of Locke's *Essay*, this analysis would say that what Locke terms 'primary' or 'original' qualities are causal powers either actually exerted or capable of being exerted or manifested. To say of some bit of matter that it *has* the property of figure or bulk is the same as to say it *has the ability* to, and that under suitable conditions it will, produce an idea of figure and bulk in our awareness. The bulk and figure of the bit of matter just is this power or ability to cause me to have those ideas. (2) Under the second analysis, to say that it *has* some property is to say that that object has the ability to produce a relevant idea in our awareness *and* also to say that object has the property, not just the causal power. Under (1), the sentence 'the desk is brown' would be given the following *hypothetical* form: 'If a perceiver looks in a certain direction under suitable conditions, he will have a brown sense quality in his visual field.' The object is the cause of my visual experience of brown but the object does not have something over and above the causal power to produce the visual experience, something called the property 'brown'. Under (2), the sentence 'the desk is brown' would be given some *categorical* form, such as the form of the sentence itself, stressing the 'is', ascribing the quality 'brown' to the desk. When I perceive the colour of the desk, there is a causal relation between me and the desk but the desk has the colour brown as well as the causal power to produce my perception of brown. To *have* a causal power is not the same as to *have* a property like brown.

Locke's analysis of properties like colour, sound, or taste is in terms of analysis (1): these properties are only powers of bodies to effect certain changes in perceivers.[1] His analysis of the proper-

---

[1] Locke's concept of power was dispositional but it was deepened by his acceptance of the corpuscular hypothesis. That is, the powers of objects are the actions of the particular group of cohering particles constituting the real essence of the

ties he calls 'original' is in terms of the categorical language of
(2). Both the parent body and the insensible particles moving
from the parent to the perceiver have, in the categorical sense, the
original properties whether they are perceived or no. The difficulty of trying to conceive of or to analyse physical objects as
nothing more than bundles of powers was not one Locke had to
face. There are many difficulties about such an analysis of body,
not the least of which is to find a subject for the power. An object
which is *nothing but* powers has at best an odd ontological status.
Locke did not avoid this dispositional analysis of body because
he saw this or other difficulties inherent in that analysis; he
followed (2) simply because this was the view that made most
sense to him and the view adopted by the scientists he respected.
The exact nature of the operation of the causal powers of bodies
on other bodies or on perceivers was a question Locke left to
science.[1] For his purposes it was sufficient to call attention to the

object. The specific qualities which an object is able to produce at the secondary
level are determined by the nature of that object's real essence. For a discussion
of this deepened sense of 'power', see M. R. Ayers' *The Refutation of Determinism*.
Also, R. Harré's 'Powers and Qualities', forthcoming in *British Journal for the
Philosophy of Science*.

[1] Locke did make a change under Newton's influence. He told Stillingfleet that
his remark in 2.8.11 that bodies act by impulse would be changed to allow for
gravitational attraction (*Works*, IV, 467–8). Locke did not mention gravitation in
the change made in the 4th edition, he simply took out the sentences which said
bodies act on each other by impulse. He did not remove the remark that the only
way we can conceive bodies acting is by impulse. The passage in the first three
editions reads as follows: 'The next thing to be considered is, how *Bodies operate*
one upon another, and that is manifestly *by impulse*, and nothing else. It being
impossible to conceive, that Body should operate on what it does not touch
(which is all one as to imagine it can operate where it is not) or when it does touch,
operate any other way than by Motion.' In the fourth edition, this is shortened to:
'The next thing to be considered is how *bodies* produce *ideas* in us; and that is
manifestly by *impulse*, the only way which we can conceive bodies operate in.'
The significance of the change is further questioned by the fact that impulse was
inserted in the fourth edition in a later passage. In the first three editions, 4.10.19
reads: 'We do not deny other effects upon this ground, because we cannot possibly
conceive their productions, we cannot conceive how Thought (or any thing but
motion in Body) can move Body...' In the fourth edition, 'motion' is replaced by
'impulse' as, 'We cannot conceive how anything but impulse of Body can move
Body'. What Locke took out of 2.8.11 has been inserted, in the same edition, in
4.10.19. The counter to impulse for moving body given in this latter passage (in
all editions) is thought moving bodies, not gravitation. It may be relevant to
note that the same example—thought moving body—was one of the examples
Newton used (in unpublished MSS) for formulating the concept of active, immaterial principles at work in nature. *Vide* J. E. McGuire, 'Force, Active Principles,

great division between the relational and the non-relational qualities of bodies. The division between primary and secondary qualities does not quite coincide with that between the observable qualities of objects, with respect to which any object is but a retainer to all other objects (at least to some finite set of environing objects), and the qualities which objects have in themselves, because primary qualities are observable when they qualify objects large enough to be sensed. Nevertheless, the two ways of dividing the qualities of objects are close enough for the purpose in hand, i.e. to see what Locke's view of the nature of things themselves was. The qualities of bodies are (*a*) primary qualities which are non-relational and categorical properties, (*b*) sensible qualities which are powers that bodies have to affect our senses in such a way as to cause us to see colour, have smells, tastes, etc., and (*c*) powers which are the abilities a body has 'by reason of the particular constitution of *its primary qualities*, to make such a *change* in the *bulk, figure, texture, and motion of another body*, as to make it operate on our senses differently from what it did before' (2.8.23). An alternate vocabulary for (*b*) and (*c*) is, respectively, secondary qualities immediately perceivable and secondary qualities mediately perceivable (26. Cf. 2.23.7,9). What these ways of classifying qualities obscure is the very important fact that primary qualities are also sensible. That fact about them does not turn them into powers, however. Locke's classification is meant to summarise the relational/non-relational distinction.

The list of primary qualities given in 2.8 varies, but the composite from that chapter is the following: solidity, extension, figure, motion, rest, bulk, number, texture, size, situation. Portions of this composite are found elsewhere in the *Essay*. Locke thought this list too long, or thought it capable of reduction. Encompassing minds as well as bodies, he offered a list of eight original ideas from which all the rest are derived (2.21.73). This curious passage is reflected in only a few other places in the *Essay*. Its position in the *Essay*, coming at the end of the very long chapter on 'power', is odd, though it seems meant as a summary of the programme of

and Newton's Invisible Realm', in *Ambix*, xv (1968), 171, 192, 205. See also below, p. 140 n. 1, and Koyré's discussion of this change, *Newtonian Studies*, pp. 154–5.

derivation so far presented. It does not, however, summarise the analysis of the genesis of ideas in the previous chapters. Rather, it appears to suggest a quite different kind of derivation. It may be Locke's attempt to suggest an explanatory structure for our knowledge of nature, but it seems also to be his ultimate reduction to original qualities. The eight original ideas cited in this passage divide into three groups. Since the first group, extension, solidity, and mobility, are given in 2.8 as primary qualities of body, we might think that the eight ideas here listed are ideas of qualities in the primary and original sense. But these eight original ideas do not all fit easily into the non-relational classification, though they almost do. The fact that Locke extends the concept 'original' to spirits as well as to bodies may alone account for the difficulties of this listing of original qualities. What this curious passage explicitly offers is a list of ideas causally basic for all other ideas.

The eight ideas are offered as those a philosopher (i.e. natural scientist) might give as the causes of all other ideas, just as the list of original qualities of body given in 2.8 accounts causally for all sensible ideas of body. The first group arises from the senses. Reflection yields two more original qualities, qualities of mind, perceptivity (the power of perception or thinking) and motivity (the power of moving). This passage is one of three where Locke draws a parallel in original qualities between body and spirit. In 2.22.10 thinking and motion are said to 'comprehend in them all actions', to be those qualities from which 'actions are conceived to flow'. In 2.23.17–19, the original ideas 'proper and peculiar to body' are said to be the cohesion of solid and separable parts and a power of communicating motion by impulse.[1] The ideas peculiar to spirit are thinking and will, 'will' being defined as 'a power of putting body into motion by thought'. (2.23.30 repeats this coupling of original qualities for body and spirit.)

The third group in 2.21.73 is existence, duration, and number. In 2.10.6, existence, duration, and number are listed as 'the affec-

---

[1] Henry Power (*Experimental Philosophy*, 1664) suggests that the 'Minute particles of most (if not all) Bodies are constantly in some kind of motion', adding that motion may be 'as unseparable an attribute to Bodies, as well as Extension is' (Preface). Cf. Hooke, *Micrographia* (1665), p. 54: '...it seems very manifest, that there is no luminous Body but has the parts of it in motion more or less'.

tions of all kinds of beings' which 'almost every object that affects our senses, every thought which employs our minds, bring along with them'. (Cf. 2.21.3; 2.23.18 gives existence, duration, and mobility, the latter seemingly out of place and number forgotten.) The three are said to belong to both the other groups, meaning I take it that anything which *is* has the properties of existence, duration, and number, whether that thing be a body or a spirit, as 2.10.6 says.[1] These three qualities are not, however, original qualities of body in precisely the same way that extension, solidity, and mobility are original qualities. Existence is later cited as the *principium individuationis* since it is existence 'which determines a being of any sort to a particular time and place' (2.27.3). The existence in a time and place which constitutes any one thing, is found everywhere on the scale of being. That scale can be divided into single particles of matter, a collection of particles making a mass of matter (or an inanimate body), particles of matter united together in such a way as to form a living body (plant or animal), and persons or spirits (2.27.3–7). Wherever we look on the scale of being, there are some properties which belong to the objects on that scale in themselves, not by virtue of extrinsic causes.

The original qualities of body and spirit are causally basic for the derivative and relational qualities. The insensible particles of masses of matter are epistemologically important in initiating processes which lead perceivers to become aware of the primary qualities of that matter. Insensible particles also play an important ontological role in Locke's speculative account of the nature of body. The heart of any material thing is a configuration of insensible particles. The internal constitution of a thing can be said to be the *essence* of the thing, providing we are careful not to think of 'essence' as referring to classes or kinds, to genus and species. In explaining to Stillingfleet what he means by 'essence', Locke said they are 'in every thing that internal constitution, or frame, or modification of the substance, which God in his wisdom and good pleasure thinks fit to give to every particular creature'

---

[1] Existence, duration, and unity were three properties commonly cited by the scholastics to characterise being. If Locke was consciously borrowing from that tradition, we have additional support for thinking of these eight ideas as his attempt at a general metaphysical classification.

(*Works*, IV, 82; cf. p. 83). There were several notions of essence current at that time. The more rational opinion about the nature of things is that 'all natural things...have a real, but unknown, constitution of their insensible parts, from which flow those sensible qualities' (3.3.17). Not only is this the more rational opinion, it is past doubt (15; cf. 3.6.11,12; 3.10.21). This core or foundation of body is the '*essentia* or being of the thing itself' (3.3.18), it is what Locke terms the 'real essence'. Locke also said there is no 'real constitution of the sorts of things', all things that exist are particular (3.3.15,16). The particularity of things themselves is an important feature of Locke's metaphysic of nature. He, of course, recognised the similarities and likenesses of things (3.3.13) and he had a clear account of classes. Classes were a function of our classification in terms of the observable likenesses of objects. The nominal, not the real, essence becomes the basis of our class concepts. Does Locke mean us to take his dictum about the particularity of things to the point of denying classes or species of nature? What Locke was opposing can be helpful in answering this question.

There was a notion of essence held by some of his contemporaries which Locke (and Boyle) found as obscure as the talk of substance as substratum. The doctrine of *substantial forms* was not so much a theory of how observable qualities are produced, though it accounts for that (albeit very generally) in passing, as it was a theory about *kinds* of things. The doctrine of substantial forms said that there are 'a certain number of those essences [forms], according to which all natural things are made and wherein they do exactly every one of them partake, and so become of this or that *species*' (3.3.17). Real essences on this doctrine are a 'certain number of forms or moulds wherein all natural things that exist are cast'. The 'certain number' means a fixed, finite number. Nature, not man, on this theory makes the classes and species, 'prefixes the bounds' of things (3.6.30). Those forms 'are all ingenerable and incorruptible' (3.3.19), they are the 'unmovable boundaries' of species (3.6.27).

Locke confesses to having no idea of a 'substantial form', save the idea of the sound 'form' (2.31.6). He does have the idea of insensible particles, because they were thought of as like observed bodies, only very tiny. Setting aside the obscurity of the notion of substantial forms, we would have to know at least three things before we could say such a doctrine was correct: (1) We would have to know that 'nature, in the production of things, always designs them to partake of certain regulated established *essences*, which are to be the models of all things' (3.6.15). (2) We must know whether nature is always successful in this mode of production, that she does not sometimes mix up forms or depart from them (16). (3) We would need to know whether monsters are a distinct species.

Locke was fascinated by, and convinced of the truth of, reports on the 'production of monsters in all the species of animals, and of changelings, and other strange issues of human birth' (3.3.17). He gave some examples in 3.6.22: creatures that 'have shapes like man, but are hairy and want language and reason'; others that have language, reason and a human shape but 'have hairy tails'; men with no beards, women with beards. He suggests that reports of women conceiving by drills may be true, cites mules and jumarts, and a case Locke claims to have seen himself of the 'issue of a cat and a rat' as other examples of what appear to be the mixing of species (23). Locke offers these monster examples in evidence against the substantial-form doctrine, as well as evidence that we do not distinguish species of things according to the real essence, in Locke's sense of the internal constitution of particles. Monsters count against the substantial-form doctrine since they show a mixing of species. They are clear proof of the fact that we do not know the real essence since, if we did, we would not be puzzled about how to classify these monsters, we would know whether they are men or no (3.3.14).

On the substantial-form doctrine, the species of things were determined by the forms which nature (or God) copies in producing things. Those species are the kinds of things we readily find about us in our environment. There was, for this doctrine, no insensible aspect of objects, at least none came into the analysis of objects offered by its proponents. Species-characteristics were the observable properties, species-determination was a matter of the way nature works, not a function of the internal mechanism of objects. In rejecting the substantial-form doctrine, Locke (with

Boyle) was rejecting that account of species-determination. His doctrine of substance serves both to explicate the concept of thing which he believed all men have and to explain our grounds for species-determination. Locke (like the Royal Society scientists) was interested in particular things mainly for their shared properties, the tables in the natural histories of phenomena were to be of *kinds* of things. It is the ideas of particular *sorts* of substances that 2.23 is concerned with (see sections 3, 4, 6, 7, 37). He was not interested in collecting coexisting qualities that do not characterise sorts or kinds of things. Observation presupposes classes. The particular parcel of matter which makes the ring on my finger has a real essence in so far as it is gold, a *kind* of thing (2.31.6). But Locke's account of kinds appears to assign them to language or thought, not to reality. All that exists is particular, '*general* and *universal* belong not to the real existence of things, but *are the inventions* and *creatures of the understanding*', the concern only of signs, not of things. The nominal essence, the collection of qualities, is our epistemic basis for classifying into kinds. 3.3.13 might be seen as contrasting the epistemic with the ontic basis of sorts of things; but the more typical passages find Locke denying any ontic sense of 'kinds': genera and species are nothing but abstract ideas (3.3.9). 3.6.1 distinguishes real essence from the sortal concepts making up the nominal essence and the name. There is no mention of sorts or kinds in the real essence. 3.6.4 says that the ordinary use of 'essence' is for sorts, but these are ideas.

The real essence, as Locke terms the *essentia* of each thing, seems, then, not to be a 'class' or 'kind' feature of things but the causal basis of the thing. Whatever any particular thing is is a function of that thing's internal constitution of particles. It is necessary for each object to be as it is, since God and nature have made it that way (3.6.4). The *essentia* or being is necessary: if it were otherwise, the thing would not be that thing. Another way of putting this point is to say that particulars have all their qualities equally essential, every feature in each individual is essential to it (3.6.5). Having said that all features of individuals are equally essential, Locke adds, 'or, which is more, nothing at all'. To say everything is essential is the same as saying nothing is essential. Locke might be thought to be making the familiar point about the wholesale use of any term lacking meaning. He may have had this notion in mind; but the example he goes on to use, and indeed the context of his discussion, indicates that the claim 'Individuals have all their qualities equally essential' does not contradict the claim 'There is nothing that is essential to any individual'. Rather, these two claims use 'essential' in two different ways. The use in the first claim is that of the *essentia* or being of a thing. The use of 'essential' in the second claim is the class notion. To say rationality is essential to me requires that I have some notion of individuals like myself with whom I compare myself. In the first sense of 'essential', if I am rational, that is part of my nature which, if changed, would make a different individual. In the second sense of 'essential', rationality may or may not be essential to me as a man, as an individual of this sort. To ask whether rationality is essential to me or extension essential to body is to ask whether these properties are included in our concepts of man and body. Similarly, the pen in my hand is what it is, all its properties are equally essential to being the pen that it is. But as lead, iron, or plastic, some of its qualities are essential, with reference to some sortal idea of lead, iron, or plastic. The two senses of 'essential' are not entirely distinct, since the causal basis of all the features of any individual is the basis for *all* the other features, including the observable qualities in terms of which we classify particulars as to kinds. Thus, Locke's real essence, the internal constitution, relates to a sort, though it is not itself a sort (3.6.6). But the sort which real essence supposes is the nominal essence. Real essence is responsible for the observable qualities by means of which things are classified into kinds, but the kinds of things that there are are a function of our ideas, not of the real essence. 3.6.7 asks directly the question, which essence is it that determines substances into sorts? The answer is the nominal essence. Section 8 does qualify this by saying that '*the species of things to us*' relates to the nominal essence. He offers as evidence for this remark about 'to us', the fact that bodies which we classify under the same sort often have many different qualities. If 'things were distinguished into *species*, according to their real essence, it would be as impossible to find different properties in any two individual substances of the same *species* as it is to find different properties in two circles'. Section 9 carries on with this epistemic qualification: *we* can only rank things according to the nominal essence.

The relation between real and nominal essence is causal, but there is also a stronger relation than that between them, a relation which, could we have an adequate knowledge of the insensible particles, would enable us to know all the properties of gross objects without observation. Is Locke saying or allowing that there are sorts of things at the real-essence level and that an intelligence different from ours might discover real sorts by knowing the real essences? Or is he saying that, if we could classify according to real essence, it would be because we had a deductive or necessary knowledge of all the qualities an object would have as produced by that real essence and could then classify with certainty? If the second alternative, the sorts would not be at the real-essence level, though the difference between the alternatives may not be great. It looks as if Locke is still saying in these passages that there are no classes in nature (an ontic denial); that classes are our invention; that we now classify as best we can in terms of observed qualities without any knowledge of how the real essence determines those qualities; and that, could we have real-essence knowledge, we would then know for certain which are the qualities that flow from the real essence of objects and could then classify, still in terms of features other than the real essence, without mixing up two qualities which flow from different real essences. All of this may still presuppose types of real essence, but the species of things would not be species of real essences. However, if A (x, y, z)—some internal constitution—produces B (a, b, c)—some set of qualities and powers discovered via observation—and if that relation is not only causal but logical or necessary, the classification in terms of B may be the same as in terms of A. In his list of the conditions which would have to be met if substances were to be classed into species according to precise essences or forms (the substantial-form doctrine) Locke says under the fifth condition that, could we know *all* the properties that flow from the real essence, we might then be said to have distinguished the bodies into species according to the real essence (3.6.19). Moreover, the 'great chain of being' doctrine (which Locke clearly accepted) may be evidence that, at least in his metaphysic of nature, there are in fact species, even though the boundaries between species are gradual and continuous.[1] Also, in pointing out that nature makes particular things agree with each other in their sensible qualities, Locke conjectures that they also probably agree 'in their internal frame and constitutions' (3.6.36), though it is not that real essence that *distinguishes* (an epistemic term?) them into sorts. Section 37 makes the same point, but brings out into the open that sorting *by men* is done by means of sensible qualities. Locke does not avoid the conclusion that his account means that *for us* there are as many sorts as we have different general names.

The conclusion I wish to draw from these passages on species is that Locke's doctrine makes species a function of observable qualities. This fact may not make species epistemic and nominal, since presumably what a knowledge of real essence would reveal would be the total list of coexisting qualities dependent upon each kind of essence. In saying this, I have perforce already talked of *kinds* of real essence. Thus, the ontic truth may be that kinds occur on both the level of real and of nominal essences. Real-essence kinds would consist of different sorts of groupings of particles of varying sizes, shapes, and motions. There may be no problem about conceiving of such real-essence kinds for a superior intelligence, but I rather think that, even though Locke's account of substance and species entails species on the real-essence level, he was not able to articulate what that would mean, nor was it of course of much importance, since he rejected the possibility that man could achieve such an *a priori* science. The science of observable qualities was the one Locke saw as possible and important, it is there that useful species distinctions can be made. I am inclined to think Locke would say that even were we able to know real essence, natural history classification would be in terms of the qualities

---

[1] The 'scale of being' doctrine may, however, be seen as tending to deny classes, in that the gradations were so gradual and the differences so small (no gaps or chasms) that species distinctions do not exist. Lovejoy, in fact, says that the principle of continuity in this doctrine did lead 'some of the greatest naturalists of that age' (the 18th century) to reject 'the concept of species' (*The Great Chain of Being*, p. 229). Locke accepted the 'scale of being' doctrine but kept the species distinctions. At least, species of spirits are 'as much separated and diversified one from another by distinct properties' as are 'the *species* of sensible things' (3.6.12).

and powers caused by the real essence, not in terms of the qualities of particles.

When Locke is making the point about class-essential features of objects referring to class concepts, he makes what appears to be an odd remark, namely, that properties belong only to species, not to individuals (3.6.6). The word 'property' is frequently used interchangeably with 'quality', so it cannot be a technical term applied only in reference to kinds. Since Locke clearly states individuals have relational and non-relational qualities, his remark about properties belonging only to species could be misleading. At best, this remark could be true of the observable properties, in that it is those (not the unobservable core) by which we classify things into kinds. The solution of this remark lies, I think, in seeing that there are two senses of 'property' which correlate with the two senses of 'essential'. While there is no real constitution of the *sorts* of things, as the doctrine of fixed kinds and moulds held, the internal constitution of particles of any given object does give rise to classes indirectly: they are the causal basis for the qualities in terms of which men classify perceptual objects. Moreover, in saying that God and angels could have a deductive knowledge of nature, Locke presumably means that those deductions would be made from a knowledge of the internal constitution of particles. That deduction might be to each particular object, rather than to class features, but the examples Locke gives are to kinds of things.[1] Thus the internal essence is closely bound up with class properties. Whether the particularity of the essence itself is violated by the relation between essence and properties is not clear. If all things that exist are particular, but if particulars have properties only in relation to other particulars, those particulars would not have the non-relational properties Locke has firmly said they do have. The relation of resemblance would not, I think, count against the non-relational feature of these properties. He reaffirms at this point that bodies do have non-relational properties, identifying them with the internal constitution: 'that particular constitution which everything has within itself, without any relations to anything without it' (3.6.6). The unobservable or unknown collections of particles

---

[1] See below, pp. 80–5, for a discussion of the method of deducing from essence.

making up the internal constitution of each individual thing have
the original qualities: they are figured, extended, have bulk, etc.,
but none of these to a degree to make them sensible to the naked
eye. Behind, as it were, 'the appearance and outward scheme of
things', there lies 'the minute particles of bodies' which make
'the real constitution on which their sensible qualities depend'
(2.23.12, 11). In his *Elements of Natural Philosophy*, Locke concludes by saying that 'the great and visible parts of the universe'
are made up 'of unconceivably small bodies or atoms, out of
whose various combinations bigger moleculae are made: and
so, by a greater and greater composition, bigger bodies; and out
of this the whole material world is constituted'.[1] The theory
found its most elaborate and detailed exposition in Boyle.[2] The
dependence of sensible qualities on insensible particles Locke had
in mind is not only that of the dependence of the immediately and
mediately sensible qualities. Rather, it includes the dependence of

[1] *Works*, III, 330. Boyle's eighth principle of his corpuscular hypothesis deals with
change, with generation, corruption and alteration. In tracing all changes to the
behaviour of corpuscles, he builds up the sensible world from insensible corpuscles.
From single corpuscles, clusters of corpuscles (still insensible) are formed, and
from several clusters sensible objects are formed (*Origine*, pp. 47–9). Cf. Newton:
'Now the smallest Particles of Matter may cohere by the strongest Attractions,
and compose bigger Particles of weaker Virtue; and many of these may cohere
and compose bigger Particles whose Virtue is still weaker, and so on for divers
Successions, until the Progression end in the biggest Particles on which the Operations of Chymistry, and the Colours of natural Bodies depend, and which by
cohering compose Bodies of a sensible Magnitude' (*Opticks*, Dover Books, 1952,
p. 394; quoted by J. E. McGuire, 'Transmutation and Immutability: Newton's
Doctrine of Physical Qualities', *Ambix*, XIV, June 1967, 82). Axtell has brought
forth evidence to suggest that Newton had a hand in the composition of the
Elements, 'Locke, Newton, and The Elements of Natural Philosophy', *Paedogogica
Europaea*, I, 235–45.
[2] The relations between Boyle and Locke have been generally recognised but not
enough emphasis has been placed upon the close similarity of passages in Boyle's
books and passages in Locke's *Essay*. Locke had in his library over sixty titles of
Boyle's publications, many of them given to Locke by Boyle. See Harrison and
Laslett, *The Library of John Locke*. Most of the ingredients in Locke's science of
nature are found in Boyle, especially in the *Origine*. The verbal similarities are often
striking. As in most matters, to discover the issues and doctrines Locke had in
mind, we need to look close at hand, to his own English friends or English writers,
rather than to the main philosophical tradition. Reading the theoretical part of
Boyle's *Origine* alongside Locke's *Essay* (in particular, those passages in the latter
on real and nominal essence, on insensible corpuscles, on primary and secondary
qualities, and on classification), the conclusion is inescapable that Locke had his
copy of this work by Boyle open beside him when writing out these portions of
the *Essay*.

the original qualities of body upon the particles of that body.[1] The extension of body 'is nothing but the cohesion of solid parts' (2.23.24), 'the cohesion or continuity of solid, separable, moveable parts' (2.4.5). It is the behaviour of the particles which determines whether water will be fluid or solid (2.23.26). Because particles cannot share the same space at the same time, bodies cannot (2.27.2). The identity of an inanimate body is dependent upon the sameness of the minute parts (2.27.3). The behaviour of the particles (what Locke calls, after Boyle, their 'mechanical affections', 4.3.25) is responsible for the causal operations of their bodies, e.g. for the ability of rhubarb to purge, hemlock to kill, or opium to 'make a man sleep'. In short, what a body is known as, what it does, and what it is are all functions of minute particles.

The minute particles are thus more basic and original than the larger objects we more normally encounter, those particles have only the non-relational qualities (though they have as well powers to affect). An important difference between the large-scale and the insensible bodies is that the former are frequently perceived, *their* primary qualities come mixed with secondary ones. We must resist the temptation to think that perception somehow taints the primary qualities of ordinary objects. The primacy of the original qualities is something we can convince ourselves of through sensory as well as conceptual tests, as we saw Locke saying in 2.8. The solidity, extension, figure and mobility we see in a grain of wheat are the same qualities the particles of that grain have when it is ground in a mill (2.8.9). Fire and snow have these qualities whether we perceive them or no (17), 'a piece of *manna* of sensible bulk is able to produce in us the *idea* of a round or square figure, and by being removed from one place to another, the *idea* of motion' (18). The ideas of these qualities which I have from that sensible piece of manna represent those qualities as they really are: 'a circle or square are the same, whether in *idea* or existence, in the mind or in the

[1] Cf. Boyle: '...when many of these insensible Corpuscles come to be associated into one visible Body', their motion will cause new qualities in that body (*Origine*, p. 49). Just in coming together and adhering the corpuscles affect the size and shape of visible bodies. There are many other passages in the *Origine* in which Boyle shows how through the behaviour of corpuscles, sensible bodies and their observed qualities are produced.

manna'. When bodies are of a size that we can perceive, 'we have by these an idea of the thing as it is in itself' (22). Porphyry is taken in 19 as an example, an almond in 20. Throughout the *Essay* Locke's examples are ordinary objects: clocks, ice, sugar, a rose, a pump, a diamond, marble, gold, a football, a flint, a snowball, chalk, milk (a few examples selected at random from Book 2). 3.3 gives a sample list of 'the particular things we meet with': bird, beast, tree, plant, soldier, sheep, crow, persons, countries, cities, rivers, mountains (2, 5). Any of these particular things has a shape or figure and is extended, some move, all have bulk. These objects are of an 'observable bigness', their 'extension, figure, number, and motion' is 'perceived at a distance *by* the sight' (2.7.12). It is because bodies act on perceivers by impulse and because sighted objects are at a distance, i.e. 'be not united to our minds', that Locke says 'it is evident some singly imperceptible bodies must come from' those objects to the eyes.

Insensible particles play two causal roles in Locke's speculative account of bodies. It is the behaviour of those particles which produces extended bodies of an observable bigness. It is also the behaviour of those particles which causes us to have visual experiences.[1] In the latter role the particles are acting in a dispositional way. In the former role their action is not dispositional. Neither causation is explained in any detail, we no more understand how it is that the action of corpuscles on our nerves produces now a colour perception of such a shape, now of another shape, than

---

[1] It is useful to keep these two features of the corpuscular theory separate, since Locke seems to have been much less wedded to that theory as an account of perception than he was as an account of matter. The corpuscular theory of matter more nearly fits later and even recent theories than does the corpuscular theory of the causation of perception. Taken seriously and consistently, there are many difficulties with that theory as an account of perception, whether taken in its seventeenth-century form or in its Greek version. For one, how are we to explain the apparently inexhaustible supply of corpuscles that bodies have and can send out to sense organs? For another, if (as Locke held) the particles may be observable via microscopes, the particles I see through the microscope cannot be the same particles that are causing my perception. The fact that Locke said the corpuscular account of the physical nature of perception is thought to be the most intelligible account indicates that he would be willing to relinquish it if self-defeating difficulties in the theory were discovered. There would be no major change required in his account of perception and knowledge of body, were the physical and physiological features of perception brought up to date.

we understand how the behaviour of particles gives the sugar its shape or size. Neither speculation nor the science of his day had adequate answers to such details, though Boyle tried to suggest some detailed explanations. It was sufficient for Locke to suggest that different perceptions were caused by differences in the figure and bulk of the particles that strike our nerves, 'different degrees and modifications of their motions' (2.8.13) or by a difference in the texture of the surface of the light-reflecting objects (texture itself being due to the configuration of the particles) (19). For the differences in the qualities of bodies of observable size, it sufficed Locke to suggest that observed differences reflect some difference in the inward nature of bodies; where the 'outward frame so much differs, the internal constitution is not exactly the same' (3.6.22).

Attempts to sort out Locke's views on the nature of physical objects and our perception and knowledge of them tend to get lost in the traditional philosophical concepts. Locke is labelled a 'representationist' and then interpreted in the light of what such a position must say. Reginald Jackson's influential 1929 article, 'Locke's Distinction between Primary and Secondary Qualities',[1] frequently obfuscates in this way. Some of Jackson's claims are especially relevant to my concerns in this and the following chapters. Even when the text fails to support him, what Jackson says, together with the necessary textual corrective, is helpful in aiding us to see what Locke was saying. Not every dispute I have with Jackson can be settled unequivocally by reference to Locke's text, but a number of claims central to Jackson's reading can quickly be rejected. One of the main claims advanced by Jackson is that Locke's distinction between primary and secondary qualities is a way of distinguishing between qualities and powers. The only qualities objects have are the primary ones which are, 'in accordance with the Representative Theory of Perception, necessarily imperceptible' (p. 55). Jackson also thinks that these qualities, the only real and proper qualities, are indeterminate. He arrives at this conclusion from Locke's remark that primary qualities are those that 'are utterly inseparable from the body,

---

[1] *Mind*, xxxviii. Recently reprinted in *Locke and Berkeley, A Collection of Critical Essays*, ed. Martin and Armstrong (Doubleday Anchor, 1968). All references are to this reprinting.

in what state soever it be' (2.8.9). A specific or determinate quality cannot satisfy this definition of primary quality, since it is not utterly inseparable from the object: particular qualities change. Shape but not square or round is a primary quality; similarly, motion but not a specific motion, hard but not a precise hardness. That Jackson is textually wrong in identifying primary qualities with the qualities of insensible parts should be clear from my earlier discussion and references to the kind of objects that we perceive. Jackson himself comes to talk of our being 'acquainted with the primary qualities of the sensible parts' (pp. 64, 66). The primary qualities of the insensible parts differ from those of the sensible parts of body, according to Jackson, in being indeterminate. Jackson believed there was an uneasy tension between what he takes to be two different features of Locke's quality talk. One kind of talk requires indeterminate qualities as the defining trait of body, not of particular bodies, and these could only belong to imperceptible parts. Another kind of talk is of determinate and perceptible qualities. But Locke has insisted that everything that exists is particular; hence even imperceptible particles must be particular and have a determinate shape, size, motion, etc.[1] What Locke is saying about the primary qualities being defining traits of body is that a body always has, in the important non-relational sense, some shape, size, motion or rest, etc. Moreover, it has these properties whether we perceive them or no, and the particles at least have these properties independently of their relations to other objects. The characterisation of body as body is a function of these qualities. The characterisation (better, the individuation) of any body as the particular body that it is is a function of its real essence, of the particular grouping and cohesion of its corpuscles.

Even though Jackson recognises that Locke talks of macroscopic primary qualities, he says that Locke denies 'that if they are of a sufficient size bodies are perceptible' (p. 66). This conclusion is again one that follows for Jackson from the representative theory of perception, since that theory says we do not see objects.

[1] Such was Boyle's doctrine also. He says that all matter, the smallest bit and large masses, has its own peculiar bulk and shape. Boyle explains that he does not mean quantity in general, in speaking of bulk and shape, but a *determinate* quantity (*Origine*, p. 6).

But there are a number of passages in the *Essay* showing Locke saying that objects are sensible. We have already seen that the bulk of Locke's examples are of ordinary perceptual objects.[1] When bodies are of perceptible size, Jackson thinks Locke must say that the causes of our ideas of those macroscopic qualities cannot be the insensible particles. How to account for apparent size and shape by reference to insensible particles?[2] Earlier, Jackson identifies 'sensible quality' with 'secondary quality' and says 'The power of a body to act on the senses in a given way by means of its qualities is called a "secondary" or "sensible quality"' (p. 56). If 'sensible quality' does not include 'primary quality', it would seem that our ideas of primary qualities would be uncaused. The corpuscular theory did not restrict 'sensible' to 'secondary', and it explained all perceived qualities by reference to the behaviour of insensible corpuscles. I find no basis in the text for saying 'Locke holds, therefore, that some powers to produce ideas depend on macroscopic qualities' (pp. 66, 67). Jackson refers to the heading (the content entry) for 2.8.11 and 12 which reads, 'How primary qualities produce their ideas'. The text of 11 simply says, 'How *bodies* produce *ideas* in us', the answer being 'by impulse'. Section 12 does single out primary, or as Locke refers to them here 'original', qualities; but its text proves Jackson's claim quite wrong, since Locke is dealing with bodies of an 'observable bigness'; his account of the causation of ideas of these observable qualities is in terms of the corpuscular theory. There can be no question, then, that Locke's account of the origin of sensible ideas, both of primary and secondary qualities, is in terms of insensible corpuscles or particles.

Jackson later admits that there are, in the *Essay*, 'many passages in which bodies and their qualities are said or implied to be perceptible' (p. 71). But lest we be encouraged to suppose that these passages show 'the primary qualities themselves become ideas by being perceived', Jackson reminds us that such a

---

[1] As one example only, recall Locke's definition of primary qualities as 'such as sense constantly finds in every particle of matter which has bulk enough to be perceived' (2.8.9; cf. 2.23.9).

[2] Jackson always speaks, as does Locke also, of the causes of our ideas of secondary qualities being the microscopic primary qualities. But it is not the primary *qualities* which are the causes of perception; it is, according to the corpuscular theory Locke accepted, the *behaviour* of the insensible *particles*.

supposition is 'inconsistent with the whole doctrine of Representative Perception'. Hence Locke cannot have held that bodies and their qualities ever are perceptible. It is misleading to speak of qualities *becoming* ideas, but that Locke believed objects and their qualities to be perceptible cannot be doubted on the basis of his texts. Only if we burden ourselves first with a theory of representative perception (and interpret that theory in a specific way) can we be led to ignore what Locke says. Locke was read as a sceptic in his own day as well as in ours. The text is *not* unequivocal on the question of immediate ideas and mediate knowledge of things.[1] It is explicit, however, that Locke talks of ordinary perceptual objects and of our seeing and perceiving those objects.

Boyle had offered the corpuscularian hypothesis as an explanation of the operations of observed bodies, especially of their qualities. Boyle claimed that 'the Corpuscularian will show, that the very qualities of this or that ingredient, flow from its peculiar texture and mechanical affections of those corpuscles it is made up of'.[2] Boyle was a patient and thorough investigator of nature, recording his many experiments with care. It was this careful experimentation and observation which yielded a knowledge of the nature of things and qualities. Locke saw this procedure as the only way to acquire accurate information about things. While Locke may be seen on occasion as lamenting man's inability to have a deductive knowledge of perceptible things and qualities (he read 'flow from' also as 'deducible from'), he firmly advanced the method of 'following things themselves' as the only sound alternative to the *a priori* and disputative method of the Schools. It is '*the consideration of things themselves*' which is the fountain of knowledge (2.4.24). 'Things themselves are to be considered as they are in themselves, and then they will show us in what way they are to be understood. For to have right conceptions about

---

[1] There are many problems about Locke's definition of knowledge and its implications for perceptual consciousness. In a later chapter I try to sort out the difficulties. By looking closely at the four kinds of knowledge-relation cited by Locke, by noting the many examples he uses of perceiving physical objects, and by paying attention to the difference between the existential question 'are there bodies?' and the epistemic question 'can we know body?', I hope to have shown a way of reading Locke which is more faithful to the text and less burdened with labelled doctrines.

[2] Quoted by M. B. Hall, in *Robert Boyle on Natural Philosophy* (1965), p. 205.

them, we must bring our understandings to the inflexible natures and unalterable relations of things, and not endeavour to bring things to any preconceived notions of our own' (*Conduct*, in *Works*, III, 246). Whatever universal truths man has discovered 'result in the minds of men from the being of things themselves, when duly considered' (2.5.25). The best way to come to truth is to 'examine things as really they are, and not to conclude they are as we fancy of ourselves or have been taught by others to imagine' (2.11.15). The process of forming class concepts is to 'collect such a number of simple *ideas* as, by examination, we find united together in things existing' (3.6.21). A complex idea or nominal essence is the class concept which emerges.[1] Locke carefully contrasts the formation of this sort of idea with those mixed modes which do not have to follow nature. The nominal essence must be faithful to things themselves; in this it stands in sharp contrast to mixed modes which can be their own archetypes. The things to which the nominal essence must be faithful are the large-scale objects of our experience. It is ordinary objects again which serve Locke as examples. 'Nobody joins the voice of a sheep with the shape of a horse, nor the colour of lead with the weight and fixedness of gold, to be the complex *idea* of any real

---

[1] There are several passages on kinds and species in Boyle's *Origine of Formes and Qualities* which are found almost verbatim in Locke's *Essay*, e.g. 'We may now advance somewhat farther and consider, that Men having taken notice that certain conspicuous accidents were to be found associated in some Bodies, and other Conventions of accidents in other Bodies, they did for conveniency, and for more expeditious Expression of their Conceptions agree to distinguish them into several Sorts, which they call *Genders* or *Species* ...' (p. 39). Again, 'that upon whose account' men 'really distinguish any one Body from others, and refer it to this or that *Species* of Bodies, is nothing but an aggregate or Convention of such accidents, as most men do by a kind of Agreement (for the Thing is more arbitrary than we are aware of) think necessary or sufficient to make a Portion of the Universal Matter belonging to this or that Determinate Genus or Species of natural bodies' (p. 41. Cf. pp. 39–46). The only way we can give an answer to a question like 'what is gold?' is to show a piece of metal that is heavy, very malleable, ductile, yellow, etc. (p. 40). We cannot answer this question by reference to a substantial form. It is also relevant to note that Boyle's 'form' is very much the same as Locke's 'nominal essence': it is, Boyle said, a technical word or term of art standing for some one thing, '*some conspicuous Phaenomenon that is exhibited*, or *some particular use* to which it is applicable upon whose account this or that Form is attributed to this or that natural Body, and only upon the recesse or abolition of which it is said to loose its *Forme*, or if you please, *Denomination*' (pp. 294–5). Or again, 'the Forme of a body being really no more than a convention of Accidents whereby the Matter is stampt and denominated' (p. 318; cf. p. 101).

substances, unless he has a mind to fill his head with *chimeras* and his discourse with unintelligible words' (3.6.28). What we discover by paying attention to things themselves are coexisting and successive qualities which we classify and name as kinds of objects. Locke's analysis of any such object is, as we have seen, into an inner but unobserved (and hence unknown) core of insensible particles and the mediately and immediately perceivable qualities caused by the operation of those insensible particles. Both the particles and the macro-objects have primary qualities whether we perceive them or no. As in so much else, Locke was replacing an older and metaphysical doctrine by a recent and scientific hypothesis. The talk of substratum is imprecise and unclear, that of insensible particles making up the internal constitution of an object is conjectural, though having the weight of Boyle and his applications of this corpuscularian hypothesis behind it. Just as Locke rejected the talk of substantial forms and finite kinds, so he tried to replace the talk of substratum and subject by the notion of an internal, insensible configuration of particles. We do not know how those particles operate, except to say they cause through cohesion a certain extension, through the texture they create a certain reflection of light, etc. Since the link between observed coexisting qualities and the insensible particles was theoretical, we cannot claim to know the entirety of a thing. We neither have sensory ideas of the internal being of body nor deductive knowledge of the sensory qualities from the behaviour of insensible particles. Those were the only uses of 'know' recognised by Locke, sensory or deductive (the latter depending upon intuition). In criticising obscure philosophical traditions, Locke borrowed from experimental science. Nevertheless, his account of the nature of things themselves goes beyond what we can learn from experience. Locke's *metaphysic* of nature sets the context for his account of the *science* of nature.

2

THE SCIENCE OF NATURE

Working in close proximity with science and scientists, Locke knew that a science of nature was possible.[1] His concern was with characterising that science, with showing what scientific knowledge was entitled to claim, how it is achieved. His analysis of these matters began with the account of the nature of things shared by theologians and corpuscularians, the great chain of being and insensible particles. The appeal of observation and experimentation was strong, the Baconian prescription was in fashion, especially with innatism and *a priorism* the only alternatives. Along with the method of observation, Locke made use of the corpuscular hypothesis. The appeal for Locke of the corpuscular hypothesis was due not only to the eminence of and his respect for Boyle, it supplied him with a more significant content for the concept of body than philosophical tradition offered. There is a conceptual necessity about our concept of body which is more meaningfully filled by 'insensible particles' than by 'substratum'.

What we learn through careful attention to nature is the order of coexisting qualities; but, since we cannot imagine how those qualities 'can subsist by themselves, we accustom ourselves to suppose some *substratum* wherein they do subsist' (2.23.1). When we say of a particular body that it is a thing which is extended, figured, capable of motion, or of a spirit that it is a thing capable of thought, the word 'thing' captures what we feel is necessary over and above the observed properties. Such an idea of a subject for the qualities is neither clear nor informative, but we cannot conceive how qualities can subsist alone, so we find

---

[1] According to the Harrison–Laslett tabulation, Locke had in his library 240 titles of books in natural science, comprising 6.6% of his collection. Nevertheless, there are some surprising omissions. For example, there are no entries in his catalogue for the following: Gilbert, Kepler, Copernicus, Tycho Brahe, Ptolemy. He did have Galileo, Harvey, Huygens, Boyle, and almost all of Bacon, some in different editions.

ourselves caught with the unclear notion (4). Locke retained the formula, 'a collection of qualities plus something I know not what', but used the corpuscular hypothesis to suggest what the unknown and unobserved portion of body is. Theory and hypothesis fill in what thought requires but experience fails to supply.

Most of 2.23 is concerned to get the reader to realise that the only clear idea of a thing (whether it be material or immaterial) which he has is made up of the observable (or reflective) and behavioural properties he finds coexisting in his experience. Locke takes ordinary objects—man, horse, sun, water, iron, bread—and challenges the reader to produce any content for these objects which is not an observable property or a power inferred from observed behaviour (e.g. the power of a magnet to attract iron). The best answer we can give to the question, what is the subject of these observed qualities and inferred powers, is 'the solid extended parts', meaning, I would suggest, the observable parts (2). We cannot, without theory, find a subject for the sensible solid, extended parts. Locke does not shy away from theory. He has clearly formulated the corpuscularian hypothesis in 2.8, he uses it throughout 2.23 (especially in sections 8–14, 23, 26). The discussion of substance in 3.6 makes extensive use of particle talk and asserts unequivocally that (1) 'every substance that exists has its peculiar constitution whereon depend those sensible qualities and powers we observe' (13), and (2) 'it is evident the internal constitution, whereon their properties depend, is unknown to us' (9). The main bent of 3.6 is to argue that our classification of objects is not done in terms of the internal constitution but in terms of the observed properties. Whether we are talking of thinghood in general or of particular objects, the internal, causally basic, cohering particles are unknown. The corpuscularian hypothesis enables us to articulate a plausible account of that inner constitution; that account nevertheless is hypothesis, not knowledge.

There is a difference between *observing* and *knowing* the internal constitution of an object. Knowing is used here in the sense of understanding the workings of that inner configuration of particles. Locke did not think the particles were unobservable in principle. He considered that microscopes had made some progress

in extending the range of our observation of bodies. He believed
that such progress was limited in practice, would be disorienting
for man, and would never lead us to an understanding of the
essentia of any body. Locke raises the possibility of our senses
being acute enough 'to discern the minute particles of bodies'
and asserts, these 'microscopes plainly discover to us' (2.23.11).[1]
Under these conditions, the colour of gold disappears, being
replaced by 'an admirable texture of parts, of a certain size and
figure'. Similarly, the opaqueness and whiteness of sand becomes
pellucid, hair loses its colour, blood shows 'only a few globules of
red, swimming in a pellucid liquour' (11).[2] With more powerful
lenses, the red globules of blood would very likely appear different
still. Magnification of '1000 or 100,000 times more acute than it is
now by the best microscope' would enable us to see things
'several millions of times less than the smallest object' of our
sight (12). Under these conditions we would 'come nearer the
discovery of the texture and motion of the minute parts of
corporeal things, and in many of them probably get *ideas* of their
internal constitutions' (12).

Despite the passages I have cited which unequivocally say the

[1] The microscopist Henry Power had made this claim in 1664. Writing in the Preface
to his *Experimental Philosophy*, Power said that 'the Minute Atoms and Particles
of matter, were as unknown' to Adam 'as they are yet unseen by us', but he says
microscopes will remedy this: 'for herein you may see what a subtil divider of
matter Nature is; herein we can see what the illustrious wits of the Atomical and
Corpuscularian Philosophers durst but imagine, even the very Atoms and their
reputed Indivisibles and least realities of matter'. Power went on to suggest that
in time we will be able to 'see the Magnetical Effluviums of the Loadstone, the
Solary Atoms of light...the Springy particles of Air, the constant and Tumultuary
motions of the Atoms of all fluid Bodies, and their infinite, insensible Corpuscles'.
Microscopes will, Power claimed, continue to support the atomical hypothesis,
even as to 'the necessary Attributes, or essential Properties of them [atoms],
as motion, Figure, Magnitude, Order, and Disposition' (p. 82). Another microscopist, Robert Hooke, was a bit more cautious, saying that microscopes will
probably help us to discover the 'subtility of the composition of Bodies, the
structure of their parts, the various texture of their matter' (*Micrographia*). Glanvill
repeated these claims: microscopes enable our eyes 'to look into the *minutes* and
subtilities of things, to discern the otherwise *invisible Schematisms* and *Structures* of
Bodies, and have an advantage for the finding out of original Motions' (*Plus
Ultra*, p. 56). Newton too 'expressed the hope that improvements in microscopes
would bring such particles within the limits of the sensation of sight' (Cohen,
Franklin and Newton, p. 145; cf. pp. 159, 164. Cohen refers to the *Principia*).
[2] Cf. Power, p. 72: 'Under the microscope, most bodies lose their colours and grow
diaphanous.'

particles are in principle observable, Mandelbaum denies that Locke holds to this view: 'that which exists independently of us, and causes our ideas of the primary qualities of an object, is not itself capable of being perceived' (*op. cit.* p. 18). This bold claim is tied to Mandelbaum's rejection of the resemblance relation as being likeness or imaging. The textual evidence is overwhelming that Locke meant precisely 'image' or 'likeness' by 'resemblance', though not for the relation between my ideas and the specific shape, size, etc., of particles. I cannot determine what Mandelbaum's views are on Locke's notion of macroscopic objects, but his objection to a likeness between idea and quality is based mainly on that relation holding between idea and microscopic particle. For Mandelbaum, it is inconsistent for an atomist to hold 'that the specific qualities which we perceive when we look at or when we touch material objects are identical with the qualities which those objects, when considered as congeries of atoms, actually do possess' (p. 15). The reason given for this general thesis about atomism is that 'the continuous contour which characterises the precise shape of an object such as a table cannot be considered by an atomist to be a wholly adequate representation of that object's true shape' (p. 15). If 'true shape' is the 'shape of the particles', of course the contour of the perceptual object is not identical with the shape of the congeries of particles, nor with the shape of any individual particle. If this is how we interpret the resemblance relation, then it does not hold between idea and particles. Locke surely did not mean that I can learn what the specific shape of the collection of particles is by attending to the shape of macroscopic objects. What he meant was that my idea of shape, size, motion, solidity reveals the kind of properties the particles have, as well as the actual specific primary qualities of perceptual objects.[1] Particles have shape, size, motion

---

[1] Harré's way of putting the resemblance relation for Locke is to say that the perceived 'quality is the perceptual counterpart of the property' of the object, e.g. the 'objective counterpart of the sensation, quality or idea of resistance is mechanical impenetrability, that is physical resistance. Both real property and perceptual counterpart are resistances' (*op. cit.* p. 101). The notion of 'perceptual counterpart' needs elaboration but I take it to indicate that my perception discloses the nature of the quality of the perceived object. In discussing Newton's views on the 'perceptible and tangible aspects of matter', J. E. McGuire interprets Newton in a similar way: 'These qualities [hardness and resistance] have as an objective

in the same way that perceptual objects do. Mandelbaum is of course correct in saying the resemblance relation is not like an image or like a plaster-cast when we are talking of ideas and particles. The move Mandelbaum makes, from his general thesis about atomism to the claim that Locke did not hold that particles are in principle observable, is obscure. He offers Locke's comments about microscopical observation in support of the general thesis. I would think those comments of Locke clearly tell us not only that they are observable in principle but indicate some of the perceptual changes that occur under the microscope.

Locke points out that under the microscope some of the secondary qualities would change, e.g. what we take to be the colour of blood with the naked eye alters when examined under the microscope. Mandelbaum says that Locke said the particles would change shape too, but I cannot see that the passage Mandelbaum cites (2.23.12) says anything about shape; it mentions texture and motion (p. 19). Mandelbaum of course wants to say the shape changes from the shape of the perceived object. This may be true, but Locke does not say so. Mandelbaum discredits the perceived object in Locke's account; at least, he identifies the real shape of the object, as well as the real object, with the particles.[1] In talking of resemblance between idea and quality (including quality of particles) Locke is 'putting forward a doctrine concerning the relation between the perceived shape of an object' (p. 24) and the shape quality of the particles, though it is not a relation that reveals the specific shape of any particle. Mandelbaum draws this conclusion eventually: the ideas of primary qualities vis-à-vis particles 'represent features of an independent physical world' (p. 26). 'Physical world' is taken by Mandelbaum to be the particles only. The relation is more properly between idea and quality, but if my idea of shape resembles the shape of the perceived object, and if there is a similar though less specific relation between my idea of shape and the shape of particles, I would think this second relation must

counterpart in the physical world solid and tangible bodies which can interact with one another' ('Body and Void and Newton's De Mundi Systemate', *Archive for History of Exact Sciences*, v.3, 1966, 234).

[1] For a further discussion of this feature of Mandelbaum's analysis and of Locke's concept of object, see below, pp. 124–6.

hold between perceived object and particles. I do not want to give the impression that I think the resemblance relation is entirely clear or without its difficulties, but it does seem to me that Mandelbaum has misled his readers. Perhaps clarity could be achieved only if we talked of two resemblance relations: (1) *resemblance as likeness* and (2) *resemblance of kind*, the former holding between idea and perceptual object, the latter between the same idea (and also between the quality of the perceptual object) and the particles.

That the relation between ideas and particles is not resemblance as likeness is clear from Locke's commenting that, if we were to think of ourselves or of angels as having microscopical eyes, we would find ourselves in 'a quite different world from other people', the 'visible *ideas* of everything would be different', the 'appearance and outward scheme of things would have quite another face to us' (2.23.12).[1] Microscopical eyes (and other similarly intensified sense organs) would handicap if not paralyse us for action. Discovery by microscopes is useful only when we can relate those discoveries to our ordinary world, in particular when those discoveries would enable us to understand why bodies have and present the qualities they do. Extension is one of the original qualities of body, a quality caused by the cohesion of particles. Microscopical investigation of the minute particles of body will be helpful only if it reveals 'how the solid parts of body are united and cohere together to make extension' (2.23.23). Locke recognised that *explanations* of cohesion are, in a limited sense, possible. For example, 'the pressure of the particles of air may account for the *cohesion of several parts of matter* that are grosser than the particles of air', but our explanation cannot, as it must if it is to be an adequate one, tell us how the particles of air themselves cohere. If we resort to 'the pressure of the aether, or any subtiler matter than air', as a way of explaining how the particles of air are held together, we have then to account for the cohesion of the parts of the aether. Thus, the hypothesis that cohesion of parts is to be explained in terms of the pressure of external insensible

---

[1] Cf. Hooke, 'The Present State of Natural Philosophy', p. 8: 'if there were another Species of Intelligent Creature in the World, they might have quite another kind of Apprehension of the same thing'. Given other kinds of sense organs, we would, Hooke suggests, have different conceptions of things (p. 9).

bodies is inadequate because it leaves the cohesion of the external bodies unexplained. The external pressure hypothesis is inadequate on other grounds: '*the pressure of any ambient fluvia*, how great soever, *can be no* intelligible *cause of the cohesion of the solid parts of matter*' (24). His reason for rejecting external pressure as sufficient is that this would not prevent the separation by a motion in a line parallel to the pressure. Thus, 'if there were no other cause of cohesion, all parts of bodies must be easily separable by such a lateral sliding motion'. To understand the extension of body requires us to understand how the particles are held together. It is a matter of fact that the parts of bodies I observe do cohere, how this is done is far from clear (25). The microscope has not made such a discovery and, Locke suggests, such a discovery is far off, perhaps not even being a matter of discovery but of hypothesis, requiring as it does an explanation of the consolidation of 'the least particle of matter that exists' (26).

Locke was close to saying the *understanding* of matter is of a different order from the observation of body. Holding that we no more understand how spirit communicates motion than we do how body does, Locke comments: 'Constant experience makes us sensible of both of these, though our narrow understandings can comprehend neither' (28). He speaks throughout these passages on cohesion of 'making it intelligible', ending by asserting that it is incomprehensible.[1] Matter and motion were as much as the

---

[1] Cf. *Second Reply to the Bishop of Worcester, Works*, IV, 465–6: 'If God cannot join things together by connexions inconceivable to us, we must deny even the consistency and being of matter itself since every particle of it having some bulk, has its parts connected by ways inconceivable to us.' Locke considered several explanations of cohesion—external pressure, the infinitude of matter—rejecting them, as we have seen, as inadequate. He does not cite the accounts Boyle gave. In opposition to the appeal to a substantial form as a way of keeping the parts of body united, Boyle said 'That the contrivance of conveniently figured parts, and in some cases their juxta-position, may, without the assistance of a substantial Form, be sufficient' (*Origine*, p. 95). The 'roughness and the irregularity of corpuscles' was also said to be that on which cohesion depends (*Mechanical Origin of Volatility and Fixedness*, 1675, *Works*, IV, 306, quoted by M. Boas, 'The Establishment of the Mechanical Philosophy', *Osiris*, X, 1952, 474). Boyle also claimed motion was adequate for cohesion, a very slow motion of the particles being adequate (see M. Boas, *ibid.*). Locke followed Boyle on most aspects of the account of matter, but it is clear that these attempts at accounting for cohesion by Boyle would not meet Locke's demand for an account of how the least particle coheres. Hooke and Newton also offered explanations of cohesion or 'congruity'. Locke's

corpuscular theory could contribute to our understanding. An explanation of the solidity of matter was lacking. Locke may seem to be too cautious in concluding that 'the simple *ideas* we receive from sensation and reflection are the boundaries of our thought' (29), since he made use of theories which went beyond those boundaries, but in point of fact the corpuscular theory did not go beyond the possible boundaries of sense and reflection. The entities postulated by that theory differ only in size, not in kind, from sensible objects. The qualities they were said to have were the same as macro-objects have. The insensible particles are beyond the reach of our ordinary perception, the microscope had not revealed the particles of every object. Even did we have microscopical eyes, and hence actually saw (or otherwise sensed) the internal constitution of bodies, our sensation and reflection would still be the boundaries of our thought about body, since we would not have penetrated to the cause of consolidation and cohesion of the particles (that 'which ties them together', 4.6.9) we were then seeing. The conclusion is tempting: that this feature of body is not observable in principle. Two conclusions *are* clear: (1) we in fact do not observe the inner workings of the bodies we meet with, and (2) we do not, even with Boyle's help, understand those workings. It is this double conclusion that Locke has in mind when he says that we do not know the real essence of any body (3.6), that we have no clear distinct idea of the 'supposed something' (the substratum) to which the observed qualities of body belong.

Mandelbaum thinks it 'fundamentally mistaken' to ascribe substratum talk to physical objects. The notion of a substratum is, he suggests, 'an indeterminate notion connected with our sensible

objections would seem to cut against their explanations as well (cf. Galileo's references to 'a gluey or viscous substance which binds' the parts of body; also his citing the principle that nature abhors a vacuum. *The Two New Sciences*, 1954, pp. 11–13). The explanation of cohesion seems to have been a problem up to and even after Newton. Millington points out that by 1690 (i.e. with the publication of Huygens's *Traité*) 'Speculation...was...reaching a deadlock, successive elaborations of aether theories and mechanical theories leading no nearer the solution of the problem of cohesion. None saw this more clearly than John Locke' ('Studies in Cohesion from Democritus to Laplace', *Lychnos*, 1944–5, p. 68). Millington points out as well that the objection which Locke raised, about external pressure not precluding a lateral displacement, was raised by Huygens against Papin. (I am indebted to Mr Russell Keat for calling this article to my attention.)

ideas of such qualities' (p. 41, note). What he seems to mean is that the idea of substratum is 'a surrogate for what in the object is material and exists independently of us' (p. 39). Mandelbaum even cites 2.23.3 as evidence that Locke did link the notion of substrate with that of the inner atomic constitution of things, though Mandelbaum thinks this not conclusive evidence and he himself seems not to want to accept it. But Mandelbaum's notion of a surrogate, ambiguous as that notion is, to stand for that which is material and independent of us in objects supplies all we need to reach the conclusion about substance which I have suggested. We know that Locke's analysis of matter is corpuscular. Thus, if 'substance' is a term which stands for matter, substance must be corpuscular. There is for Locke a conceptual necessity in our idea of quality, requiring a subject to which qualities belong. That is the epistemic side to the analysis of body. On the ontological side, qualities and properties do not exist by themselves, they flow from and belong to matter. Locke did not find substratum talk informative for this ontological point. He sought to find a meaningful substitute for it in the talk of particles cohering together. In this scientific translation, it is the cohesion of the particles which is unknown and unknowable for man. There is nothing fundamentally mistaken in saying the real essence is 'hidden away in the unknowable but necessary substratum', though it is more precise to talk of the unknowability of real essences because of our inability to understand how particles cohere.

Whether my interpretation of what it is in bodies that is unknown for Locke is accepted or not (and whether the reader is satisfied with my identification of substance with the inner constitution of particles), it is quite clear that for Locke our knowledge of body is inadequate for a deductive science of body.[1]

---

[1] Whether a knowledge and understanding of cohering particles of a body would be adequate for providing Locke with the deductive knowledge of body he was at pains to deny that man can have is a question I examine in the next chapter. It was of course commonplace after Locke to assert a scepticism of substance (see my *John Locke and the Way of Ideas*, chapter IV, sect. 2). Cf. Newton: 'What the real substance of anything is we know not. In bodies we see only their figures and colours, we hear only the sounds, we touch only their outward surfaces...but their inward substances are not to be known either by our senses, or by any reflect act of our minds.' (*Principia*, 1713, p. 483. Quoted by Koyré, *Newtonian Studies*, p. 159.)

Locke does not regret this lack in man's knowledge because he does not think we need it for action, action being one of the main concerns for Locke, the second main division of the sciences. Moreover we are able to see the importance of studying nature carefully, rather than trying to find some principles from which to derive truths about nature. Experiment and observation become all-important. An observational science of nature is not only possible, the Royal Society had been advancing that science since its beginnings around 1660.[1] The aims of that society were to replace the 'Philosophy of discourse *and* disputation', as one of its members, Robert Hooke, explained, because it pays too much attention to '*the subtility of its Deductions and Conclusions*' and too little attention to the first ground-work of knowledge, sense and memory.[2] Another member of the society, Henry Power, referred to the 'old Dogmatists and Notional Speculators', saying that instead of 'Solid and Experimental philosophy' these dogmatists and rational scientists wrangled about 'Perepatitick Qualities'.[3] These men, Power went on to say, 'daily stuff our Libraries with their Philosophical Romances and glut the Press with their Canting Loquacities'.[4] Power ends his detailed study of microscopic, mercurial and magnetic phenomena with an expression of the spirit of the Royal Society: 'These are the days that must lay a new Foundation of a more magnificent Philosophy...that will Empirically and sensibly canvas the *Phaenomena* of Nature, deducing the Causes of things from such originals in Nature, as we observe are producible by Art, and the infallible demonstration of Mechanicks...' (p. 192). In his *History of the Royal Society* Thomas Sprat also complained of the 'Notional Warr' of dis-

---

[1] Locke was elected a member in 1668. The most useful discussion I have discovered of the early period of the society is C. Webster's long review article of Margery Purver's *The Royal Society, Concept and Creation* (1967), in *History of Science,* ed. Crombie and Hoskin, VI (1967), 106–28.

[2] *Micrographia* (1665), Preface.

[3] *Experimental Philosophy* (1664), p. 186. E. Maynwaring, *Praxis Medicorum* (1671), speaks of such a person as a 'meer *notional* man, a *Prescribe,* a *Book* Physician, that draws all his skill out of his *Library*'(p. 95). A good discussion of Power's philosophy is found in C. Webster's 'Henry Power's Experimental Philosophy', *Ambix,* XIV (1967), 150–78.

[4] Cohen points out that for Newton, the phrase 'philosophical romance' referred to 'an hypothesis that produces an arbitrary theory in the absence of experience' (*Franklin and Newton,* p. 139). J. E. McGuire tells me that Huygens used it against Descartes' *Principles.*

putants where too much attention was paid to 'general Terms, which had not much foundation in Nature' (pp. 16–17). The members of the Royal Society have 'turn'd their thoughts, from Words, to experimental Philosophy' (p. 56, cf. p. 105). Sprat characterised disputing as 'a very good instrument, to sharpen mens wits, and to make them versatil, and wary defenders of the Principles, which they already know: but it can never much augment the solid substance of Science itself...' (p. 18). Molyneux contrasts the experimental method of the new societies (the Royal Society and the Dublin Society to which he belonged), a method which he says was concerned with actions instead of words, with the method of the Schools which was more concerned with 'Dispute and Verbose empty Stuff, than in any Curious Discovery of Natures Actions' (Sciothericum Telescopium, 1686, Epistle). The common charge against the traditional philosophers of nature made by the defenders of science as practised by the members of the Royal Society was twofold: (1) they get lost in words and language, mistaking, as Locke later said, words for things and (2) they occupy their time with disputing about trivial or general theories unchecked by observation. The vanity of dogmatising (the title of one of Joseph Glanvill's defences of the Royal Society) rather than the solidity of discovering what there is and how it works by going to the things themselves: such was the frequent form the polemic took.

Notional conjecture was to be replaced by experimental and observational knowledge, 'raising a Structure of Natural Philosophy, by the Collections of Experiments of all sorts',[1] a persistent theme in all of the writing about science by those on the side of the moderns. Glanvill said there are two ways whereby knowledge can be advanced: '(1) By enlarging the History of Things: And (2) By improving Intercourse and Communications'.[2] Natural history is said by Glanvill to report 'the Appearances, and is fundamentally necessary to all the Designs of Science' (p. 51). Instead of the old way of turning inwards upon itself and conversing with its own ideas, science must now 'be raised from the Observations and Applications of Sense, and take its Account from Things as they are in the sensible World' (p. 52). Instances 'must be aggregated,

---

[1] Simpson, Hydrologia Chymica, Preface.   [2] Plus Ultra (1668), p. 9.

compared, and critically *inspected'.* Boyle speaks repeatedly of 'natural histories of qualities'. Any object or event whatsoever could be put into the natural history, as Hooke remarked in 'The Present State of Natural Philosophy' (p. 21). Natural histories were not restricted to medicine (as Mandelbaum seems to suggest) or to the collections of naturalists (as Givner appears to think).[1] A history was a careful recording of observations of objects, of their properties under different conditions, and of their behaviour. To record and tabulate these observations was considered to be the first important stage in any science. Boyle's histories of qualities and Hooke's descriptions of microscopical phenomena were only two of the more important instances of Royal Society scientists who asserted and practised this Baconian doctrine.[2]

Hooke prefaced his account of his microscopical discoveries on plants, hair, wood, stone, and many other objects by saying that what is needed in science is not so much imagination or exact method as '*a sincere Hand, and a* faithful *Eye, to examine, and to record, the things themselves as they appear'.*[3] His intention was to employ his senses aright. '*The truth is, the Science of Nature has been already too long made only a work of the* Brain *and the* Fancy: *It is now high time that it should return to the plainness and soundness of* observations *on* material *and* obvious *things.'*[4] In presenting his work to

[1] See Givner, 'Scientific Preconceptions in Locke's Philosophy of Language', *Journal of the History of Ideas,* XXIII (1962), 345. Givner cites A. R. Hall's *The Scientific Revolution* where Hall identifies fact-gathering and natural histories with 'the biological sciences' (pp. 167, 304) and with botany (p. 281).

[2] In characterising this doctrine as Baconian, we must be careful not to confuse the method of natural histories with Bacon's inductivism, with his account of the way hypotheses and explanations will emerge from the collected information of the histories. Webster thinks the Baconian attitudes were a façade employed by the Royal Society, 'a defence mechanism against critics', rather than 'a genuine expression of the natural philosophy of its members' ('Henry Power's Experimental Philosophy', *loc. cit.* p. 177). There was of course much diversity among the members, but I think there can be little doubt that Boyle and Hooke in particular did collect information with the intent to build natural histories.

[3] Unless noted, the citations from Hooke are to the unnumbered pages of the Preface to *Micrographia.*

[4] The concern with ordinary objects is also an important feature of the programme of constructing natural or philosophical histories. The publisher, H. Hall, of Boyle's *Origine* complains (in his Preface) that the speculations of the Schools failed to explain '*the ordinary* Phaenomena *which* Nature *every day presents the world with'.*

the more general public with the official approval of the Royal Society, Hooke avowed a modesty very similar to (even verbally so) Locke's under-labourer claim.

As for my part, I have obtained my end, if these my small Labours shall be thought fit to take up some place in the large stock of natural observations, which so many hands are busie in providing. If I have contributed the meanest foundations whereon others may raise nobler superstructures, I am abundantly satisfied; and all my ambition is that I may serve the great Philosophers of this Age as the makers and grinders of my Glasses did to me...[1]

Hooke saw his microscopical observations and descriptions contributing to the overall aim of the Royal Society of increasing the natural histories of bodies. Locke viewed his epistemological analysis as playing a similar, modest role in explaining what the new science was doing. While Locke accepted the corpuscular hypothesis, it is observation not theory which he praised as the way of acquiring knowledge of body. Locke thought that a man 'accustomed to rational and regular experiments, shall be able to see further into the nature of bodies and guess righter at their yet unknown properties than one that is a stranger to them' (4.12.10).[2] He also allowed that hypotheses, 'if they are well made, are at least great helps to the memory and often direct us to

[1] Whether Hooke (or Locke) was sincere in this statement of humility may be doubted, the modesty-trope was a standard literary device (see Rosalie Colie, 'The Essayist in his Essay', in *John Locke: Problems and Perspectives*, pp. 243–5). The under-labourer theme was common also at the time. That theme was used by Glanvill in defending the Royal Society (*Plus Ultra*, pp. 91–2) and Thomas Sprat found some praise for the 'modern dogmatists' who 'have made the ground open, and cleer, for us: they have removed the rubbish' (*op. cit.* pp. 28–9, 94). There are other Lockean sounding phrases in Hooke's short Preface. He talks of 'the true nature of things themselves', says that nature is too large to be comprehended, that our thoughts are confined to a small space. Besides being fellow members of the Royal Society, Locke had both Power's and Hooke's books in his library. Hooke records in his Diary a number of meetings with Locke (see *The Diary of Robert Hooke*, ed. Robinson and Adams, 1935, pp. 5, 11, 16, 44, 54, 65, 155, 185, 401, 412, 416, 449). These meetings range from 1672 to 1680. In a later portion of his Diary, Hooke records speaking to Locke in May 1689, and other entries indicate his interest in the published *Essay* (*The Life and Work of Robert Hooke*, Part IV, by R. T. Gunther, in *Early Science in Oxford*, 1935, X, 122,
[2] 177, 232, 254).
Hooke thought that those well skilled in all the sciences, who were acquainted with the various hypotheses, suppositions, collections, and ways of reasoning in the sciences, would be better able to explain phenomena: 'For by this Means the Mind will be somewhat more ready at guessing at the Solution of many Phenomena almost at first sight' ('The Present State of Natural Philosophy', p. 19).

new discoveries' (13). Any hypothesis we accept must not be taken up

> *too hastily* (which the mind, that would always penetrate into the causes of things and have principles to rest on, is very apt to do) till we have very well examined particulars and made several experiments in that thing which we would explain by our hypothesis and see whether it will agree to them all, whether our principles will carry us quite through and not be as inconsistent with one *phenomenon* of nature, as they seem to accommodate and explain another (13).[1]

Early in Book 2, Locke warns against the improper use of hypotheses. There he considers the question whether the soul always thinks, a consequence of the Cartesian doctrine that thought is the essence of the soul. Locke did not consider this question a metaphysical one; rather, it is a question about a matter of fact. The Cartesian definition becomes an hypothesis which settles the question out of hand. We could just as well suppose that 'all watches, whilst the balance beats, think, and it is sufficiently proved and past doubt that my watch thought all last night' (2. 1. 10). Locke issues a warning about hypotheses similar to the one in 4. 12. 13: 'But he that would not deceive himself ought to build his hypothesis on matter of fact and make it out by sensible experience and not presume on matter of fact because of his

---

[1] Hooke referred to the rules of the Royal Society, expecially that of 'avoiding *Dogmatizing*, and the *espousal* of any *Hypothesis* not sufficiently grounded and confirm'd by *Experiments*'. Boyle was equally cautious about hypotheses: 'And whatever applause is wont in this age to attend a forwardness to assert hypotheses, yet, though fame were less to be sought than truth, this will not much more be, whilst I observe, that hypotheses hastily pitched upon do seldom keep their reputation long; and divers of them, that are highly applauded at the first, come, after a while, to be forsaken, even by those that devised them' (*Works*, II, 239, quoted by Jones, *op. cit.* p. 314 n. 71). In *Certain Physiological Essays* (1661), Boyle says that one of the best services that natural philosophers can perform for mankind is 'to set themselves diligently and industriously to make Experiments and collect Observations, without being over-forward to establish Principles and Axioms, believing it uneasie to erect such Theories as are capable to explicate all the Phaenomena of Nature, before they have been able to take notice of the tenth part of those Phaenomena that are to be explicated' (p. 8, quoted by Jones, p. 313 n. 69). Jones also quotes from a letter of Cudworth to Boyle: 'The writers of hypotheses in natural philosophy will be confuting one another a long time, before the world will ever agree, if ever it do. But your pieces of natural history are unconfutable, and will afford the best grounds to build hypotheses upon' (p. 315 n. 79). These remarks are all representative of what one finds throughout most of Boyle's works.

hypothesis, that is, because he supposes it to be so;...' (2.1.10). It is not clear what sort of hypothesis might aid in answering this particular question about the soul's thinking, since Locke seems to insist that the only ground for saying the soul always thinks is that he perceives it to be so: 'no definitions that I know, no suppositions of any sect, are of force enough to destroy constant experience; and perhaps, it is the affectation of knowing beyond what we perceive that makes so much useless dispute and noise in the world' (2.1.19). This injunction about not going beyond what we perceive is a general rule for Locke about discovery, even though in the particular case of the soul's always thinking, for Locke it is a conceptual truth that to think is to be conscious that I am thinking (18, 19). It may be that he has in mind some hypothesis which would suggest how the soul operates, similar to the corpuscular hypothesis about matter which offered an account of how matter operates. Locke thought the corpuscularian hypothesis a useful one in explaining the observed properties and operations of body, although it did not give any insight at all into the matter of cohesion or consolidation. But the aspect of science which interested Locke was not the formation of hypotheses, however carefully they were constructed. There is in the *Essay* no analysis of knowledge by hypotheses, no account of the formation of hypotheses; there is extensive material on classification in terms of observable properties. Repeatedly Locke tells us how to enlarge our knowledge, but in only a few instances does he cite the formation or use of hypotheses.[1] We are to 'be informed by observation and experience, and not make [our] own hypotheses the rule of nature' (2.1.21; cf. 4.12.14). The enlargement of our knowledge of bodies is done by noting coexisting qualities.

Locke's stress upon collecting information rather than using hypotheses was perhaps an over-reaction to the Schools' predominance. The pretence that discoveries could be made without

---

[1] Writing of Hooke, M. B. Hesse remarks: 'It is noticeable that the various discussions of "method" which he puts before the Royal Society in the early 1660s go no further than a "Method of making Experiments" and the like, and contain no commitments about a method of constructing theories. This is understandable, in view of Hooke's evident anxiety at this time, expressed in the preface to the *Micrographia*, to avoid bringing upon himself the strictures against speculation and hypothesis-making which were frequently heard in the early Royal Society' ('Hooke's Philosophical Algebra', *Isis*, LVII, 1966, 75).

observation, that principles of reason and logic could yield deductions true of the world was, of course, the main opposition against which Locke and most of the writers on science wrote. A more effective reaction might have been to show how good hypotheses should and could be constructed and used. Locke appreciated the fact that when hypotheses are to be used, they must be carefully based upon observation. Nevertheless, he remained wary of hypotheses. His hesitation about, even distrust of, hypotheses and general theories appears in a letter to Molyneux. Locke speaks of general theories as a 'sort of waking dreams'. He stresses again that any useful hypotheses must be built upon 'the established history of diseases' (he was there discussing Sydenham).[1] Knowledge of bodies (which typifies science for Locke) starts with noting coexisting qualities and ends with some tentative generalisations about their coexistence. No hypothesis is used in the *Essay*, save the corpuscular one. Locke does discuss several hypotheses about the cohesion of matter, setting them all aside after showing that they were all incomplete, that they left some bit of matter still unexplained. His treatment there is rational and analytic, not empirical. Locke also advances the occasional conjecture which goes beyond experience and observation. For example, he suggests that perception marks man off from animals (2.9.15); that bodily states affect our memories (2.10.5); that the speed of succession of ideas through the mind has both

[1] See letter of 20 January 1692/3, *Works*, IX, 463–4. Sydenham's diagnostic methods attracted Locke (they were friends from 1667) just because they moved away from the traditional attitudes of relying upon maxims and principles. Sydenham insisted upon getting 'as genuine and natural a description, or history of all diseases, as can be procured' (*Works*, ed. John Swan, 1842, p. iii). This historical method will enable the physician to reduce all diseases to certain and determinate kinds' (p. iv). The description of diseases must be done 'with the utmost accuracy; imitating in this the great exactness of painters, who, in their pictures copy the smallest spots of moles in the originals' (p. v). Hypotheses are accepted only when they arise out of the careful observation of diseases, their symptoms and circumstances (pp. v, 474). It is 'experience derived from the solid testimony of the senses' that we should seek; all the knowledge of nature we can acquire 'is to be had only from experience', human knowledge being 'restrained to the narrow limits of knowledge, derivable from the senses' (pp. 484–6). Sydenham, in other words, employed what Locke called the argument from the nature of things themselves. Locke praised Sydenham's method to Molyneux in several letters, see *Works*, IX, pp. 459, 461, 464–5. For an informative and detailed discussion of Sydenham's views on method, see R. M. Yost, 'Sydenham's Philosophy of Science', *Osiris*, IX (1950), 84–105.

an upper and a lower limit (2.14.9, 10); that thinking is the action of the soul, not its essence (2.19.4); that created spirits are not totally separate from matter (2.23.28). The programme of the Royal Society did not exclude the formation and use of hypotheses, although that was more a future goal than a present practice. The need was for careful observations. Boyle frequently offers explanations of what he has discovered in the laboratory by reference to the corpuscular hypothesis. Hooke and Power hardly ever use that hypothesis, though they often seek to explain what their microscopes have recorded in terms of physical, physiological and biological mechanisms.

Hooke frequently offers suggestions about the causes of observed phenomena, explanations of what his microscope had disclosed. These explanations are always based upon careful observation. In fact the reasons or explanations for some phenomena refer, in most cases, to features of the objects seen through the microscope. For example, in Observation III ('Of fine lawn, or Linen Cloth'), Hooke discusses a manufactured silk flaxen. When this flaxen is twisted into threads, it loses its lustre 'and becomes as plain and base a thread to look on, as one of the same bigness, made of common Flax' (*op. cit.* p. 5). The reason for this phenomenon is that, whereas the parts of ordinary silk are '*small, hard, transparent*, and to their bigness proportionally *stiff*' so that each part or filament preserves its figure and reflection entire, even when twisted into thread, the parts of manufactured flax are '*flat, limber, softer*, and *less transparent*, and in twisting into a thread they joyn, and lie so close together, as to lose their own, and destroy each others particular reflections' (p. 6). A similar observation (his Observation V) on watered silks notes the way in which this kind of cloth appears dark in one part, light in another, and how those dark and light patches change. These are phenomena observed with the naked eye. With the microscope, we can easily discover the reason for this phenomenon: it

proceeds onely from the variety of the *Reflections* of light, which is caus'd by the various *shapes of the particles*, or little protuberant parts of the thread that compose the surface; and these parts of the waves [of the cloth] that appear the brighter throw toward the eye a multitude of small reflections of light, whereas the darker scarce afford any (pp. 8–9).

He goes on to give a detailed account of how watering affects those parts and hence their reflecting powers. In Observation VIII, what the fiery sparks are that result when steel is struck with flint, the microscope reveals to be bits of the steel. Hooke calls this an 'hypothesis' but it is in effect a discovery of what is the case by observation with the microscope.[1] At the end of his remarks on his account of petrified wood and other bodies (Observation XVII), after having suggested ways in which petrification probably takes place, Hooke raises a question about nature's designs in this process, about the function such a process may serve. Confessing man's ignorance of the purpose or function of these processes, he says:

> It were therefore very desirable, that a good collection of such kind of figur'd stones were collected; and as many particulars, circumstances, and informations collected with them as could be obtained, that from such a History of Observations well rang'd, examin'd and digested, the true original or production of all those kinds of stones might be perfectly and surely known... (p. 112).

The scientific scene in the seventeenth century was diverse; mathematical and deductive techniques ran alongside empirical and experimental ones. Hypotheses about the causes of specific phenomena appear along with careful recording of observations.

By the latter part of the seventeenth century, physical scientists were becoming wary of 'thought experiments'. Boyle, Hooke, and Newton —major exponents of the British empirical school—took pains to describe in detail all aspects of their experiments: the nature and con-

---

[1] Hooke also used the method of hypothesis and sometimes argued by analogy to explanations. In Observation VI, 'Of Small Glass Canes', the explanation for the fact that water rises less quickly and less high in small tubes of glass than in large ones is that the unequal heights are caused by the difference of pressure of air outside and inside the glass tube. He then describes an experiment which shows that there is an unequal pressure and that the height of the water does vary with that pressure. This was done by showing that water is attracted more to glass than is air, the concept of congruity (cohesion) being appealed to. The congruity of air to glass is greater for water than for air. Congruity is then explicated (I do not think it is explained) by means of an analogy with a swirling dish of sand (pp. 11–16). That Hooke had no intention of resting with natural histories, or even with causal explanations of specific phenomena, is clear from a number of his observations (e.g. the thirteenth) and also from the announced programme of a philosophical algebra. Hesse is confident that that algebra was to be the deductive testing of hypotheses extracted from or stimulated by the natural histories (*op. cit.*).

struction of their apparatus and instruments, the very steps taken and the minutiae of observation...[1]

Cohen has the Newton of the *Opticks* in mind more than of the *Principia*. There was a marked difference between Newton generally and others like Boyle and Hooke.

The difference, in short, can be boiled down to an extremely characteristic trait of Newton: the fact that he measures, whereas Boyle and Hooke do not. They describe, admire, and explain the lovely colors of birds' feathers, of metals, of mica—and, though Hooke's explanation of the appearance of colors in plates of mica...and soap bubbles is remarkably good, it is not based on measurements.[2]

Newton was just as good an observer, even more precise because of the measurements he made. The Bacon–Boyle approach, incorporated into the Royal Society, was for 'the systematization of knowledge and the collection of "histories" of all sorts of natural phenomena and of trades'.[3] A clear formulation of the method is found in a letter of Newton to Oldenburg:

For the best and safest method of philosophizing seems to be, first, diligently to investigate the properties of things, and establish them by experiment, and then to seek hypotheses to explain them. For hypotheses ought to be fitted merely to explain the properties of things, and not attempt to predetermine them except in so far as they can be an aid to experiments.[4]

The official policy of the Royal Society, in so far as that can be gleaned from the statements of some of its more active members (Boyle, Hooke, Power) and from Sprat's account, was for natural histories, the collection of data. Sprat characterised observation as 'the great Foundation of knowledge' (p. 20), said the purpose of the members was 'to make faithful *Records*, of all the Works of *Nature*, or *Art*, which can come within their reach' (p. 61; cf. pp. 85, 89, 97, 99). Hypotheses and explanations about the causes and operation of the objects and events recorded were of course offered, and were carefully debated at their meetings. But it was the making of natural histories which Sprat said was their main

[1] Cohen, *Franklin and Newton* (1966), p. 8. Cf. Koyré, *Newtonian Studies*, pp. 11–12.
[2] Koyré, p. 42.   [3] Cohen, p. 108.
[4] Letter of 2 June 1672, quoted by Cohen, pp. 155–6.

intent. 'And as their purpose was, to heap up a mixt Mass of *Experiments*, without digesting them into any perfect model: so to this end, they confin'd themselves to no order of subjects; and whatever they have recorded, they have done it, not as compleat Schemes of opinions, but as bare unfinish'd Histories' (p. 115).[1] Sprat's formulation is something of an exaggeration of some of the actual practices of the members of the society, although many of the virtuosi of that group did in fact proceed just as Sprat describes. Locke had the virtuoso's curiosity about a wide range of phenomena.[2] It was the stress upon the need for careful histories of observations which attracted Locke's attention when he came to ask himself questions about knowledge and reality.[3]

Just as Hooke and Boyle sought to explain the phenomena they observed, so Locke was not rejecting explanation and hypothesis from the science of nature. In part, he was objecting to the notion common at this time that all knowledge, whether of the physical world or not, was to be derived from basic axioms or maxims.

[1] Another member of the Royal Society and friend of Locke, writing in 1692, William Molyneux, emphasised this same aspect of science. Natural philosophy, he said, proceeds by observation, experiment and history as a method of obtaining 'the Knowledge of the Properties and Affections of Natural Bodies'. Molyneux recognised that some people say that natural philosophy is also concerned with assigning 'the true Reasons or Causes of these Properties'. But he is very sceptical of the success of this attempt, suggesting that all sorts of conjectures can be made but says 'these deserve not the Name of Natural Philosophy; they serve only for Chat and Diversion' (from the Dedication to his *Dioptica Nova*).

[2] Cf. Laslett, 'The Great Recoinage, and the Origins of the Board of Trade', in *John Locke: Problems and Perspectives*, p. 157: 'Locke was a virtuoso and a savant rather than an applied scientist as we now know them.'

[3] Certainly in their statements, but also I think in much of their practice, the making of natural histories was a more characteristic feature of the Royal Society scientists than was the appeal to the corpuscular theory of matter. The corpuscular view was the general framework within which the scientists operated. In this sense, Cohen is right in saying 'The "new science" or the "new philosophy" which Newton called "experimental philosophy" was simply a "Corpuscular philosophy"' (*op. cit.* p. 145). Boyle may have been alone, as Mandelbaum suggests, in trying to support or justify the corpuscular theory. Most of the other scientists simply accepted it and got on with the task of observing and recording. It is the programme of natural histories which caught Locke's eye. Mandelbaum suggests that to read Locke as concerned with natural histories only may be a result of looking at Locke's historical method in the context of his interest in Sydenham's techniques in medicine (pp. 7–8). I am suggesting that this is a misreading of Locke and overlooks the announced method of the Royal Society. It is also a misunderstanding of what a 'natural history' was for the seventeenth century.

Such was what a rational science of nature (as opposed to an experimental science) meant for Locke. This method of deducing from principles was not, Locke believed, a fruitful one for discovery. The method of deducing from principles was not, of course, the same as the method of hypothesis. Having so clearly accepted the corpuscular hypothesis, did Locke not also grant the usefulness of hypotheses in explanation and discovery? As Laurens Laudan points out, there are a number of statements in the *Essay* which show Locke's awareness of the nature and use of hypotheses.[1] Laudan's article is useful in directing our attention to Locke's account of the science of nature, but he is not as clear as he might be about the difference between (*a*) accepting the corpuscular hypothesis, (*b*) recommending that hypothesis as a tool for empirical discovery, and (*c*) accepting the role of hypotheses in scientific explanation and discovery. Laudan moves easily from (*a*) and (*c*) to (*b*). The *specific* issue raised by Laudan is whether Locke used the corpuscular hypothesis, or whether he saw it as being used, in the science of discovery. The more *general* issue Laudan raises is whether Locke found any room in his account of science for hypotheses, whether Locke was opposed 'to the use of virtually all hypotheses in science' (p. 211).

There can be no question about Locke's acceptance of the corpuscular theory as an account of the nature of matter and as an explanation of the causation of perception. I can find no evidence that the account of the science of nature Locke gives recommended using the corpuscular hypothesis as a way of discovering new observable qualities of bodies. Nor did Locke's account urge us to use, or say that scientists were using, that hypothesis to explain all phenomena in the natural histories. R. M. Yost, against whom Laudan writes,[2] is correct in denying that Locke believed 'that the employment of hypotheses about sub-microscopic events would accelerate the acquisition of

---

[1] 'The Nature and Sources of Locke's Views on Hypotheses,' *Journal of the History of Ideas*, XXVIII, no. 2 (April–June 1967), 211–23.

[2] In an earlier publication ('The Science of Nature', in *John Locke: Problems and Perspectives*), I mistakenly said that Laudan identified Aaron, Gibson, and myself as among the anti-hypothesis interpreters of Locke. None of these three has of course ever denied that Locke accepted the corpuscular hypothesis, though none has given any discussion of Locke's account of scientific method.

empirical knowledge'.[1] In making this denial Yost does not mean Locke rejected the corpuscular hypothesis: Yost explicitly says Locke accepted it (p. 121). Yost's denial refers to a programme of scientific discovery, using the corpuscular hypothesis. Locke was not interested in, and certainly found no room in his account of knowledge for what Mandelbaum calls 'transdiction', the attempt to confirm the corpuscular hypothesis or to make inferences from observed to unobserved phenomena. As Yost says, Locke denied 'the possibility of discovering...the *specific* sub-microscopic mechanism that corresponds to observable species' (p. 123). Yost is correct in this remark, as he also is in saying that 'Whenever he [Locke] spoke of the method of increasing empirical knowledge, he recommended the "historical" method, not the "speculative" or "hypothetical" method' (p. 127).

Laudan cites 4.12.13 in evidence that Locke understood the 'true use of hypotheses', a passage in which Locke says hypotheses 'are at least great helps to the memory and often direct us to new discoveries'. In that passage Locke also remarks on the need to check any hypothesis against a variety of phenomena to be sure it is not falsified by some instance. Laudan is even more impressed by 4.16.12 where Locke cites the use of analogy in the construction of hypotheses. Locke speaks of the 'rule of analogy' and refers to the probability of hypotheses: 'This sort of probability, which is the best conduct of rational experiments, and the rise of hypothesis has also its use and influence; and a wary reasoning from analogy leads us often into the discovery of truths and useful productions, which would otherwise be concealed.' Laudan interprets this statement as explicitly saying 'that the use of corpuscular hypotheses could' lead to the discovery of truths (pp. 216–17). The total passage may possibly be construed that way, though that final statement does not mention the corpuscular hypothesis. It comes at the end of a discussion of the chain of being. Locke applies the rule of analogy to a wide variety of conjectures. 4.16.12 constitutes Locke's discussion of those probabilities not concerned with matters of fact, with things that can be observed. These unobservables range from 'finite

[1] 'Locke's Rejection of Hypotheses about Sub-Microscopic Events', *Journal of the History of Ideas*, XII (1951), 111.

immaterial beings without us; as spirits, angels, devils', to material beings remote from us, as 'plants, animals, and intelligent inhabitants in the planets and other mansions of the vast universe'; to the causes of observed objects. The corpuscular hypothesis is cited as an explanation of the sensible effects of objects.

At this point Locke gives two examples of the move from observed effects in bodies to corpuscular causes.

Thus, observing that the bare rubbing of two bodies violently one upon another produces heat, and very often fire itself, we have reason to think that what we call heat and fire consists in a violent agitation of the imperceptible minute parts of the burning matter; observing likewise that the different refractions of pellucid bodies produce in our eyes the different appearances of several colours, and also that the different ranging and laying the superficial parts of several bodies as of velvet, watered silk, etc., does the like, we think it probable that the colour and shining of bodies is in them nothing but the different arrangement and refraction of their minute and insensible parts.[1]

Just before these examples Locke had referred to the generation, nourishment, and motion of animals, to the attraction of iron to a lodestone, and to a burning candle that gives light and heat. The causes of these phenomena are all unknown but can be probably conjectured. Causal explanation in terms of unobservables can 'appear more or less probable only as they more or less agree to truths that are established in our minds and as they hold proportion to other parts of our knowledge and observation'. It is not clear to me what the truths might be to which the corpuscular hypothesis agrees. The analogy in the example of heat appears to be between the rubbing of bodies and the agitation of particles.[2]

[1] Locke must have had Hooke's observations on watered silk in mind in this last example.
[2] This analogy is somewhat curious, since if sensed heat is to be explained by the behaviour of particles it cannot be true that 'the bare rubbing of two bodies violently one upon another produces heat' and fire. Thus, the analogy between rubbing and agitation may help in the *conceiving* of particles, but the analogy of rubbing *causing* heat or fire and the agitation of particles *causing* the same, really cannot be used. Similar remarks hold for the 'light' example. If the different appearances of colours are produced in our eyes by the 'different ranging and laying the superficial [i.e. the observed] parts' of bodies, they cannot also be caused by the different arrangements and refractions of insensible parts. However

Assumed also perhaps is an analogy between observed bodies and unobserved particles, though elsewhere Locke says we do not have clear ideas of minute particles. 'In matter, we have no clear *ideas* of the smallness of parts much beyond the smallest that occur to any of our senses' (2.29.16). We have clear enough ideas of division and divisibility, 'yet we have but very obscure and confused *ideas* of corpuscles or minute bodies so to be divided, when, by former divisions, they are reduced to a smallness much exceeding the perception of any of our senses' (*ibid.*).

It is, according to Laudan, just 'because we can never get inside of nature's clock', that 'we must be content to hypothesize about the probable arrangements of its parts on the basis of its external cortex' (p. 217). But in those passages where Locke refers to the 'famous clock at *Strasbourg*' (a favourite example in the century), he does so to comment that did we have such a knowledge of the internal workings of bodies we would have an *a priori* knowledge of the observable effects of bodies (4.3.25) and be able to classify according to real essences (3.6.9). As it is, 'we can give no reason of the different qualities we find in them', e.g. 'what makes lead and antimony fusible, wood and stones not...what makes lead and iron malleable, antimony and stones

Locke may be distinguishing the *sensed* colour of bodies (i.e. the ideas) from 'the colour and shining of bodies', and the heat *felt* from the heat of bodies. If so, we may have to modify the usual reading of secondary qualities (see below, pp. 129–30). Elsewhere, Locke was more careful in his recommendation of analogy in natural philosophy, pointing out that we must 'take care that we keep ourselves within that wherein the analogy consists'. Concluding that because the acid oil of vitriol is good for certain uses, therefore the spirit of nitre or vinegar will also be good for the same purposes is a proper conclusion only if 'the good effect of it be owing wholly to the acidity of it' (*Conduct*, sect. 40). The other use of analogy in 4.16.12 has nothing to do with the science of nature. It deals with the 'scale of being' doctrine, claiming that that doctrine is made probable from the fact that 'in all parts of the creation that fall under human observation...there is a gradual connexion of one to another'. Analogy here might only permit us to say that, if there are other beings, the differences between them will likely also be small and gradual; but 3.6.12 (as also less explicitly, 4.16.12) does say that the notion that 'there should be more *species* of intelligent creatures above us than there are of sensible and material below us is probable to me from hence: that in all the visible corporeal world we see no chasms or gaps'. Just why this fact about the visible *corporeal* world lends probability to a claim about a further *incorporeal* world is not explained by Locke, but it is clear that this claim receives some support from two other sources: (1) that the supposition is not inconceivable or repugnant to reason and (2) that the supposition 'is suitable to the magnificent harmony of the universe and the great design and infinite goodness of the Architect' (3.6.12).

not?' (3.6.9), and our classifications are based on observed properties only. There is no suggestion in either of these passages (or
anywhere else in the *Essay*) that, because we lack this knowledge of
the internal structure of matter, we should hypothesise about
that structure, or that an hypothesis about the cohering particles
can in any way aid in our classifications of body or in the discovery of coexisting qualities. Locke was content to accept the
general claim of the corpuscular hypothesis—that the observable
features and behaviour of bodies are caused by the insensible
particulate structure—but there is nowhere in his writing any
attempt to suggest a specific arrangement of corpuscles to account
for some observed effect. Far from Locke's denial of any knowledge of real essence leading to conjectures about real essence,
that denial leads him to locate the science of nature with observation and experience.

The remarks Locke makes about general principles and maxims
are also relevant to the question about his recognition of hypotheses. The *Conduct of the Understanding* has some useful remarks on
the relative merits of observation and general maxims in discovery. It also contains the one explicit mention of Newton's
principle of gravitation. Section 13 says that particular matters of
fact are the foundation for civil and natural knowledge. Civil
knowledge would be our knowledge of man fetched from a study
of history: what we would today rank under sociology, psychology
and anthropology. There are for Locke three kinds of facts: facts
of natural agents (bodies), recorded via observation, either
ordinary or experimental; facts of voluntary agents, the actions of
men in society; and facts of opinion, the beliefs men hold (*Works*,
III, 249). Locke observes that some who study man in his past
social structures merely collect facts, derive no instruction from
the 'crowd of particulars' thus amassed (p. 234). Such collections
of facts only produce a 'heap of crudities'. Contrasted with these
part-time sociologists are those who also fail to benefit from the
matters of fact they discover because they 'are apt to draw
general conclusions, and raise axioms from every particular they
meet with'. The middle path between these two methods is the
one praised by Locke for properly benefiting from matters of
fact.

Between these, those seem to do best, who taking material and useful hints, sometimes from single matters of fact, carry them in their minds to be judged or, by what they shall find in history, to confirm or reverse these imperfect observations; which may be established into rules fit to be relied on, when they are justified by a sufficient and wary induction of particulars (p. 234).[1]

A later passage makes the same point.

General observations drawn from particulars are the jewels of knowledge, comprehending great store in a little room; but they are therefore to be made with the greater care and caution, lest, if we take counterfeit for true, our loss and shame be the greater when our stock comes to a severe scrutiny (pp. 253–4).

Section 34 urges us to allow our opinions to be influenced and guided by evidence: assent should only be upon evidence from things themselves. Examination of received opinions by reference to things themselves should be done with a perfect 'indifferency'.

Locke does not cite instances of the sorts of rules he sees being extracted from particulars. They might be hypotheses suggested by observation or even anticipating observations, later confirmed by induction. The rules also might be general statements like 'lead sinks in water but floats in mercury'. What they are not, I suggest, are general explanatory theories like the corpuscular hypothesis. The general rules Locke has in mind emerge from classification of coexisting qualities which careful observation discovers. 'The collection of several things into several classes gives the mind more general and larger views' (p. 261). Here, too, over-hasty generalising from every particular leads to useless general rules. Discovery is impeded if one makes too many artificial and scholastic distinctions. Discovery is more advanced if we can uncover those 'fundamental truths that lie at the bottom' of things. At this point, Locke cites Newton's principle that 'all bodies gravitate to

[1] Despite his other remarks (see above, p. 63) which seem to place the Royal Society scientists among the first group cited by Locke, Sprat characterised the attitude of the members of the society in terms similar to those used by Locke of the third or middle path: 'They have striven to preserve it [the knowledge of nature] from being overpressed by a confus'd heap of vain, and useless particulars; or, from being straitened and bounded too much up by General Doctrines' (*op. cit.* p. 62). But cf. M. B. Hesse, *op. cit.* p. 67, who speaks of 'the unproductive amassing of uncoordinated facts and experiments visible in some of the phases of the early Royal Society'.

one another' (p. 282). This rule or principle is said to be 'the basis of natural philosophy' in the same way that the rule, 'we should love our neighbours as ourselves', is the basis for civil knowledge. This civil principle enables us to regulate human society, Newton's principle aids (is constitutive of?) our understanding of nature. In the *Essay*, Newton is praised for discovering general truths which have pushed mathematical knowledge forward.

In all of this Locke is urging us to avoid trifling propositions, such as the ones that were cited by many of the rational scientists (the deductivists of his day), e.g. 'What is, is', 'The same thing cannot both be and not be'. These principles were not, and could not be, derived from careful observation of phenomena. In this passage in the *Conduct*, Locke is looking at the relation between proper principles and the facts to which they relate. What he calls 'bottoming' of our knowledge of matter of fact, whether it be in civil or natural knowledge, will illuminate most of the difficulties that arise. 'For example, if it be demanded, whether the grand seignior can lawfully take what he will from any of his people? This question cannot be resolved without coming to a certainty, whether all men are naturally equal...' (p. 283). Discovering the truth of this principle about equality would constitute 'proper bottoming' of our civil knowledge. The truth of that principle cannot be discovered by observation; it is probably (though Locke does not say so) one of those fundamental moral principles which he called laws of nature. Its function in civil and moral knowledge is to disclose the truth of other propositions. How Locke viewed the status of Newton's principle of gravitation is not clear from what he says. What is clear is that it functions in a 'bottoming' way by explaining and shedding light on other propositions (perhaps facts) in science. The maxims of the Schools are not, as had been claimed, principles of science, they can lead to no discoveries, nor can they explain phenomena. They produce at best verbal, not real, truth (4. 7. 16). 'Instruction lies in something very different, and he that would enlarge his own or another's mind to truths he does not yet know must find out intermediate *ideas*, and then lay them in such order one by another that the understanding may see the agreement or disagreement of those

THE SCIENCE OF NATURE

in question' (4.8.3). Locke recognised (more in the *Conduct* than
in the *Essay*) that some general principles, like Newton's on
gravitation, can help us see new agreements of ideas; but the
main concern (the only examples he gives) has been with the
relation of coexistence and with the generalisations of particular
coexisting groups. Principles of restricted generality, in other
words, are the ones Locke cites and shows us how to discover.
It is these upon which he thinks the science of body must be
based. Only an 'incomparable Newton' has the genius to uncover
and use principles of wide generality.

If the hypotheses to which Laudan refers are taken to be those
of wide generality, like Newton's principle of gravitation, Locke
does not reject such hypotheses, but neither does he fit them into
his own account of our knowledge of body. He *says* they can help
our understanding, but what he stresses is the observation of
coexisting qualities. If the hypotheses to which Laudan refers are
those of restricted generality which Locke cites repeatedly—silver
dissolves in *aqua fortis*, lead sinks in water, etc.—then obviously
Locke finds room for hypotheses though they play no role in
discovery. Locke sees such general statements as the result of our
careful classifications of qualities. The concept of 'hypothesis'
did not have a univocal meaning in the seventeenth century.
Koyré finds two senses of the term in Newton, the good sense of
a 'plausible though not provable conception', and the pejorative
sense of a gratuitous fiction (p. 36). Cohen has discerned nine
different senses of 'hypothesis' in Newton's writings, ranging
from axioms, postulates, and premises, to philosophical romances
(*Franklin and Newton*, pp. 138-40).[1] Locke was undoubtedly
sensitive to these various uses of the term, especially to the
hypothesis which was constructed to explain observed phenomena
and to the more encompassing type, such as Newton's principle of
gravitation.[2] Nevertheless, with the two exceptions of hypotheses

[1] Koyré and Cohen (among others) have finally scotched the notion that Newton
was against using hypotheses, though the explication of the famous *hypotheses non
fingo* given by Koyré differs slightly from that given by Cohen. For a bibliography
of other discussions of this issue, see Mandelbaum, pp. 71-5, n. 12.

[2] Two statements on hypotheses by scientists Locke knew clearly indicate that there
was a firm recognition of hypotheses as explanatory, as well as a recognition of
the criteria for a good hypothesis. 'Because to me it seems rational that Hypotheses
...by which the Phaenomena can more clearly and genuinely be solved ought

of wide generality, the corpuscular and the gravitational, Locke does not mention hypotheses, nor does either of those he mentions function in his account of scientific discovery. The hypotheses on cohesion are cited only to be rejected. While relying on the corpuscular hypothesis as explanatory, the kind of discovery Locke stressed concerned the observable properties of bodies.[1]

To discover the properties of bodies, neither maxims, principles, nor hypotheses can replace the analysis of things as we observe and experience them. Any of these could and has led us astray in our quest for knowledge of things. Certain qualities are observed to be always 'joined and existing together'. The making of ideas of things is not simply a listing and noting of all the qualities that go together, since not all qualities that coexist in things are used in the class ideas we form of things (3.6.32). But those ideas which we do put into our class concepts or particular ideas of things must accurately follow the qualities of things. Some observers are better than others. It is only by a patient observation of the nature and properties of things themselves

of right to be prefer'd before the rest; for if I mistake not, to render any hypothesis such, it is indispensably requisite that the principles concluded on, be of a competent number, teeming nature, perspicuous, and the most universal, well grounded upon Mechanical Experiments...' (pp. 8–9, *Philosophical Dialogues concerning the Principles of Natural Bodies*, 1677, W. Simpson). The second statement is from Boyle: 'For, the use of an *Hypothesis* being to render an intelligible account of the Causes of the Effect or Phaenomena propos'd, without crossing the Laws of Nature or other Phaenomena, the more numerous and the more various the Particulars are, whereof some are *explicable* by the assign'd Hypotheses, and some are *agreable* to it, or at least are not dissonant from it, the more valuable the Hypothesis and the more likely to be true' (p. 16, *The Mechanical Origin of Heat*, 1675). No one was opposed to hypotheses. The point is that they were careful to distinguish a stage of observation and gathering of facts from a stage of explanation of what had been observed. They were, it might be said, only pointing out that one does not explain before one has made careful observations. The talk of stages may separate observation too sharply from theory and hypothesis. No one was denying that observation is theory-laden, or at least theory-guided, though those modern terms are misleading if used to characterise attitudes in the seventeenth century. But the needs of the time were such that the rational excesses of the theory of knowledge advocated by the Schools' philosophers necessitated a stress upon observation and a de-emphasis upon hypotheses.

[1] There is some possible ambiguity about speaking of the 'hypothetical method'. We must not, of course, conclude that Locke recognised hypotheses in explanation and/or discovery because, like others around him, he stressed the hypothetical and tentative character of all our generalisations about body. To say that scientific knowledge is merely probable is not to say that hypotheses are employed in that knowledge.

THE SCIENCE OF NATURE

that we can improve our knowledge and remedy the imperfections and abuses of language.[1] With his sensitivity to the force
of language, Locke set language analysis aside also as a guide to
the nature of things. When we argue about 'natural bodies and
substantial things' it is insufficient to 'have learned, from the
propriety of the language, the common...*idea* to which each
word is applied' (3.11.24). The grammar rules of the language are
an improper and untrustworthy guide to the nature of things
(cf. 3.9.8.). Instead, we must acquaint ourselves 'with the history
of that sort of things' (3.11.24).

Locke even proposed by-passing language by constructing a
natural history dictionary consisting of little pictures of the things
named. Such a dictionary would be drawn up by 'men, versed in
physical inquiries and acquainted with the several sorts of natural
bodies' (25). Locke cites the naturalists who have used this sort
of reproduction of the objects named in their vocabulary: 'he
that has occasion to consult them will have reason to confess
that he has a clear[er] *idea* of *apium* or *ibex*, from a little print of
that herb or beast, than he could have from a long definition of the
names of either of them. And so, no doubt, he would have of
strigil and *sistrum* if, instead of a *currycomb* and *cymbal*, which are
the English names dictionaries render them by, he could see
stamped in the margin small pictures of these instruments as
they were in use amongst the ancients' (3.11.25). Locke thought
that such a *Petit Larousse Illustré* would

require too much time, cost, and pains to be hoped for in this age,
yet methinks it is not unreasonable to propose that words standing
for things which are known and distinguished by their outward
shapes should be expressed by little draughts and prints made of them.
A vocabulary made after this fashion would perhaps, with more ease
and in less time, teach the true signification of many terms, especially
in languages of remote countries or ages, and settle truer *ideas* in men's

[1] Hooke, Boyle and the Royal Society scientists started with objects and then
sought by careful observation to discover their properties. Locke is not saying
that we establish what kinds of objects there are by noting coexisting qualities.
He too starts with objects already defined or specified. The coexistence relation
is not offered as a way of justifying our species divisions. It is rather offered as a
way of formulating the knowledge we have of the qualities of things, the familiar
and ordinary objects of our everyday experiences, as well as the chemical objects
of gold, silver, lead, etc., about which Boyle was so much concerned.

minds of several things, whereof we read the names in ancient authors, than all the large and laborious comments of learned critics.

It is the outward shapes of observed objects which would be captured in the natural history dictionary.

In the absence of such a natural history dictionary, Locke enjoins each of us to check his ideas of things against themselves. '*Experience here must teach me* what reason cannot' (4.12.9). Arguments from the nature of things themselves give us the probability which experience provides (4.16.6). Those arguments involve the general consent of all men in all ages concurring 'with a man's constant and never-failing experience, in like cases'. 'For what our own and other men's constant observation has found always to be after the same manner, that we with reason conclude to be the effects of steady and regular causes.' Propositions like 'fire warms a man', 'fire makes lead fluid and changes the colour or consistency in wood or charcoal', 'iron sinks in water but swims in quicksilver' are propositions about particular facts which agree to our constant experience and hence may be taken as near certainties. Experience and history give us the only science of bodies we can have.

In the knowledge of bodies, we must be content to glean what we can from particular experiments, since we cannot from a discovery of their real essences grasp at a time whole sheaves, and in bundles comprehend the nature and properties of whole species together. Where our inquiry is concerning coexistence or repugnancy to coexist, which by contemplation of our *ideas* we cannot discover, there experience, observation, and natural history must give us by our senses and by detail an insight into corporeal substance (4.12.12).

In physical things, it is 'useful and *experimental* philosophy' which alone can advance our knowledge (4.3.26). We should try to be good observers 'and with an intent application endeavour to observe accurately all that is visible' in any object (4.13.2). Experience, experiments and 'historical observations' are the methods to follow in discovering the nature of things themselves (4.12.10. In 4.6.16 Locke speaks of 'experiment or observation', in 4.3.28 of 'observation and experiment'). A knowledge of the nature of substance must be 'grounded on experience' (4.7.15).

We can have only 'an experimental knowledge' of the connexions, i.e. coexistences, of the qualities of objects (4.3.29). Such experimental and historical knowledge takes time and skill and long examination (3.6.30), not all observers are equally skilful or careful (31), but nature must be copied by 'observing certain qualities always joined and existing together' (3.6.28). Only in this way can we form proper and accurate ideas of the substances in nature. The historical observation of this method to knowledge gives us the 'collections of sensible qualities' on which the science of nature is founded (3.6.24. The language of 'collections and observations' is found elsewhere, e.g. 4.7.16; 4.11.9).

In his admiration for Boyle, Newton, and Sydenham, Locke was praising these men for this method of carefully observing and recording (as did Power and Hooke also) the observed coexistence of qualities. In his own scientific interests Locke practised this method also.[1] Theory and hypothesis must find their place in the context of experience and history. The scientists of the day had been making new discoveries and advances by using the method praised by Locke. Locke's role in these methodological changes was equally important, though different in kind from the scientists': he exposed the older techniques and claims (for innate principles, maxims as the foundation for knowledge, substantial forms and finite kinds) as unfounded and unfruitful. Moreover, Locke placed the new method of experience and history in the context of philosophical debate. He gave a philosophical foundation for the new science.

[1] Locke's own involvement in the science of his day and his close association with the leading scientists is well known, though the details are just now being revealed. See Dewhurst, *John Locke, Physician and Philosopher*; James Axtell, 'Locke, Newton, and the Elements of Natural Philosophy', in *Paedagogica Europaea*, I, 235–45; Axtell, 'Locke's Review of the *Principia*', *Notes and Records of the Royal Society*, xx, 2 (1965); Axtell, 'Locke, Newton and the two Cultures', in *John Locke: Problems and Perspectives* (1969), ed. J. W. Yolton, pp. 165–83. Some of the material in this chapter appeared as my contribution to this last-named volume.

3

THE METHOD TO SCIENCE

For the discovery of non-necessary coexisting qualities, there can be no substitute for careful observation. Such is the first task of the science of nature. The next stage after natural histories in the programme of science was not always discussed or filled in by the apologists for the Royal Society. That there was a clear understanding of the nature and role of hypotheses in explanation is evident in some of the writings of the men I have been referring to. Moreover, the method of hypothesis was of course used and discussed by Galileo, Kepler, and Copernicus in astronomy. That Locke did not own the books of Kepler and Copernicus may suggest that he was much less informed and interested in astronomy than he was in chemistry, medicine, and physics. The method of hypothesis, together with mathematical calculation and deduction, was more appropriate, certainly more used, in astronomy and celestial mechanics than in the theories of matter. This fact may help to explain why Locke followed the method of natural histories, rather than the method of hypothesis, in his account of the science of nature. These two methods were not incompatible. The programme of the scientists of this period to whom I have referred, the ones that Locke knew, always included the construction of hypotheses, but only after sufficient observation and histories of phenomena had been collected and tabulated. Laudan is surely correct in rejecting the view that the development of scientific method in England in the seventeenth century can 'be understood simply as a series of footnotes to, and commentaries on, Bacon's *Novum Organum*'.[1] Even after correcting this reading of scientific method in that century, it is equally important to point out, as Laudan goes on to do in this article, that most writers on science in the latter half of the century also rejected

---

[1] 'The Clock Metaphor and Probabilism: The Impact of Descartes on English Methodological Thought, 1650–65', *Annals of Science*, XXII (1966), 73.

Bacon's inductivist notion of the way hypotheses are constructed. Laudan speaks specifically of Boyle. While recognising that, like Bacon, Boyle 'envisaged the compilation of vast histories of nature which would summarize and codify the information gleaned from experiment' (pp. 86, 87), Laudan remarks that Boyle then saw the next stage in method to be the construction, not the induction, of hypotheses: 'Boyle does not believe that theories will arise ready-made from the data, or that the data will uniquely determine any single theory...it is the faculty of reason which constructs theories from the data; they do not spring full-blown from the histories' (pp. 87–8).

There is an important difference in the accounts Boyle and Bacon give of the way theories and hypotheses are made. Nothing Locke says indicates that he followed Bacon on the formation of hypotheses, or that he rejected hypotheses from the method of science. What I have tried to show is that the account Locke gives of the science of nature predominantly concerns the natural history stage. In that respect he was following the general programme accepted by many scientists. Even Laudan recognises that Boyle's clear acceptance of and his attempts to use the stage of hypothesis was not shared by all the members of the Royal Society: there were some members of the society 'who were so obsessed with the new experimental philosophy that they denied any role to speculation or conjecture'. Laudan also contrasts Boyle's views with 'the trenchant empiricism of many members of the Royal Society' (*ibid.* pp. 94–5). Even more, commenting on the views of Power, Hooke, Newton, and Cowley that the new microscopes will in time be able to disclose the corpuscular mechanism of nature, Laudan notes that 'As the faith in the unlimited magnifying powers of the microscope grew, English hypotheticalism waned' (*ibid.* pp. 102–3). Laudan had earlier in the same article said that 'Once one accepts the corpuscularian theory of matter, and with it the theory of knowledge which makes corpuscles unobservable in principle, then it is altogether natural to adopt a hypothetical methodology' (p. 96).[1] He ends by

---

[1] Since Locke believed the particles of matter were in principle observable, it would follow from Laudan's remark that Locke would reject the use of hypotheses in science. The fact that there was a feature of particles which was unintelligible if not unobservable, cohesion, may place Locke on the side of those who thought

reasserting the close tie between the belief in particles being observable in principle and the rejection of the method of hypothesis:

The demand for a science free of all hypotheses, which was widely circulated after Newton, could never have gathered such enthusiastic adherents if the hypotheticalism of Descartes, Boyle, and Glanvill had not died such a quick and needless death at the hands of those who thought nature's clock had no secrets which man's instruments could not seek out and know with certainty (p. 103).

Whether or not there is, either historically or logically, this link between hypotheticalism and the belief that the corpuscular structure of matter is unobservable in principle, the scientific literature of many of the Royal Society members clearly reveals a firm and pervasive belief that the important task for science at that time was the careful compilation of histories of phenomena. Boyle also accepted this programme while insisting (as Hooke and others did) on the role of hypotheses after adequate observations had been made.

Newton seems to have agreed on the value of natural histories, but he also effectively used the method of hypothesis, both as a way of explaining what had been observed and as a way of bringing together a variety of phenomena which observation might not have found coexisting. New relations between objects were in this way discovered, e.g. that all bodies, far distant ones as well as minute and insensible ones, gravitate towards one another. Even if I am correct in saying that, while Locke did not reject hypotheses, even saw roughly how they could be used, he nevertheless gave the preponderant role in the method to science to natural histories, we can rightfully wonder why his friendship with Newton did not lead him to modify his account of the science of nature, to throw much more stress upon hypotheses and calculations. As we have seen, gravitation as one of the properties of body, certainly as one of the ways in which bodies operate, was not an entirely easy notion for Locke. He tried to add it to impulse as one of the ways in which body acts on body, though

the particles (or some feature of them) unobservable. On either reading of Locke it is still true that he did not reject hypotheses, he merely gives much greater prominence to the formation of natural histories.

he was not sure we could conceive this mode of action. He did not reject gravitation. Moreover, Locke cited magnetic attraction as a feature of iron. One would have thought those passages giving impulse as the only way that bodies act would have been modified to take account of magnetic attraction, although of course it does not apply, as does gravitation, to all bodies. It is the breadth of application of the principle of gravitation which sets it off from magnetic attraction; but the significant difference in Newton's application of gravitation is the exactness of the calculations he was able to make of bodies by means of it. There is a striking difference between this method to science and the one Locke singles out for analysis in his epistemology of science. Not only did Newton's calculations employ a technique to science other than observation, they sometimes required the assigning of numerical values to ideal, not real, bodies. Nevertheless, those calculations had astounding relevance to the ordinary world of gross objects. Even granting that Newton began with observation of the behaviour of ordinary objects, his use of some hypotheses of wide generality and his numerical calculations and derivations would appear to be a method to science different in kind from the simple observation and recording of data Locke praised. It would, in fact, seem in some sense to be a discovery of the qualities and behaviour of bodies independent of observation. Was Newton's method an instance of deriving (perhaps via deduction) a knowledge of bodies from their real essence?

In detailing the method of relying upon the observed nature of things themselves for our discoveries of coexisting qualities and for the basis of generalising to probable propositions about bodies, Locke carefully contrasted this method with that of deducing from real essence. Rejecting the doctrine of fixed kinds, Locke argued that each object has a specific internal configuration of particles from which flow all its properties and effects. While Locke followed other microscopists in saying that the particles may become observable through the microscope, an understanding of the real essence of any object requires more than observation of the particles: it requires an intelligible account of the cohesion of each particle and of the cohesion of the group comprising each object. It is at least the lack of this understanding of cohesion which prevents man from having a knowledge of the real essence and hence from being able to follow (in the knowledge of matter) *the method of deducing from essence*. That Locke saw that an understanding of the real essence of any object would be different from the observation of the minute particles making up the internal essence of that object, is most strongly shown by his careful, extensive, and repeated remarks about what we would know had we that understanding. Necessary connexion is the epistemic analogue of the cohesion of particles. If we had an idea of the real essence of any object, the observed properties would be deducible from that idea, thereby disclosing the necessary connexion between observed properties and real essence (2.31.6). The comparison is with the dependence of all the properties of a triangle and their deducibility from 'the complex *idea* of three lines including space'. If our ideas of geometrical figures were acquired by examining particular figures, learning only some of the properties of that kind of figure, we would be in the same position in geometry as we are in physical knowledge, i.e. we would not see any necessary relations. Starting with 'the whole essence' of an ellipsis, for example, we can from that discover its properties 'and demonstratively see how they flow and are inseparable from it' (11). Just as the essence of geometrical figures 'lies in a very little compass', that is, in a few ideas (e.g. that of a triangle consists of three lines enclosing space), so Locke conjectures that the real essence of substances 'lie in a little compass, though the properties flowing from that internal constitution are endless' (2.32.24). A knowledge of the *essentia* of man, for example, would show us how 'his faculties of moving, sensation, and reasoning and other powers flow' from that *essentia* (3.6.3).

Philosophers before and after Locke have claimed to have produced such a deductive metaphysic of nature. Locke suggests that this is the sort of knowledge God has of all objects; it is possible that angels also have a deductive knowledge of things (3.6.3).[1] In saying we are incapable of such a knowledge of

---

[1] 'Though yet it be not to be doubted that spirits of a higher rank than those immersed in flesh may have as clear *ideas* of the radical constitution of substances as we have of a triangle, and so perceive how all their properties flow from thence: but the manner how they come by that knowledge exceeds our conceptions' (3.11.23. Cf. 4.3.6). It is very likely also that angels have much better memories

nature, Locke does not deny there are necessary connexions in nature. God's deductive knowledge of bodies and their properties presupposes a necessary connexion in bodies. But to say there are necessary connexions in nature just means that bodies are such that, had we an understanding of their internal constitution, we would also be able to know the qualities and operations of bodies without observation and with certainty. The necessary relation would hold between the real essence and the observable qualities and perceived ideas; it would also hold between the coexisting qualities. What for us is only a contingent connexion between yellowness, malleableness, etc., of gold would, for the discerner of real essence, be apprehended as a necessary connexion. Would an understanding of cohesion be sufficient for yielding such knowledge, for bringing about the epistemic change in us from perceiving contingent to perceiving necessary coexistence? What precisely is required for such necessary knowledge?

The coexisting qualities we discover and in terms of which we classify objects into kinds carry 'no visible necessary connexion or inconsistency' with each other (4.3.10). We cannot know which qualities

have a necessary union or inconsistency one with another; for, not knowing the root they spring from, not knowing what size, figure, and texture of parts they are on which depend and from which result

than we do, are able to 'retain together and constantly set before them, as in one picture all their past knowledge at once' (2.10.9). There is a suggestion in this same passage that God's omniscience holds all things—past, present and future—in view in the same way that a man (Locke cites the stories of Pascal's memory) or an angel holds all past knowledge in one view. Angelic and divine knowledge may thus dispense with reasoning and demonstration, intuition replacing the need for discursive thought. Locke also suggests that 'the spirits of just men made perfect shall have, in a future state', an intuitive knowledge 'of thousands of things which now either wholly escape our apprehensions or which, our short-sighted reason having got some faint glimpse of, we, in the dark, grasp after' (4.17.14). W. Simpson, in *Hydrologia Chymica* (1669), attributes to Adam an intuitive knowledge of all things (p. 239). Now, for imperfect man, knowledge is inverted: 'For the order of our knowledge is inverted, since it was intuitive, since now we only know *a posteriori* from the products and effects of things; whereby then we knew from the very essential causes themselves' (p. 203). Thomas Browne, *Religio Medici* (4th ed. 1656), suggests that angels 'know things by their forms, and define by specificall difference what we describe by accident and properties; and therefore probabilities to us may bee demonstrations unto them' (pp. 70–1).

those qualities which make our complex *idea* of gold, it is impossible we should know what other qualities result from or are incompatible with the same constitution of the insensible parts of *gold*, and so consequently must always co-exist with that complex *idea* we have of it, or else are inconsistent with it (11).

In this passage, knowing the size, figure, and texture of the particles of gold which cause the observed qualities would also tell us what other qualities result from and are incompatible with that same size, figure, and texture of particles. But I must *know* that particles of that size, figure, and texture do cause those observed qualities, not merely establish some correlations between particles and qualities. To know that those qualities depend on and flow from those particles will not result from discovering the particles. We must discover certain and indubitable rules of connexion between secondary and primary qualities, and between primary qualities and sensations (13). Even if we did 'discover the size, figure, or motion of those insensible parts' which immediately produce sensations in us, we would not have a deductive knowledge of body nor find necessary connexions among its qualities because 'there is no conceivable *connexion* betwixt the one and the other'. The term 'connexion' means 'necessary connexion', as Locke immediately explains in 14. The criterion of essential knowledge here is there being a *conceivable* connexion between the size, figure, and texture of the particles and the perceived qualities. That is, not only can we not *discover* the certain and indubitable rules of connexion: we cannot even *conceive* what they would be like.

There are a few qualities which do have a necessary connexion with other perceived qualities, as 'figure necessarily supposes extension, receiving or communicating motion by impulse supposes solidity' (4.2.14), but those connexions are very few. We do not discover these necessary connexions by observation, but rather through intuition or demonstration. The two examples Locke cites here might better be termed 'conceptual necessities'. He cites several more such necessities in 15: that each particular extension, figure, number of parts, and motion 'excludes all others of each kind', that 'no one subject can have two smells or two colours at the same time'. A better formulation of this last conceptual necessity is 'it is as impossible that the very same particle of any body should at the same time differently modify or reflect the rays of light, as that it should have two different figures and textures at the same time' (15). In 4.7.5, 'that two bodies cannot be in the same place' is cited as self-evident. Some *ideas* also 'require others as necessary to their existence or conception', e.g. 'Motion can neither be nor be conceived without space', solidity is inseparable from the idea of body (2.13.11). These examples of necessary connexions ought to give us some understanding of what we should have to conceive of, if we were to conceive of necessary connexions between all the observed coexisting qualities and between those qualities and the insensible particles which cause the qualities. The task of conceiving is less an impossible one than it is inapplicable or implausible. We have examples of conceptual necessities and impossibilities, but the nature of our knowledge of bodies is such that those relations do not hold. The situation is, however, stronger than this. What Locke is denying is that we are able to conceive the non-necessary coexistences to be necessary. We cannot conceive of the coexistences discovered by observation becoming conceptual connexions. We cannot, that is, understand what it would be like to say the yellow colour of gold could not exist without gold's malleableness, or to say that its solubility in *aqua regia* is impossible without its friability. We cannot understand these possibilities just because it is not contradictory to affirm one discovered coexisting quality to be absent while finding the others. We can never 'from consideration of the *ideas* themselves, with certainty affirm or deny, of a body whose complex *idea* is made up of yellow, very weighty, ductile, fusible, and fixed, that it is soluble in *aqua regia*: and so on for the rest of its qualities' (4.6.9. Cf. 7, 10; 4.9.1; 4.12.9). Similarly, there is no 'conceivable connexion between any impulse of any sort of body and any perception of a colour or smell which we find in our minds' (4.3.28). Aside from the few rather obvious and uninteresting conceptual necessities cited by Locke, our knowledge of bodies (and of spirits) does not reach any further than experience; sense and reflection are our boundaries. Whatever hypothesis about the nature of body we accept (Locke says the corpuscularian hypothesis is 'thought to

go farthest in an intelligible explication of the qualities of bodies',
4.3.16), 'our knowledge concerning corporeal substances will
be very little advanced by any of them, till we are made to see
what qualities and powers of bodies have a *necessary connexion or
repugnancy* one with another; which in the present state of philosophy I think we know but to a very small degree' (*ibid.*). The
rational, non-experimental character of this sort of knowledge is
stressed even more, later in the same chapter, where Locke remarks that if we knew the mechanical affections of the particles
of any object we would 'know without trial several of their
operations one upon another' (25). We would be able, for example,
'to tell beforehand that *rhubarb* will purge, *hemlock* kill, and *opium*
make a man sleep'. The method of deducing from essence would
free us from observation. With such knowledge, we would
understand why silver dissolves in *aqua fortis* and gold in *aqua
regia*, and not the other way around. As it is, our reason carries
us 'very little beyond particular matter of fact' (25). Certainty and
demonstration do not extend to our knowledge of substance,
universal truths of body cannot be had, *experimental* philosophy
replaces *scientifical*, this latter term being Locke's word for rational,
deductive, certain knowledge. 'The things that, as far as our
observation reaches, we constantly find to proceed regularly, we
may conclude do act by a law set them, but yet by a law that we
know not' (29). That law must be not some generalisation from
coexistences but rather some certain and indubitable rule.

The method of deducing from essence would not entirely
remove the need for observation, since a knowledge of the
particular size, figure, texture, motion and configuration of
particles comprising each object is needed for such derivations.
That knowledge is necessary but not sufficient. Thus, that method
would not be *a priori*, though it would involve deductions or
intuitions. Nevertheless, the paradigm is conceptual or linguistic
truth where, for example, a proposition like 'all gold is malleable'
is certain if malleableness is part of our definition of gold. But
the certainty of that proposition is no different from the certainty
of 'a centaur is four-footed': what we have said is 'that that
sound stands for an idea in which malleableness is contained'
(4.6.9). Such linguistic truths are common, but they should not be

mistaken for the *real* certainty Locke is discussing, of knowing the necessary connexions of qualities, not just of ideas. Real, as opposed to linguistic or conceptual, certainty may be possible only from an understanding of cohesion, from knowing what 'ties the particles together'. I have stressed in the previous chapter Locke's insistence that observation of the particles is inadequate for knowing the real essence. Cohesion seems to have held the secret of nature for Locke, in the sense that only with that could our knowledge of body cease in any way to be observational and become conceptual. Were it possible, a rational science of bodies (and of spirits), based on the method of deducing from essence, would give us a knowledge of all the properties of bodies (and likewise of spirits) quite independent of and prior to the observation of coexisting qualities. We would acquire such knowledge by an analysis of our ideas, not by an analysis of things. Were we able to use the method of deducing from essence, 'to know the properties of *gold*, it would be no more necessary that *gold* should exist and that we should make experiments upon it than it is necessary, for the knowing of the properties of a triangle, that a triangle should exist in any matter' (4.6.11). Such a knowledge would yield universal principles necessarily true of body. The connexions between qualities, and the connexions between primary qualities of particles and our ideas of both primary and secondary qualities would also be necessary. An analysis of our ideas (starting with the idea of the real essence of any particular object) would reveal to us, by intuition and demonstration, the necessary connexions which must hold among qualities. To reach such a state of knowledge and understanding would be to have 'a perfect *science* of natural bodies (not to mention spiritual beings)' (4.3.29).[1]

---

[1] The source of such a deductive knowledge of body is easier to conceive than is the source for a perfect science of spirits. Our knowledge of the workings of bodies and spirits may be equally sparse, but with bodies Locke had available the corpuscular theory which gave some account of the nature and operations of matter. Hence, one can begin to see that at least a knowledge of the particles and an understanding of cohesion might be able to give us a basis for a deductive knowledge of body. There is much less to go on for conjecturing how Locke might have thought the method of deducing from essence would work for spirits. It should be clear from the analysis in this chapter of what the method of deducing from essence would be that Harré's interpretation of Locke's denial of a science of bodies is too weak. By saying a science of nature is not possible for man, 'Locke means no more than what is usually meant by saying that every law of nature

Newton, of course, made no claims to have followed this method to science, although he did produce universal propositions about the nature and behaviour of body. His calculations gave precision to many of the general laws and predictions made from his principles and hypotheses. Newton's techniques clearly go beyond the recording of phenomena. They are not so systematic or formal as to be labelled 'hypothetico-deductive' nor are they the method of deducing from essence such truths as 'rhubarb purges' or 'hemlock kills'. Still, one might think that Locke would have incorporated into his account of the science of nature some of the mathematical method used by Newton and other scientists. That Locke's analysis of the science of nature stayed with the natural histories of the scientists I have discussed may in part have been due to the fact that Newton's *Principia* did not appear until 1687, after the *Essay* was all but complete. The more probable explanation is that, in addition to the fact that Locke agreed with those who believed natural histories were an important and necessary under-labourer exercise in science, he himself was concerned to show that feature of physical science and its method which could be characterised by his epistemology. The recording of observational data finds a place in the cognitive relations which constitute knowledge for Locke, the coexistence relation yields certainty.

Quite apart from the epistemic status of our knowledge of coexisting qualities in the science of nature, Locke was aware of Newton and seems to have understood the significance of his different method to science. Axtell has recently argued that Locke's 'characterisation of science changed over his lifetime', from science primarily as natural history to science as following the 'mathematico-deductive method of Galileo'.[1] Axtell credits

is stated under the limitation of induction, that is that we can have no *general* guarantee that the course of nature will not change radically at any time' (*Matter and Method*, pp. 103–4). I suppose that the necessary or conceptual knowledge of nature which a rational science would provide might give us the guarantee Harré cites, but providing that guarantee would be far from the main result of such a science. Nor is the consequence of our not having such a science captured by saying we lack that general guarantee. The consequence is, as we have seen, that we must use the method of observation in order to learn the nature of things themselves.

[1] *The Educational Writings of John Locke*, ed. Axtell, pp. 72, 73–4.

this change in Locke's account of scientific method to Newton's *Principia*. It used to be thought that Locke was unable to follow the mathematics of the *Principia*. Axtell argues for a better estimate of Locke's mathematical ability.[1] Axtell's case is largely circumstantial but not without some force. There is evidence pointing to Locke as the reviewer of the *Principia* in the *Bibliothèque Universelle* (March 1688), a review that did not skirt round the more difficult parts of the book. Axtell's argument that in preparing his *Elements of Natural Philosophy*, Locke asked for and received from Newton a summary on physical science, which was incorporated into the *Elements*, is more circumstantial but still probable.[2] More importantly, Locke's reading after 1690 included mathematical books directly relevant to Newton's work. He made detailed notes in his journals of this reading.[3] Nevertheless, even with this new evidence of Locke's reading in mathematics, I think it doubtful that Locke was skilled in the subject. He did, however, have an appreciation for the general value of mathematical techniques. The *Conduct of the Understanding* praises mathematics as a way of reasoning, even as the model of reasoning. 'For, in all sorts of reasoning, every single argument should be managed as a mathematical demonstration; the connexion and dependence of ideas should be followed, till the mind is brought to the source on which it bottoms' (*Works*, III, 222). Demonstration for Locke was just the revealing of the connexions or relations between ideas. His notion of demonstration was informal, opposed to the logic of the syllogism. But there is something else in this comment from the *Conduct* which is of importance in understanding Locke's views on the method to science: his reference to principles on which are 'bottomed' some series of ideas.

[1] See his 'Locke's Review of the *Principia*' and 'Locke, Newton, and the Elements of Natural Philosophy', *loc. cit.* Also chapter 4 of his edition of Locke's *Educational Writings*.

[2] Axtell's claim that the *Elements* follows 'the axiomatic-mathematical method of Newton's *Principia*' in its organisation is puzzling ('Locke, Newton, and the Elements of Natural Philosophy', *loc. cit.* p. 244 n. 26). The *Elements* is written in terse, outline form, chapter 1 being a point-by-point presentation of the laws of motion, but there is certainly no axiomatic-mathematical method in any of the chapters of this work. It is a short, discursive account of information on dynamics, astronomy, geography, animal and plant life, etc.

[3] See Axtell, 'Locke, Newton and the Two Cultures', in *John Locke: Problems and Perspectives*.

Newton's principle of gravitation is said by Locke to be the 'basis of natural philosophy', a fundamental and not an incidental truth (*Conduct*, pp. 281-2). It is important to note, however, that it is not observational truths, the truths of natural histories, to which these fundamental verities are opposed: it is rather the trivial and uninstructive truths of logic which are criticised. Locke warns against young men throwing their time away 'in purely logical inquiries', comparing the logician with the painter who, instead of painting, spends 'all his time in examining the threads of the several cloths he is to paint upon, and counting the hairs of each pencil and brush he intends to use in the laying on of his colours' (*ibid*. p. 281).[1] Logicians mistake their 'airy useless notions for real and substantial knowledge, and think their understandings so well furnished with science, that they need not look any further into the nature of things, or descend to the mechanical drudgery of experiment and inquiry' (p. 282).[2] The logic of the syllogism is impotent with respect to new knowledge, it is inept with respect to disclosing the relations of ideas. Proper demonstration was always part of Locke's method to knowledge; in the science of nature the main task is to acquire clear ideas from things themselves. Demonstration, whether axiomatic-mathematical or just syllogistical, has to do with the relation of ideas, but it cannot reveal the non-necessary coexistence relations. Had Locke changed his views on the method to science after the publication of Newton's work, there is no reason why he could not have incorporated any such changes into the various editions of his *Essay*, showing how or where demonstration might come into the science of nature. That he did not make such changes does not, of course, show that his views did not change. The passages in the *Conduct*, the *Elements*, and one or two places in the *Education* at

[1] This comparison may have been a common one in attacks against formal logic. S. J. Curtis quotes Juan Luis Vives as saying (in his *In pseudo dialecticos*) against the practice of dialectics: 'Does an artist spend all his life preparing his brushes and colours?' (in *A Short History of Educational Ideas*, Curtis and Boultwood, 1966, p. 134).

[2] In the *Education*, Locke had warned parents not to let their sons practise or to admire the practice of logic, since it breeds the habit of never taking any answers as final, of always arguing further. The goal of this kind of logic was to 'maintain what he has once affirm'd', with an indifference to truth. For Locke, 'Truth is to be found and supported by a mature and due Consideration of Things themselves, and not by artificial Terms and Ways of arguing' (p. 297).

least give some indication that Locke recognised the usefulness of principles and demonstrations in science.

Whether or not Locke would have said that gravitation was part of the essence of bodies (Newton firmly denied it),[1] it is quite clear that the principle of gravitation does not enable us to make the kind of deductions Locke describes in the method of deducing from essence, since it does not provide us with the basis for deducing all the qualities and effects of objects, including the ideas produced in perceivers. The method of deducing from essence requires a quite specific starting place for the deduction. It is not characterised by its deductive nature but by the specific entities from which the deduction would be made, as well as by the qualitative features of objects that would be deduced. I think it safe to say that Locke recognised the value of the sorts of axioms, rules, principles and hypotheses used by Newton, a value of uniting and bringing together a range of phenomena; that these principles did increase our knowledge by disclosing new relations and making possible precise calculations of the behaviour of bodies; and that this method of principles and demonstration was possible only after or in conjunction with careful observation. It may also be true that the example of Newton's *Principia* convinced Locke that there was a much more powerful method to science than the one praised by Sprat, Glanvill and Molyneux and practised by Power, Boyle, Sydenham and Hooke. If so, he was unable or unwilling to adjust his theory of knowledge and his account of the science of nature to take account of this new understanding. Of the four specific knowledge relations cited by Locke, identity and diversity are the preliminaries to any kind of knowledge, not unique to knowledge of body; the catch-all category Locke called 'relation' seems meant for necessary connexions only; necessary connexion, as a separate relation, sometimes paired with but clearly different from coexistence, can have no place in the science of nature without turning that science into a conceptual, not an empirical, discipline; and real existence only articulates the existential conviction generated by sensation and perceiving.[2] The cognitive relation of necessary

[1] Koyré, *Newtonian Studies*, pp. 149–64.
[2] These cognitive relations are given an extended discussion in the next chapter.

connexion could of course cover the deductions made from hypotheses, perhaps mathematical calculations as well; but what is lacking in Locke's list of knowledge relations is one for hypotheses themselves. They would, I presume, come under probability. Whether he would allow that deductions made from *probable* hypotheses would yield *knowledge*, is doubtful. That fact may only be a result of his strict definition of knowledge. Had he given more attention to the interconnexions between probable generalisations and hypotheses *and* knowledge claims, Locke might have been led to modify his list of knowledge relations so as to include a relation more specific to such a hypothetical method in science. Even if we say that the few remarks he does make about hypotheses, together with his comments on probability (belief and assent), warrant concluding that Locke saw the method to the science of nature as including the use of hypotheses, the important fact to keep in mind is that his account of knowledge does find room among the cognitive relations for the knowledge yielded by the natural histories, while it does not make room for the results of the hypothetical method. Whatever he absorbed and accepted from Newton did not lead Locke to change his analysis of our *knowledge* of body.

There was a method claimed for science by men of this period— John Sergeant is one, whose book, *The Method to Science* (1696), lends its title to this chapter[1]—a *method of deducing from principles,* which Locke was careful to attack and reject. This was a method to knowledge used by the Schoolmen and claimed to apply to all knowledge, including knowledge of nature. Their methodological dictum was 'ex praecognitis et praeconcessis' (4.7.8). These were the people identified by Power, Hooke, Sprat, and Glanvill as the 'old dogmatists', who were more concerned with disputing than with increasing human knowledge. They would defend any conclusion by their disputative methods, tracing all truths back to the principles of logic. There were two main evils for Locke in this method of deducing from principles. One evil was in the selection of principles, all of the ones cited by the scholastic philosophers being trivial and uninstructive (e.g. 'what is, is',

---

[1] For a discussion of this aspect of Sergeant, see my *John Locke and the Way of Ideas*, pp. 76–87.

'the same thing cannot both be and not be'). These logical principles contrasted sharply with those physical ones employed by Newton. The second evil of general principles for Locke was their use as the grounds for syllogistic inferences. In logic, Locke was an informalist.

Margaret Wilson has pointed out that Locke's anti-formalism extended to any formal schema.[1] Whereas Leibniz viewed the principle of identity as a formal schema relevant to any instance of identity, Locke argued that maxims (the formal schema) and instances are 'separate and independent truths, connected only extrinsically' (p. 350). Perceiving the truth of any identical proposition, including that of general maxims, requires and is dependent upon our seeing the agreement between the two ideas in that proposition. 'To know that a "man is a man" is a true proposition is a matter, then, of perceiving the "agreement" of the idea of man (subject) with the idea of man (predicate); in precisely the same way, to know that "whatsoever is, is" is a matter of perceiving the agreement of the idea of "being" (subject) with the idea of "being"(predicate).' In other words, Locke's anti-formalism leads him to the position that 'We recognize the truth of an identity not by recognizing a valid formal schema, but by intuiting a relationship between the subject and predicate "ideas"' (p. 351). Even more forcefully, 'Locke has resolutely turned his back on the whole notion of a formal order. There is no aspect of a proposition which is in any way independent of the character of the ideas involved: i.e. there is no isolable formal aspect which it is the purpose of a general axiom to express' (p. 354).[2]

[1] 'Leibniz and Locke on "First Truths"', *Journal of the History of Ideas*, xxviii (1967).
[2] Miss Wilson thinks formalism creeps into Locke's account of the principle of identity since he says that all that the maxim, 'whatsoever is, is', proves 'amounts to no more than this, that the same word may with great certainty be affirmed of itself, without any doubt of the truth of any such proposition' (4.8.2–3). Miss Wilson argues that 'the same word may be affirmed of itself' is a *general* truth, and hence a formal schema (p. 363). In addition, Miss Wilson does not see how Locke could distinguish '2 + 2 = 4' from '2 is 2', the latter being trifling and uninstructive while the former is non-trivial and instructive. If in both cases the truth is apprehended by comparing subject and predicate, the difference can be drawn only by covertly introducing 'the notion of a formally valid principle or schema' (p. 364). I would think, however, that the difference lies in the fact that '2 is 2' affirms an idea of itself while '2 + 2 = 4' does not, although I realise all the problems facing us about analytic statements. What needs to be given is a clear criterion saying when an idea has been affirmed of itself. Locke's point is

Miss Wilson is, I believe, the first to recognise the antiformalist and informalist character of Locke's attack on the method of deducing from principles. His informalism is even more pronounced in his theory of demonstration. The ruling thought behind Locke's theory of demonstration is, as Miss Wilson characterises the general doctrine of the relation of ideas, that 'the true connection between ideas is exactly what we apprehend it to be by our intuition, and not something that is formally expressible' (p. 361). Demonstration as a mode of knowledge was recognised by Locke, even stressed; but, while demonstration included deduction (limited at that time to the rule of syllogism), demonstration meant primarily for Locke just the uncovering of conceptual connexions. Locke has repeatedly stressed our inability to discover conceptual connexions between sensory ideas: there, only experience and careful observation can reveal the agreements or lack of agreements of ideas and qualities. Demonstration has to do with general knowledge (4.17.2; 4.6.16) and with those cognitive relations which deal with necessary connexions. It is restricted even more properly to what Locke calls 'mixed modes', those ideas that are their own archetypes. In short, demonstration produces conceptual truths. The Schoolmen were wrong in their belief that factual discoveries about the nature of things themselves could be made by demonstration. They were also wrong in restricting demonstration to deduction. Locke mounted a sustained attack against these deductivists, objecting to the artificiality of the formalism of the syllogism. Locke was in no way opposing demonstration. What he was doing was recommending a revision of the notion of demonstration, not to include generating new factual discoveries but to extend to the enlargement of our conceptual understanding. The method of the syllogism is not suited to dealing with all conceptual connexions, only those that are deductive.

The two main terms 'demonstration' and 'deduction' need

that in affirming an idea of itself, we are not adding to our knowledge: certainly not in the same way that other propositions mark an addition to knowledge. Even Locke says identities come first, if we do not perceive that our ideas agree with themselves we can make no progress at all in knowledge. It may be wrong for Locke to say identical propositions yield only a verbal truth, but I do not see that he must admit any formal schema.

careful watching. To deduce a principle or a conclusion frequently means simply to derive the conclusion by means of formal deduction. Locke frequently uses both terms in a non-deductive sense. 'To demonstrate' means 'showing' or 'making clear', 'deduce' often just means 'infer'. The psychology of inferring tends to replace the logic of inference. The strict logical sense of 'deduce' was also commonly used by logicians of the time, but one finds the looser sense frequently. Throughout the early portions of the *Essay* Locke's use alternates; sometimes which meaning he has in mind is not clear. But by the time he comes to expose the limitations of the rule of syllogism and to offer a wider, more informal sense of 'demonstrate', he is quite precise about his usage. 1.2.6–9 refers to mathematicians deducing 'unknown truths from principles or propositions that are already known'. Sections 10 and 22 of the same chapter speak of 'mathematical demonstrations', and 28 of 'the masters of demonstrations'. 1.3.4 tells us that moral rules depend upon other principles from which they can be deduced, suggesting that the proposed demonstrative morality was deductive in the logical sense. Section 12 of that chapter talks of rules of action being 'the obvious deductions of human reason'; this use of 'deduction' does not need to be, and I think is not, the logical sense. The rule cited here, 'Parents, preserve and cherish your children', is a law of nature for Locke; those laws are not demonstrated but are rather those other principles from which moral rules are derived. Locke says that the idea of God is naturally deducible (1.4.9), the deduction outlined later and also in the *Essays on the Law of Nature* is a version of the cosmological argument but without any attempt on Locke's part to put it into a logically deductive form. Experience presents us with a universe of such and such a sort, our reason simply concludes there is a god. Elsewhere, Locke refers to cogent demonstration from principles (1.4.26), says that madmen make 'right deductions' from their fancies: given the delusions they have, they act and think consistently with them (2.11.13). 2.16.4 contrasts demonstration in numbers with demonstration in extension: the former may not be more evident and exact, but 'they are more general in their use, and more determinate in their application'.

The demonstrations familiar to Locke were those in which general maxims were used in the School disputes. Locke was strong in his condemnation of this technique of arguing, since the maxims used could not possibly yield new knowledge.[1] Moreover, contradictory conclusions could be derived from the same maxim. If I use the maxim, 'what is, is', and then take as my idea of body that it is 'bare extension', I can arrive at the conclusion that there is no vacuum, since space without body would have to be extended; but extension and body, on this idea, go together. If, on the other hand, I alter my idea of body to that of extension and solidity, the conclusion can be equally demonstrated that a vacuum is possible (4.7.12–13). Locke's objection here is more against the principles or maxims employed than against the demonstration. One of the defects for him of demonstration from principles is that it gives us verbal, not real truth (4.7.14, 16). Demonstration is really not applicable, certainly not useful, in the science of nature: various conclusions can be demonstrated, given the concepts, but the demonstration cannot reveal the truth of the conclusion (4.11.10; 4.11.12). It is truth which, in experimental science, we are after (4.7.17; 4.8.9). But there is a truth in the relations of ideas, too, which is not disclosed by demonstration. Here, the objection is against demonstration as a formal procedure, not only against the maxims used. In no case should we be content with verbal truth or with demonstration merely for disputative triumphs. We want to discover how in fact ideas are related. Working from the maxims of the Schools will not reveal those connexions, neither will the rule of syllogism. In fact, Locke's point is that the syllogistic schemata presuppose and rest upon our being able to perceive the relations of the ideas in the demonstration. He did not think he was introducing any new method of

[1] Locke conceded that maxims have some use, i.e. 'to silence wranglers and put an end to dispute', even perhaps in the teaching of science, but of no use in the discovery of 'unknown truths or to help the mind forward in its search after knowledge' (4.7.11). In his rejection of maxims and syllogism as tools for advancing knowledge, Locke was very close again to Hooke. 'I do not here altogether reject *Logick*, or the way of Ratiocination already known, as a thing of no use. It has its peculiar Excellencies and Uses in ordinary Discourse and Conversation: and affords some Helps to some kinds of Invention, especially of Arguments, as well as to the Memory by its Method' ('The Present State of Natural Philosophy', p. 5). Hooke adds that logic is of no use in learning about nature, since we cannot from an axiom or sentence deduce the causes of all effects and actions (p. 6).

demonstration, only emphasising a fundamental feature which had been lost since Aristotle's day or which had been ignored for the sake of the formal patterns of reasoning.

Stillingfleet had objected that in Locke's way of certainty and demonstration there were 'no antecedents and consequents, no syllogistical methods of demonstration' (quoted by Locke, *Second Reply, Works,* IV, 385). Locke's reply is significant:

> If your lordship here means, that there be no antecedents and consequents in my book, or that I speak not or allow not of syllogism as a form of argumentation, that has its use, I humbly conceive the contrary is plain. But if...you mean, that I do not place certainty in having antecedents and consequents, or in making of syllogisms, I grant I do not (pp. 385–6).

Part of what Locke means to say in this reply is that we do not need the syllogism to give us certainty: people have always found certainty in ordinary affairs without reliance upon this formal mode of reasoning. But an equally important feature of his reply is his claim that he allows the syllogistical forms of argument to have a use. This claim is misleading, if taken to say that apart from formal argument and disputation, syllogism has a use. What we learn about the relations of ideas in Locke's kind of demonstration may be capable of being put into modes and figures of syllogism, but the logic of discovery Locke has in mind operates independently of such formal reasoning.

Early in Book I Locke indicated his own notion of demonstration. 1.4.23 speaks of '*ideas* placed in order, a due comparing of them, and deductions made with attention'. The *comparing* of ideas will reveal their relations, not the *insertion* of those ideas into formal modes and figures. Knowledge of any sort for Locke results from comparing ideas, seeing their relations; it does not result from deducing truths from those general maxims of the Schools, nor from discovering what follows from premises solely as a consequence of the relation of two terms to a middle term. Increase of knowledge and understanding, beyond what is discovered by the real existence and coexistence relations, depends upon ideas being laid out 'in such order one by another that the understanding may see the agreement or disagreement of those in question' (4.8.3). Mathematics is praised in the *Essay* (as it was later in the *Conduct*) as a model for exposing the non-contingent connexions of ideas; 'The art of finding proofs, and the admirable methods they have invented for the singling out and laying in order those intermediate *ideas* that demonstratively show the equality or inequality of inapplicable quantities, is that which has carried them so far and produced such wonderful and un-expected discoveries' (4. 12. 7). The informal terms Locke uses are significant: 'juxtaposition' of ideas, showing their connexions by the 'intervention' of one or more proofs (4. 13. 1), 'illation' (4. 17. 2). This last term is most important. Together with 'sagacity', illation is identified as one of the two intellectual faculties operating in reasoning. Sagacity discovers intermediate ideas which can reveal connexions, illation 'so orders the intermediate *ideas* as to discover what connexion there is in each link of the chain' (4. 17. 2). Illation is the same as inferring.[1] In some of the in-ferences we make between ideas, we are working with certainty and necessary connexions (4. 17. 2), while in others we are working with probability. In both, we are seeking to go beyond the con-tingent connexions discovered through sensation and observation.[2]

It is in 3. 17. 4 that Locke explicitly raises the question of whether the syllogism is the proper instrument for the use of sagacity and illation. Locke's answer is no. His first reason for this answer is curious: 'Because syllogism serves our reason but in one only of the forementioned parts of it, and that is to show the connexion of the proofs in any one instance, and no more.' In other words, the syllogistic relating of ideas does not enable us to generalise from that instance, is limited to the specific ideas related by each syllo-gism. For that, we do not need the syllogism, 'since the mind can perceive such connexion where it really is as easily, nay, perhaps better, without it'. Locke is not, I think, denying that syllogistic methods rest upon a general rule, for he refers several times to the

---

[1] Matthew Hale identifies 'illation' with ratiocination or discourse (*op. cit.* pp. 50–1. Cf. p. 238 where 'Illation upon Premises' appears as part of the title to ch. XI). Under 'illation', Bishop Wilkins lists: inference, consequence, sequel, conclusion, corollary, result, follow, imply, deduction (*op. cit.* p. 48). See also Thomas Tenison, *The Creed of Mr. Hobbes Examined* (1670), p. 20.

[2] Probability does not for Locke relate to contingent connexions but rather to what we might term 'probable necessary connexions'. That is, probability (and the assent and belief that go with it) attempts to generalise beyond the contingent certainties that coexistence and real existence disclose.

rule of syllogism. What he is denying is that that general rule helps us to see the connexion of ideas. 'If we will observe the actions of our own minds, we shall find that we reason best and clearest when we only observe the connexion of the proof, without reducing our thoughts to any rule of syllogism.' Some might doubt the truth of this psychological claim, but Locke has a stronger one to make against the syllogism. What we want to discover is some specific relation of ideas, though the ideas involved are general or class ideas. The syllogistic way of connecting ideas can just as well disclose the connexions of those ideas as class concepts as can Locke's more informal ordering. If Locke is denying this fact about the syllogism, he is surely wrong. What I think he wants to say is that knowing the general inference patterns of all the modes and figures does not aid at all in revealing the connexions of ideas. We have to perceive that connexion, whether we use the syllogistic form or not. The general schemata can only reveal those connexions when they are applied to particular cases. If that is true, it is not the general rule of syllogism which makes the disclosure, but the specific application. To Stillingfleet, Locke pointed out that he agreed with Aristotle that the principle of reason or inference is 'that what things agree in a third, agree among themselves', but to know that any two ideas do agree with a third requires me to *perceive* that agreement (*Works*, IV, 383–4). Aristotle himself 'found out some forms to be conclusive and others not, not by the forms themselves but by the original way of knowledge, i.e. by the visible agreement of *ideas*' (4.17.4). This being so, the syllogism has little advantage over other, less formal ways of revealing those agreements of ideas. The 'artificial form' of the syllogism restricts its use to those specialists who have 'thoroughly studied *mode* and *figure*'.

Do those trained in figure and mode, or those versed in inference patterns and well-formed formulae, by-pass the perception of the agreement of ideas united by the formal schema? I take Locke's answer to be no, again. Spotting a standard form of inference, seeing that a schema whose validity has been established is exemplified, may play the role of the intermediate idea in Locke's account. The spotting would be a function of sagacity. We still must perceive *that* the schema does relate the two ideas, or the two propositions on either side of the intermediate one. The syllogistic form gives no help in perceiving that connexion: 'it only shows that, if the intermediate *idea* agrees with those it is on both sides immediately applied to, then those two remote ones or, as they are called, *extremes* do certainly agree' (4.17.4). This perceiving is the illation in Locke's account. Knowing that an inference schema is valid and discovering that its pattern is exemplified in some argument or claim are not sufficient for apprehending the connexion: all that I would know would be that I have in this instance a case of formally valid connexions of ideas or propositions. I could *say* that the two ideas or propositions agreed (i.e. the one leads to the other), I could even be said to *know that* they were so connected. What I would lack would be a knowledge of the content of the claim or ideas and hence how the content or meaning of the two ideas was related. Locke finds formal relation inadequate, since it is incapable of disclosing the meaning-connexions of ideas or propositions. It is thus not so much the artificiality of figure and mode to which Locke objects as it is their generality and their formality.

It is in this context that Locke made his oft-quoted remark: 'But God has not been so sparing to men, to make them barely two-legged creatures, and left it to *Aristotle* to make them rational.' We do not learn to reason by following rules, we have 'a native faculty to perceive the coherence or incoherence' of our ideas. Locke freely admits that 'all right reasoning may be reduced to' the forms of syllogism. His claim is that we do not need to reason by so reducing arguments, nor is that even a way of reasoning. 'Right Reasoning is founded on something else than the *Predicaments* and *Predicables*, and does not consist in talking in *Mode* and *Figure* it self' (*Education*, p. 296, sect. 188). Reasoning is understanding the contents of our ideas and seeing how their contents (what I am calling their meaning, though Locke does not talk this way) are related. 'To infer is nothing but, by virtue of one proposition laid down as true, to draw in another as true, i.e. to see or suppose such a connexion of the two *ideas* of the inferred proposition.' Locke does not want to know that two propositions do stand in this relation of 'deducible from' or 'follow from'; he demands that the mind make the inference correctly. To make an inference correctly is, he explains, to find out intermediate ideas and to 'take a view of the connexion of them placed in a due order'. If the mind has proceeded without such a view, 'it has not so much made an inference that will hold or an inference of right reason as shown a willingness to have it be, or be taken as such'. To have knowledge is not to know that a formal schema has been exemplified, it is to have perceived the connexions of meaning. To expose the connexions of meaning, Locke recommends that we move no faster from premise to conclusion than we are able to perceive the immediate connexion of ideas. Thus, how shall we see that the conclusion, 'Men can determine themselves', follows from the proposition, 'Men shall be punished in another world'? The lay-out Locke recommends is as follows:

(1) Men shall be punished in another world;
(2) God the punisher.

For this move, I have to see that there has to be a punisher if men are to be punished, a rather trivial point. That God is the proper punisher is a function of other ideas which Locke elsewhere relates.

(3) Just punishment.

For the punishment to be just

(4) the punished must be guilty and
(5) be able to do otherwise, which requires
(6) man is free, and hence
(7) is able to determine himself.

There is, Locke believes, a natural order of ideas which his lay-out retains, but which syllogistic form disrupts and makes more difficult for men to follow the connexions. By a natural order Locke seems to mean that there is an order in which we think of related ideas. The cluster of concepts in the example of punishment in another world could be made to reveal the connexions they have by moving through them in almost any fashion, but Locke presumably only means that the natural order is any one we find clarifying. An artificial schema like the syllogism pushes us out of our ordinary way of linking these concepts. If syllogism must be used, Locke insists that 'the natural order of the connecting *ideas* must direct the order of the *syllogism*' (4.17.4).

Moreover, he is not opposed to 'rules of art' which can aid the sagacity and illation. He only wants to say the art of the syllogism is no aid, 'The rules of *syllogism* serve not to furnish the mind with those intermediate *ideas* that may show the connexion of remote ones'. In 4.17.7 Locke cites a remark of Hooker lamenting the lack of proper and useful aids to reason. Locke does not 'pretend to have found or discovered here any of the *right helps of art*', though his lay-out might count as a preliminary, under-labourer aid.[1] The suggestion is that there are men (not the disputating logicians) who may be able to produce such rules of art. 'But I can be bold to say that this age is adorned with some men of that strength of judgment and largeness of comprehension that, if they would employ their thoughts on this subject, could open new and undiscovered ways to the advancement of know-ledge.' Algebra is cited as an example of a method in mathematics which succeeded in relating ideas not formerly believed to be related. Could there be developed a general art of reasoning, it would be similar to algebra in showing us how to find ideas which could disclose the relations of ideas not normally seen. In this way would knowledge be advanced.

Such aids would help us to find connecting ideas, they would not eliminate the need for laying-out and ordering ideas. It is the *visible* connexion, the *juxtaposition* which is for Locke the indis-pensable device for relating ideas in demonstration. The inter-mediate idea functions like the measuring yard-stick which enables us to discover that two houses which could not be brought to-gether and laid side by side are in fact of equal length (4.17.18). Draft A of the *Essay* speaks also of comparing one extension, whose length we know, with another which we do not know: 'The foundation whereof being all laid in sense, viz. sight, the certainty thereof however looked on as the greatest we can or expect to have can be noe greater then that of discerning by our eyes, which the very name Demonstration how highly soever magnified for its certainty doth signify' (Aaron and Gibb, p. 21). Later in the same draft, Locke said demonstrations 'are as the word denotes the beare shewing of the things or proposing them

---

[1] It is of some interest that Locke says what he has said about reasoning is 'to me wholly new and unborrowed' (4.17.7).

to our senses or understandings soe as to make us take notice of them' (p. 47). Locke may also have had support for this notion of demonstration from the method of superposition of figures in Euclid's geometry.

The geometry of Euclid, with its frequent appeal to the ideal super-position of one figure upon another, comprised all the mathematics with which he was thoroughly familiar, and coloured his whole view of mathematical and other knowledge. For he failed to observe that this method of superposition is not applicable beyond the region of geometry. Accordingly, the 'juxtaposition' of ideas and 'application' of ideas to one another, become terms of constant occurrence in his account of our knowledge.[1]

I have been unable to discover whether superposition as a method of demonstration in geometry was stressed in the seventeenth century, or whether Gibson's suggestion about the extent of Locke's knowledge of mathematics and geometry is correct. R. Harré has pointed out to me that the Hobbes–Wallis dispute raged, in part, around just this issue: Hobbes attempted to introduce motion into geometry. Hobbes remarked to Wallis that 'motion' occurs in some of the definitions of Euclid's *Elements*. He went on to say: 'But I must here put you in mind, that geometry being a science, and all science proceeding from a precognition of causes, the definition of a sphere, and also of a circle, by the generation of it, that is to say, by motion, is better than by the equality of distance from a point within' (Hobbes, *Works*, VII, 210). Earlier, Hobbes talked of 'the superposition of quantities', defining 'measure' as follows: '*one quantity is the measure of another quantity, when it, or the multiple of it, is coincident in all points with the other quantity*' (*ibid.* p. 196).[2] The method of superposition is explicitly cited by Euclid in 1.4 and 1.8. For example, 1.4 says: 'For, if the triangle ABC be applied to the triangle DEF, and if the point A be placed on the point D and the straight line AB on DE, then the point B will also coincide with E, because AB is

---

[1] James Gibson, 'Locke's Theory of Mathematical Knowledge and of a Possible Science of Ethics', *Mind*, v (1896), 39. See also Gibson's *Locke's Theory of Knowledge*, pp. 152, 155.

[2] It is likely that Locke knew of this famous debate although he did not have in his library any of the pamphlets in this exchange. Harré very kindly allowed me to read an unpublished paper of his on this debate.

equal to *DE*.' In his note on this and the 1.8 proposition, Heath says that it is clear that in both these passages, Euclid did mean that we actually would move one figure and place it on top of the other figure. Heath thinks Euclid was not entirely happy with this method, that he tried to replace it where possible, but that it is fundamental to the *Elements* since so much depends on proposition 1.4.[1] At least, the presence of superposition in Euclid and Hobbes's efforts at a geometry of motion show that the literal moving alongside and on top of was one sense of 'demonstration' which Locke could have had in mind. His own statements about juxta-position and seeing certainly fit into this sense.

In his constant stress (especially in the long passage in 4.17.4) upon the literal ordering of ideas by putting the words which stand for the ideas down on paper, Locke is in effect substituting a formal pattern of his own to replace the syllogistical ordering. It is a 'simple and plain order' as he saw, but it was designed to facilitate that mental perception without which no reasoning and demonstrating was possible. To demonstrate was, for Locke, not just to bring someone to understand the connexions of ideas by means of intermediary ideas, it was to write down propositions or phrases incorporating the ideas in such a way that the mind and the eye could work together in moving down or across the page in a step-wise fashion to the final conclusion. The lay-out of argument Locke recommended attempts to capture the way in which our thinking does in fact move from idea to idea. It was not a device for making explicit an association of ideas: Locke's added chapter on the association of ideas (2.33) makes it quite clear that he saw the difference between conceptual analysis and descriptive

---

1 See *The Thirteen Books of Euclid's Elements*, trans. and edited by T. L. Heath (Cambridge, 1956). Heath points out that objections to superposition have been made: it takes away the theoretical dignity of the demonstration, it introduces motion into geometry. This latter objection is perhaps the most telling: 'Since geometry is concerned with empty space, which is immovable, it would be at least strange if it was necessary to have recourse to the real motion of bodies for a definition, and for the proof of the properties, of immovable space' (pp. 226–7). Berkeley queried this method, observing that with one triangle on top of another, the under one would be nothing at all since it would not be perceived. Moreover, Berkeley remarked, lines and surfaces cannot, on the definitions given, be touched or felt (*Philosophical Commentaries*, entries 528, 514, 531). (I am indebted to Professor W. Kneale for the references to Heath's edition of Euclid.)

psychology. There are links between concepts, relations in our thought and language, which demonstration must elucidate. 'Some of our *ideas* have a natural correspondence and connexion one with another; it is the office and excellency of our reason to trace these, and hold them together in that union and correspondence which is founded in their peculiar beings' (2.32.5; section 8 distinguishes between 'natural and acquired antipathies'). An elucidation of conceptual connexions might be thought of as a kind of natural history, exposing the relations between ideas similar to the natural scientist's recording of the relations of qualities. Locke does note many conceptual connexions (his polemics often challenge by denying the connexions claimed), but his main interest was with countering the syllogistic method with one of his own, a method of demonstration which he thought would preserve the natural order and connexion of ideas and which might lead the way to a new kind of logic, an informal logic of concepts.

There are, then, two methods to science accepted by Locke. The *method of natural history* proceeds by experiment and observation, recording the experienced coexistences, working within the relation of real existence. The *method of demonstration* applies primarily to mixed modes, to those ideas not fetched from things themselves. His remarks on demonstration are clearly designed to provide a method for the knowledge and understanding of the relation between ideas. Those relations and this method were particularly useful in the science of action where, according to Locke, our concepts and ideas are not empirical. The method of deducing from essence, were we able to use it, would apply the method of conceptual analysis to material and immaterial objects, as God's understanding does. The compass of human understanding is limited, though adequate to our needs. The two methods which Locke endorses are fitted to guide our understanding to a knowledge of things as they are in themselves and to an enlargement of our knowledge of conceptual connexions.

4

RELATIONS IN KNOWLEDGE AND REALITY

At the observational level physical objects are retainers to other objects; what they are as observable objects is a function of environment and context. Relation is the important feature of things themselves as perceived and perceivable, though not all the observed relational properties of things are perceiver-dependent: some, the primary ones, are object-dependent. In both cases—observable properties that are perceiver-dependent and those that are object-dependent—the science of nature strives to record the coexistence of qualities defining objects. Coexistence is both an ontological and an epistemic relation. There *are* qualities in relation, and the groupings we select define for us the objects relevant to our needs and interests. Locke was most concerned with the epistemic role of relations, but he did not overlook their ontological status. Locke is usually read as denying the reality of relations, as his own words do frequently suggest. Relation is not, he says, 'contained in the real existence of things, but something extraneous and superinduced' (2.25.8). In this context it appears that the superinducing is done by the mind comparing one object with another; Locke is giving his analysis of the origin of our *ideas* of relations. As with qualities, Locke is not always careful to distinguish his talk about relations from the talk about the ideas of relations. In fact he is less concerned with relations than with the ideas of relations. Nevertheless, both his metaphysic and his science of nature find relations in nature. Relative ideas arise from the activity of the mind in comparing ideas or things. An analysis of relative ideas indicates the objects which stand in the specific relation designated by that idea.

If a word does not lead the mind to things and qualities other than those *in* (in the non-relative sense) the thing being considered, that word is not relative. Thus, the following are absolute, i.e. not relative, words: a man, black, merry, thoughtful, thirsty, angry, extended, because in each case I am talking about an object and the properties it has. The man is merry, thirsty, etc. On the other hand a man is not, *qua* man, a father, brother, king, husband, blacker, merrier: these are relative terms since they 'imply also something else separate and exterior to the existence of the thing' (2.25.10). The word or idea, 'husband', *intimates* some other person, 'whiter' intimates some other thing (2.25.1). Other examples of correlative terms, those with '*reciprocal intimations*' (2), are father–son, bigger–less, cause–effect. Language does not always mark reciprocal intimations with correlative terms, e.g. 'concubine' (2), 'constable', 'dictator' (2.28.3), though 'when duly considered' such names are seen to 'include evident relations' (2.25.2). A name for correlative relations which does not mark the reciprocality of the relation is called an 'external denomination'. Besides the relative terms and the external denominations, there are '*seemingly positive* terms' like 'old', 'great', 'imperfect', which do intimate beyond themselves (3). Locke speaks of the relations thus named as *observable*. Relative names do not signify 'something absolute in the' object (something non-relative), but they *denominate* or *intimate* the objects that are related. The relation itself does not wait upon our thought and language, since being a concubine or being a father involves, whether we recognise it and mark it in our language, more than one person. The relation depends upon the existence of the relata, e.g. Caius ceases to be a father upon the death of his son (5).

In saying of relation that 'it be not contained in the real existence of things, but something extraneous and superinduced' (8), Locke means only to say that relations are not positive or absolute properties of things, not properties which objects have by themselves. Relations are real, however, in the sense that objects do in fact stand in relation with other objects. He does not mean, for instance, that a man is not a husband, that he does not stand in certain relations to a wife. 'Husband' is a term we apply to certain objects when they satisfy certain conditions. Specific actions are performed when I marry, actions which constitute marriage. That those actions are called marriage is a function of our society and of our language. The role of language and thought in naming types of actions differs in some interesting ways from their role in naming physical objects. The nominal or named features of objects must be related to things as accurately as possible. The nominal essence can be real or fantastical. With actions, I can form a concept and a name of some action not witnessed by me: this is a characteristic of mixed modes. Normally my action locutions do apply to what people do. The institutional facts of actions have a basis in the behaviour of people, but they differ from relations like father–son in 'that they are most, if not all, some way or other alterable and separable from the persons to whom they have sometimes belonged, though neither of the substances so related be destroyed' (2.28.3). Even those relations Locke calls 'natural', e.g. father, son, brothers, cousins-german (blood relations), are more fitted to 'the use of common life' than to 'the truth and extent of things', since it is certain that in reality the relation is 'the same betwixt the begetter and the begotten in the several races of other animals as well as men' (2).

The 'use of common life' never diverges wholly from the way things are. Action-concepts and moral rules are directed upon what men do, physical concepts must, to be useful, be patterned after the objects they name. The relation of being a pattern or standard is one of the more important ones for Locke; it is a relation bound in with several others embedded in his account of nature and presupposed in his science of nature. Cause and effect is 'the most comprehensive relation wherein all things that do or can exist are concerned' (2.25.11). Things partake of this relation, the corpuscular hypothesis ascribes causes to things. Identity and diversity are two other relations of importance for Locke, both ontologically and epistemically, though identity is peculiar in not requiring more than one object. Things have identity by existing, being in one place at one time is the criterion of identity of a body (2.27.2). While existing things are particular, Locke points out that they are similar, their similitude is observed and forms the basis for our knowledge of things as sets of coexisting qualities. Similitude should not be confused with conformity, agreement, or pattern, even though agreement is a relation that includes resemblance. It is the relation of agreement which plays such a fundamental role in Locke's definition of knowledge in 4.1.

There is a cluster of terms Locke uses in different places for the relation of agreement: conformity, pattern, standard, archetype, copy, ectype, resemblance. The terms in this cluster are closely related to another set: real–fantastical, adequate–inadequate, true–false. The characteristics of the reality, adequacy, and truth of ideas (and of the propositions or judgments made up of ideas) are similar. A real idea is one which has 'a foundation in nature, such as have a conformity with the real being and existence of things, or with their archetypes' (2.30.1). Being 'conformable to some real existence' is not the same as being conformable to 'that real constitution and essence of anything' (2.32.4). We can never say our ideas are conformable to the real essence of an object, but every actual sense perception gives us reason for saying the sensory ideas conform to some real existence. 'Conformity' in this case does not only mean 'image', since it is only the ideas of primary qualities which exactly copy or image their qualities. All simple ideas agree with the reality of things in the sense of being caused by things.[1] Causal correspondence constitutes agreement to some real existence. Agreement to some real essence would require at least the precise grouping of the primary qualities of the insensible parts. In this way, our ideas of substances are inadequate, since they do not 'represent...that constitution on which all their properties depend' (2.31.2). Our ideas of substances can be adequate at the observational level, where they 'are designed to be pictures and representations in the mind of things that do exist, by ideas of those qualities that are discoverable in them' (6). Even here, our ideas of things are frequently incomplete (and in this sense inadequate) since the qualities and powers of body are 'so many and various that no man's complex idea contains them all' (8; cf. 13). With respect to bodies, agreement covers both 'cause' and 'pattern'.

In stating that the reality of ideas consists in the conformity with the 'real being and existence of things, or with their archetype' (2.30.1), the last phrase is important since it indicates that the conformity relation which makes ideas real is not restricted to

---

[1] Locke was careful to remark, à propos 4.4, in the *Bibliothèque Universelle* abridgement: 'Je n'entends pas une conformité de ressemblance, mais la conformité qui est entre un effet constant et sa cause.'

the relation between ideas and bodies. The conformity of any idea to its archetype makes the idea real. The conformity of my idea of murder to the concept of murder in my society makes my idea real, if I include the same simple ideas in my complex idea of murder as my society does. A fantastical idea is one that has no conformity 'with that reality to which' it is 'tacitly referred' (2.30.1; see 2.31.4). The reference of an idea is important in determining whether it is real or adequate: it is the intended (and appropriate) agreement that is relevant. Since the ideas of mixed modes and relations are not intended to be (nor need be) copies from anything, there is a second and more fundamental sense of their reality, 'a possibility of existing conformable to them' (2.30.4). These ideas are themselves archetypes and standards which measure actions. Only if they are inconsistent would they be unreal. The conformity to the ordinary signification of our ideas or words gives a derivative sense of reality and adequacy. Abstract ideas are 'something in the mind between the thing that exists and the name that is given to it', they have a double conformity to things and names. Our action-concepts also normally have a double conformity, to actions and names. For ideas of physical objects and ideas of actions (though Locke does not explicitly say the latter), 'it is in our *ideas* that both the rightness of our knowledge and the propriety or intelligibleness of our speaking consists' (2.32.8). Without such double conformity we would 'think amiss of things in themselves, and talk of them unintelligibly to others'. Similarly, a proposition that correctly stands for or agrees with ideas is verbally (or nominally) true; but, if the ideas are meant to signify or agree with things, the proposition gives real truth, a truth of things (4.5.8).

The relation of agreement or conformity, then, has at least three different meanings: resemblance, caused by, and standard (this last, as a moral rule is the standard for right and wrong, physical object and moral concepts are the standards for meanings).[1] There are a number of different kinds of agreements in

---

[1] The terms 'standard' and 'archetype' are used wherever something—word, idea, or thing—functions as the rule for our ideas. See 3.9.13 where coexisting qualities function as the standard for our ideas and names of things; 3.11.15 where mixed modes are standards; and 3.6 where the language of standards is applied to substance.

the knowledge relation. Just how many there are is, at first glance, unclear, since Locke gives two different listings of them. A close look at those lists, and at his examples and discussions of them, enables us to be precise about those cognitive relations. The two listings are as follows:

(A) *4.1.3*
  1. Identity, or diversity
  2. Relation
  3. Coexistence, or necessary connexion. (The examples of this relation cited in 4.1.6–7 are only of coexistence.)
  4. Real existence

(B) *4.3.8–9, 18, 21*
  1. Identity and diversity
  2. Coexistence
  3. Relation
  4. Real existence

The definition of knowledge in 4.1.2 speaks of the connexion and agreement *of* ideas. We might think that 'connexion' means 'necessary connexion', since its negative is 'repugnancy' and that is clearly a logical term at this time. Hence, we might expect that Locke will go on to define knowledge in demonstrative or necessary terms only. It *is* the case that he goes on to talk of connexions *and* agreements for a few lines, but the concepts of agreement and disagreement seem to be taken as the basic ones since the four kinds of agreement include necessary connexion. I do not think 'connexion' is the same as 'agreement'. What Locke seems to be doing—what one would expect him to do once one had seen his special concern with the science of nature—is to offer a definition of knowledge wide enough to cover both demonstrative (or necessary) and non-demonstrative relations.

The listings detailing the knowledge relation clearly support this suggestion. Both lists contain necessary and non-necessary relations. The agreement called 'relation' appears to be redundant on list (A), since 'necessary connexion' is cited under 3. It is not redundant on list (B), where 'necessary connexion' does not appear.[1] 'Relation' covers all instances of necessary connexions

---

[1] List B also appears, though rearranged, in 4.7.3 (identity, relation, coexistence, real existence) and in the *Bibliothèque Universelle* abridgement (Jan. 1688, VIII, 120) as identity, coexistence, real existence, relation.

between ideas. The example cited in 4.1.7 of this kind of agreement is '*two triangles upon equal bases between two parallels are equal*'. The discussion of this cognitive relation in 4.3.18 also uses the language of demonstration. The relation in this case holds *between* ideas, the aim of Locke's account of demonstration being, as we have seen, to disclose the conceptual connexions between ideas. The relation of coexistence also holds between ideas, but the connexion there is only contingent. The first relation on both lists involves single ideas alone, though in perceiving the agreement of a simple idea with itself I am enabled to perceive its disagreement or diversity from other ideas. But the first kind of agreement is that of an idea with itself. The 'or' in the phrase 'identity, or diversity' cannot be the 'or' of equivalence; it separates two sub-types of agreement and disagreement, as its replacement by 'and' in list (B) indicates. These two relations may not be separable: the agreement of an idea with itself goes along with its diversity from other ideas, the perception of one leads to the perception of the other. Nevertheless, they are two different perceptions. The fourth kind of agreement, real existence, is a relation between idea and thing (God, self, or physical object).[1]

The knowledge relation, as outlined in these brief listings of the kinds of agreement cited by Locke, does not always require two ideas, is not always *between* ideas but is in some cases a feature *of* ideas. The perception of any kind of relation between or of ideas can produce knowledge. The term 'agreement' signals an intimation of something beyond the idea itself. Sometimes the intimation is of other ideas contingently coexisting with the idea, other times it is of other ideas necessarily connected with the idea, still other times the agreement intimates some physical cause producing the idea. While the only immediate objects of the mind in thought and reasoning are its own ideas, we are able to go beyond the ideas of the present moment through the coexistence and necessary connexion relations. More importantly, we are able

---

[1] Locke only discusses the real-existence relation in connexion with our sensory ideas. The relation *there* is causal, bodies cause my sensory ideas. I know by intuition that I exist and by demonstration that God exists. In these last two cases, the real existence relation seems to be replaced by the truth relation. That is, both 'I exist' and 'God exists' are known to be true. Locke's treatment of *these* existential propositions is brief. His main concern was with existential claims for body.

to know that our coexisting sensory ideas have a basis in the physical world. Did none of our ideas intimate beyond themselves to things, we could make no claims for our knowledge being real. Our knowledge may only be 'conversant about' ideas (4.1.1) but some of those ideas stand in the agreement relation of 'caused by' to physical objects.

It has been easy to take Locke's definition of knowledge as being the perception of the agreement or disagreement *between* ideas only. Such a reading seems obvious from the emphasis Locke places upon ideas being the only immediate object of thought. Moreover, Locke does not always follow the *between* locution; only when discussing coexistence and necessary connexion. Sometimes Locke says without qualification that 'knowledge consists only in perceiving the habitudes and relations of ideas one to another' (*Conduct*, in *Works*, III, 262; cf. p. 236. Also, *Essay* 4.2.15; 4.4.12). Furthermore, when challenged by Stillingfleet that the way of ideas does not permit us to say we can 'know the actual existence of any thing by our senses' because we know 'nothing, but of the perceived agreement of ideas', Locke attempts to show how the perception of the relation between two ideas enables us to say an actual object exists. 'Now the two ideas, that in this case are perceived to agree, and do thereby produce knowledge, are the idea of actual sensation (which is an action whereof I have a clear and distinct idea) and the idea of actual existence without me that causes that sensation' (*Second Reply*, in *Works*, IV, 360). Stillingfleet had referred to 4.11; Locke suggests he missed the distinction there between an idea 'that has by a former sensation been lodged in the mind' and the 'actually receiving any idea' (*ibid.*). To sense or be aware in any way is to have some idea, it being one of Locke's principles that 'having *ideas* and perceiving ...[are] the same thing' (2.1.9). Yet, perceiving and having ideas are not identical, as if we cannot distinguish content from act. My reflective idea of sensing differs from my reflective ideas of recalling, feeling pleasure, or reasoning: the faculties and operations these ideas refer to differ from one another. The difference is not, on Locke's own account, analysable into a difference of kinds of ideas received when I sense, recall, feel pleasure, or reason, though difference of an idea is part of the difference of process. Locke's response to Stillingfleet in this matter is accordingly misleading, even on his own account of thinking, perceiving, etc. On Locke's account of the relation of real existence (4.4 and 4.11) it is not the *idea* of actual sensation which carries the agreement with physical causes but the *receiving* of sensory ideas (see especially 4.11.1–2; 4.2.14 speaks of the 'actual entrance of ideas'). To translate the real-existence relation as holding between the idea of actual sensation and the idea of actual existence of something without me leaves the nature of the agreement in this case unclear, makes it sound as if it was just that the two ideas were not incompatible, that they are consistent; it diverts attention from the clearly expressed point in the *Essay* that the agreement involved in real existence is a causal relation. The very nature of receiving sensory ideas is such that I know they have a causal origin outside me. To know this does involve having the idea of an actual existence, but that idea arises from an act of receiving a sensory idea.

A consequence of this recognition about Locke's definition of knowledge is that knowledge is not limited to certainty in the deductive or demonstrative sense of entailment. Real existence does not yield this kind of certainty, though he says it is more than probability. The third type of agreement includes, as one of two relations, the perception of coexistence or non-coexistence. Coexistence in this type of agreement is not the same as necessary connexion. It is most important to see that Locke's first examples of this third sort of agreement are only of coexistence: necessary connexion is not even mentioned. Sections 4.1.6–7 cite the familiar examples of observed coexistences which were so important in his account of the science of nature. Locke has thus explicitly included observational and non-necessary or non-deductive knowing among knowledge. The experimental, historical method yields knowledge. Locke singles out identity and coexistence in 7 where he repeats the list of four kinds of agreement but cites only coexistence as the third type, omitting entirely necessary connexion (list B). What may appear as an exception is 4.7.5, where Locke speaks of coexisting ideas that stand in a relation of necessary connexion to each other. But at the very most, all that this passage does is to remind us that ideas linked by necessary connexions do coexist, either with each other directly or via some intermediary ideas. The perception of necessary connexion, which is what demonstration consists in for Locke, requires the intuitive grasp of that connexion. For that, the ideas must be co-present to us, whether their connexion is logical or conceptual. For the most part, talk of coexistence is reserved for the non-necessary connected ideas. Put in the language of qualities, the qualities of observed objects coexist but they do not, for us at least, stand in any necessary connexions. It might help to distinguish two types of coexistence, the necessary and the non-necessary. It is the latter which Locke frequently links to the science of nature.

It may also be significant that coexistence is listed second, after identity, in the second listing of the four kinds of agreement. About this kind of agreement Locke says: 'in this our knowledge is very short, though in this consists the greatest and most material part of our knowledge concerning substance' (4.3.9). This sort of knowledge tells us what qualities go together. Section 10 points out that the knowledge of coexistence, which is a weighty and considerable part of human science, is narrow and limited since we do not have a knowledge of any necessary connexions or inconsistencies between coexisting qualities. Such knowledge is limited to experienced coexistences. We do not have a deductive knowledge of bodies, only an experimental knowledge (14; cf. 4.3.29). Nevertheless, it is knowledge that experience and observation yield. 'We see animals are generated, nourished, and move; the loadstone draws iron; and the parts of a candle, successively melting, turn into flame and give us both light and heat. These and the like effects we see and know...' (4.16.12). As far as experience reaches to the coexistence of qualities 'I may have certain knowledge' (4.12.9). We 'cannot know certainly any two to *co-exist* any further than experience by our senses informs us' (4.3.14); 'it is by trying alone that I can certainly know what other qualities co-exist with' one I have already discovered (4.12.9). But in this reliance upon sense experience, we do *certainly* know the coexistences we discover. Moreover, experimental knowledge is knowledge *about* something. Sensitive knowledge is real. Merely from co-existing qualities we cannot conclude that our knowledge is real, but from the actual receiving of ideas of sense we can (4.11.1; 4.9.1). In other words, the type of agreement called (non-necessary) coexistence is different from the type called real existence. Both are involved in scientific knowledge, though it is coexistence which constitutes that science. Our science would not be real and significant were it not *of* bodies in the world. The co-existing qualities we observe can be taken as belonging to objects. They agree with those objects in the sense that they are caused by their objects. The causal *nature* of perception—not the causal *theory*—roots the qualities we observe in the world.

If I am right in saying one of the main concerns of the *Essay* was to give a philosophical foundation (or interpretation) of the scientific practices and discoveries of people like Boyle, Hooke, and Sydenham, the coexistence of qualities yields, when carefully noted, one of the most important features of human knowledge. It is here that arises all the knowledge of things themselves which man can have. Such knowledge is not universal, except of what we mean by our physical object names. Nor is it a knowledge of the real essence, but a careful observation does yield a knowledge of the observable features of bodies.[1] The conclusions of the argu-ment from the nature of things themselves are not general propo-sitions about the world, and hence their certainty is not that of universal knowledge. Locke frequently puts the propositions which result from observation in the past tense, perhaps as a way of indicating they cannot be given validity as universal claims, e.g. 'fire warmed a man', 'iron sank in water'. We *take* such proposi-tions as true for the future, however, and allow them to 'govern our thoughts as absolutely and influence all our actions as fully as the most evident demonstration' (4.16.6). No general or universal *existential* proposition can be certain; probability enters our science at this point. The certainty of universal, non-existen-tial propositions derives from their abstraction from particularity, is a function of the conceptual connexions of the ideas in those

---

[1] Experienced coexistences are not limited to body. We acquire our complex idea of man by 'collection and observation'. The coexisting qualities of the idea of man include white colour, a specific shape, laughter, rational discourse, language user (4.7.16–18).

propositions. All '*general knowledge* lies only in our own thoughts and consists barely in the contemplation of our own abstract ideas' (4.6.13; cf. 4.6.16; 4.3.13; 4.9.1). A rational science of nature would produce propositions about body that were universally true; for this, we need to know the scope and limits of classes as real species (4.6.4). Universal propositions deal with necessary connexions. Experimental knowledge contrasts with universal or general knowledge just in the former's lack of any necessary connexions, apart from some conceptual necessities of the meanings of our physical object terms.

To deny *universal* certainty to the science of nature is not to deny it *certainty*, nor is it to say it does not yield knowledge. Not all certainty is of the necessary sort. There was in the seventeenth century a doctrine of kinds or degrees of certainty.[1] Locke has his own variation of this doctrine. The knowledge relations all yield certainty, the range of propositions said to be certain includes four different types. (1) *Intuition* yields the greatest certainty, perhaps also the first in time. A child 'knows as certainly, before it can speak, the difference between the *ideas* of sweet and bitter (i.e. that sweet is not bitter) as it knows afterwards (when it comes to speak) that wormwood and sugar-plums are not the same thing' (1.2.15). A child also 'certainly knows that a stranger is not its mother' (4.7.9). I am certain that the ideas I receive from an external object are in my mind (4.2.14). I know such truths as that white is not black, a circle is not a triangle (1). These truths are said to be *infallibly* certain (4.7.4). Locke also seems to include under intuition some metaphysical principles, e.g. that '*nothing can no more produce any real being than it can be equal to two*

---

[1] Cf. Matthew Hale, *The Primitive Origination of Mankind*, who distinguishes four different kinds of certainty: (1) the certainty of logical demonstrations which yield eternal truths; (2) 'Mathematical conclusions have an infallible certainty by Mathematical Demonstration'; (3) objects 'objected immediately to our sense have another kind of certainty by sensible evidence'; and (4) 'matters simply of fact not objected immediately to our Sense have another kind of certainty' (p. 129). Bishop Wilkins cited physical certainty (sensory knowledge), mathematical certainty (mathematical and logical truths) and moral certainty. The first and third types of certainty are said to be indubitable, the second to be infallible (*Of the Principles and Duties of Natural Religion*, pp. 5–10, 17). There is some discussion of the different kinds of certainty used by Chillingworth, Tillotson, Wilkins, Glanvill and others in Henry G. Van Leeuwen, *The Problem of Certainty in English Thought, 1630–1690*.

right angles', and that '*something* must be *from eternity*' (4.10.3, 8).
In the same way, it is certain that objects are but retainers to
other parts of nature (4.6.11). (2) *Demonstration* always has to do
with general truths which are abstract and universal. Locke
frequently terms this certainty *universal* or *undoubted* (4.4.7, 10).
(3) *Sensing* also produces certain knowledge. Such knowledge is
particular and limited to the present moment. While I write this
sentence, it is certain that this ink and this paper are not all of a
colour (4.2.5). I cannot doubt that something really exists causing
this appearance I call 'white paper' (4.11.2). I cannot be 'uncertain of the existence of those things' which I see and feel (3; cf.
4.16.12). 4.15.6 speaks of 'the certainty of observations', 5
giving as an example my seeing a man walk on ice: 'If I myself
see a man walk on ice, it is past *probability*, it is knowledge.'[1] I
cannot doubt that 'actual seeing hath a cause without' (4.11.5, 8).
'Thus, seeing water at this instant, it is an unquestionble truth
to me that water doth exist' (11). (4) *Memory* also yields certainty.
Remembering that I saw water yesterday, it will 'be always true
and, as long as my memory retains it, always an undoubted
proposition to me that water did exist 10th *July*, 1688'. Remembering that I did once demonstrate some truth, I can claim certain
knowledge of that truth (4.1.9). Remembering that I saw a man
run another man through, I certainly know now that that man
wounded that other man (*ibid,*). The truth of this memory
proposition depends, of course, upon the truth of a sensory
proposition: seeing X run Y through gives me the sensory
knowledge that X wounded Y.

The three degrees of knowledge distinguished by Locke,
intuitive, demonstrative, and sensitive (4.2.14), do not give a
separate category to memory. We cannot therefore say just
where the certainty of memory-knowledge comes in Locke's
scale. That he recognised different kinds of certainty is beyond
doubt, since in the passage just referred to Locke expressly says of
the three degrees of knowledge: 'in each of which there are

[1] The sense certainty in this example is a function of other supporting experiences,
e.g. having learned about frozen water, etc. Locke contrasts the knowledge he
can have from this sensory experience with the probability, or less, that a man
born in the tropics might have of hearing (even, presumably, of seeing for the
first time) about such an event.

different degrees and ways of evidence and certainty'. No matter what kind of agreement relation it is that we perceive *between* and *of* ideas, there we find knowledge: 'Wherever we perceive the agreement or disagreement of any of our *ideas*, there is certain knowledge' (4.4.18). Only by failing to see that the four kinds of agreement relation differ, could we make the mistake of saying all knowledge for Locke involves necessary connexions, that the only kind of certainty he recognised was logical.[1]

[1] Laudan makes this mistake: 'To know that a statement X is true is to perceive that we could not conceive things to be other than the state of affairs which X specifies' ('The Nature and Sources of Locke's Views on Hypotheses', *loc. cit.* p. 214). Laudan draws the conclusion: 'In this way we "know" the truth of mathematics. But we do not "know" anything about the physical world' (*ibid.*). He may be led into the error by identifying 'the physical world' with 'the minute parts of bodies'; since the latter cannot be known in any sense for Locke, the translation into no knowledge of the physical world follows easily. Such an identification for Locke is patently wrong. Whatever the source of the error, Laudan has failed to see that the mathematical or logical sense of 'know' does not and cannot hold for the coexistence and real existence relations. Locke says, e.g., many times that we can conceive coexisting qualities not coexisting, or more usually, that there is no discoverable necessary connexion between them.

5

KNOWLEDGE OF BODY

Locke's definition of knowledge in Book 4 of the *Essay* has usually been taken to have demonstration as its model: the cognitive relation has been interpreted as deductive and necessary. What I take to have shown in the previous chapter is that Locke carefully constructed the concept of knowledge so as to allow for both demonstrative and factual, necessary and non-necessary knowledge. The non-necessary knowledge, covered by two of the cognitive relations, real existence and coexistence, was of contingent relations in reality, but our knowledge of those relations was certain. The coexistence relation is by far the more important of these two contingent, cognitive relations. The relation which in fact holds between qualities may be necessary (in the sense that other intelligences might perceive them as necessary), contingency may just be a result of the limitations of human knowledge; that is not a matter of great importance for Locke. What he thought worth stressing is that our knowledge of those coexisting qualities can be and is, under careful observation and attention, certain. The range or extent of such factual but certain knowledge is not large, being particular and limited to present- or (with the help of memory) past-tense propositions. The basis can be found in the *Essay* for extending our factual knowledge to future-tense and even generalised claims, but only as probable, not certain knowledge. Probability does not appear in Locke's analysis of knowledge, there is no cognitive relation for it. In fact, probability applies to those demonstrations which lead to judgment, rather than to certain knowledge. His brief discussion of probability, his somewhat longer discussion of belief, assent, and judgment come only after he has charted in the nature and extent of knowledge as certainty. It may not seem that Locke has given us very much by way of factual *knowledge*: we tend to believe it is the generalisations and predictions in empirical science which are the real cognitive accomplishments. But in trying to understand Locke's account of the science of nature, and in seeing how and where his science of signs (the epistemology of idea-signs in particular) fits into and supports his analysis of experimental science, we must recognise that he was as much concerned with the knowledge of that science as with the universal and demonstrative knowledge of necessary connexions. The answer he gave to the question 'Can we *know* body?' was clearly affirmative. We know, by the relation of real existence, *that* there are bodies; and we know by coexistence what the specific qualities are that make up our idea of particular bodies.

Even if my interpretation of the way in which Locke says that we know body is accepted, there remain two fundamental questions, either one of which could defeat the affirmative answer about knowledge of body. One of these questions is 'Can we know *body*?' (as opposed to knowing only ideas and their relations). The second of these additional questions is 'What is the nature of the body that is known?'. These questions are intertwined. The second question would be useless if, as has usually been assumed, the answer to the first is 'no', because the way of ideas and the representative theory of perception have been thought to lead to scepticism. However, we could still uncover the concept of object which seems to be at work in the *Essay*. The first of these additional questions can be answered only by a further examination of Book 4, with passages from other books which deal with the nature of body.

Book 4 opens with the reminder that 'the *mind*, in all its thoughts and reasonings, hath no other immediate object but its own *ideas*'; hence, our knowledge 'is only conversant about them' (4.1.1). It ends by saying that the only things the mind contemplates or thinks about are, for the most part, not ideas (4.21.3). It is because the objects of thought frequently are not ideas and are never present to the mind (Locke means *immediately* present) that 'it is necessary that something else, as a sign or representation of the thing it considers, should be present to it'. The doctrine of signs, the third division of the sciences distinguished at the end of the *Essay*, is concerned with word-signs and with idea-signs. Those signs are employed by the mind in understanding things (idea-signs) and in expressing our knowledge and understanding of things to others (word-signs). Locke's way of talking about idea-signs, as being the things *present to* the mind, the *immediate* object of the mind, as 'whatsoever is the object of the understanding when a man thinks' (1.1.8), as that which *represents* objects, suggests that the experimental science of nature may be unable to make observations, that observations of objects have to be replaced by inspection of our own ideas. The problem Locke himself poses in 4.4 seems to indicate that he saw the way of ideas threatened with isolation among ideas, that he also thought the representative or sign function of ideas tended to undermine our knowledge of things. But the problem of 4.4 is an existential one: are there any objects, can we distinguish dreams and illusions from reality? Sensitive knowledge meets this existential difficulty, enabling us to say there *are* objects other than our ideas. The science of nature is not concerned with this existential problem: it presupposes its solution. The account of sensitive knowledge has the other important side, the account of the coexistence relation. It is this relation which is the backbone of experimental science.

The science of nature works with coexisting qualities discovered through observation. Locke's careful and repeated insistence that, in dealing with substance, we must be faithful to things themselves should leave no doubt that observation of physical objects is an important operation. There is, however, one possible source of confusion, due to Locke himself. In 2.8.7 he speaks of ideas in two senses: perceptions in our minds and modifications of matter in bodies. Modifications of matter cannot, of course, be ideas. Throughout the *Essay* Locke frequently talks (whenever he discusses physical objects) of ideas where one would expect him to talk of qualities. Sometimes he writes 'coexisting ideas' where the sense seems clearly to be 'coexisting qualities'. Locke was aware of this confusion, he remarked twice upon it. In 2.8.8 he says that if he speaks of ideas 'sometimes as in the things themselves, I would be understood to mean those qualities in the object which produce' the ideas in us. In 2.31.2 where he was talking of the secondary qualities as powers in objects, he pauses to make the point that the locution 'secondary qualities in objects' means 'a power of an object'. He also explains that when he speaks of the ideas of pain or of colour being in the object, he means to speak in the same way of the power of the object to produce pain or colour sensations in us.

Some readers are bothered by Locke's failure to go through and correct all those uses of 'idea' where he means to write 'quality'. These two passages that I have quoted seem unequivocal in telling us to make the proper changes, not to take him as wanting to say we observe *ideas* in things.[1] I see no reason to ignore Locke's instruction to rewrite those passages for him. He himself is often quite explicit about it being things and their qualities that we observe. 3.6.24 speaks of men's collections of sensible qualities, and of knowing things one from another by their sensible qualities. In 28 of the same chapter, he speaks of men 'Observing certain qualities always joined and existing together'. Section 30 says we use outward appearances of things to identify them; he talks also here of coexisting qualities (cf. 32, 35, 36). Other passages in Book 3 speak of our ideas of properties united together (10.18); of leading or key qualities as those by which we identify an object (11.19–21); of seeing animals for which we lack class concepts (10.32); of seeing objects, e.g. a drill, a man, a monstrous foetus (10.21); of observing the alterations of a base metal in fire (29.13); of examining stones and iron (6.9); elsewhere of seeing a rainbow, feeling a statue (4.13.12); of observing and naming such objects as bird, beast, tree, plant, sheep, crow, sound (Book 3.8), horse, mule, sulphur, antimony, vitriol (3.6.7, 8). There are many other passages in Books 3 and 4 where Locke uses the language of coexisting qualities and of observing things.[2] In the light of the inconsistency of this use, and in view of Locke's injunction in 2.8.8, we must say that the claim that we know only ideas on Locke's account finds no support from these terminological slips, slips of which Locke was aware and commented upon.

[1] Two sample passages where he does use 'idea' correctly are 3.6.9 and 3.6.21. There are many others. Mandelbaum notes the 2.8.8 passage and comments several times on Locke's distinction between ideas and qualities (*Philosophy, Science, and Sense Perception*, pp. 16, 30, 34–7).
[2] At one point in the controversy with Stillingfleet, Locke speaks of 'The idea which taken from the outward visible parts I give the name watch to' (*Second Reply, Works*, IV, 412).

Even granting, as it seems we must in the light of all the textual evidence I have cited, that Locke is saying we observe physical objects, there is an important question still remaining in doubt, another possible source of confusion. Jackson identifies 'sensible' with 'secondary' quality (*op. cit.* p. 56). He also says that, because we are ignorant of the primary qualities of the insensible parts of body, we have 'recourse to its secondary qualities and powers' in 'trying to describe a given body' (p. 64). Locke says in 2.8.26 quite clearly that it is the non-primary qualities (both immediate and mediate ones) 'whereby we take notice of bodies and distinguish them one from another'. A modified version of this remark is found in 2.22.8: 'secondary qualities are those which in most' substances 'serve principally to distinguish substances one from another'; they are the 'characteristical notes and marks whereby' we frame ideas in our minds of substances. Similarly, in 4.3.1, Locke says that secondary qualities are the ones about which our knowledge of substances is most employed. Jackson suggests that macroscopic differ from microscopic primary qualities in being determinate instead of general. So far as I can see, there is nothing more particular and determinate about secondary qualities than about primary ones, whether micro or macro. Yellowness (which Locke cites repeatedly for gold) is no more particular than shape. The particularisation of any object is a function of its existence in a specific time and place. The coexistence of qualities discussed by Locke is one which defines classes, nominal not real classes. Coexistence by itself does not individuate. Thus, whatever qualities are included or most frequently used in the careful noting of coexisting qualities cannot be there because of their particular and determinate character.

One of Locke's interests with primary qualities in 2.8 was with the way they play causal roles in perception. They do so as qualifying insensible particles. The insensible particles play just as much a causal role in generating ideas of primary as of secondary qualities. Primary qualities are clearly sensible in many instances, as various textual references have already made clear. Yet Locke adds, to his remark about secondary qualities being the ones most usually used in talking of and describing body, the comment that secondary qualities are usually called 'sensible' (2.8.23). The question of what qualities he cites in talking of coexisting qualities and of observing bodies is most important for an understanding of his concept of object and of our knowledge of body. How are we to take his own remarks, which seem to say that primary qualities play no role, or only a minor role, in observing and recording coexistences? We need to be quite explicit about what the text says on this point, for the bulk of the text is clearly at variance with the suggestion that primary qualities are not sensible.

2.1.2 speaks of observation employed about external sensible objects. The quality 'hard' is cited in section 3 of that chapter. Section 5 defines 'sensible qualities' (which are furnished the mind by external objects) as 'all those different perceptions they produce in us'. 'Tangible qualities' are cited in 6. Section 7 talks of the ideas of the motions of a clock, motion being a clearly designated primary quality in Locke's list. 2.2.1 speaks of a man seeing 'at once motion and colour'. Section 3 of that chapter says it 'is *not possible* for anyone *to imagine* any other qualities in bodies, howsoever constituted, whereby they can be taken notice of besides sounds, tastes, smells, visible and tangible qualities'. If these last two include qualities like shape, solidity, and other primary qualities, as they must, this passage does not support the comment in 2.8.23 about secondary qualities being the only sensible ones. 2.3.1 says that touch yields heat, cold, and solidity. Other sensible ideas generated via one sense are 'sensible configuration, as smooth and rough, or else, more or less firm adhesion of the parts, as hard and soft, tough and brittle'. Solidity is the subject of 2.4 and is there assigned to touch. 2.5 credits to diverse senses the ideas of space or extension, figure, rest, and motion, one of the clearest statements that primary ideas are sensible. These latter ideas arise from both seeing and feeling. 2.9.8 says that a round globe of uniform colour imprints the idea on our minds of 'a flat circle, variously shadowed'. Circle is a primary quality, a species of shape. Section 9 of the same chapter speaks of sight conveying the ideas of space, figure, and motion (cf. 2.13). In 2.23.9 Locke says that the ideas of 'the primary qualities of things...are discovered by our senses', adding as an example that sensible motion of a loadstone reveals to us the power it has of attracting iron. Section 14 of this chapter lists among our ideas of a swan those of white colour, long neck, red beak, etc, 'and all these of a certain size'. Section 16 speaks of the 'complex *idea* of extended, figured, coloured, and all other sensible qualities', linking primary with secondary as sensible qualities. 2.31.9 speaks of observing in a lump of gold its bulk and figure, two primary qualities again. In listing the primary qualities of solidity, extension, figure, number, and motion and rest in 2.8.22, Locke had said that these qualities 'are sometimes perceived by us, viz. when the bodies they are in are big enough singly to be perceived' (cf. 2.8.23). In pointing out that we frequently use key or leading ideas as a way of characterising certain kinds of objects, 3.6.29 says that in sensible substances, it is the shape which is the 'leading quality and most characteristical part that determines the *species*' in substances propagated by seed, e.g. vegetables and animals. An 'extended solid substance of such a certain figure usually serves the turn'. Man is singled out: a creature without the shape of a man would hardly be considered a man. For other bodies not propagated by seed (e.g. gold) it is colour which is the key identificatory quality. Finally, section 40 of the same chapter speaks of artificial things and says that their idea or essence consists 'for the most part in nothing but the determined figure of sensible parts, and sometimes motion'.

I can see no alternative, in the face of these remarks, but to say that Locke asserted both (*a*) that primary qualities can be and most often are sensible, and (*b*) that they frequently appear in the co-existences which careful observation records.[1] This conclusion has, of course, been implicit in the analysis of the science of nature: the objects and events whose histories are recorded are either gross perceptual objects and events, or objects and events perceived with the help of microscopes and telescopes: but still perceived, not inferred. Mandelbaum agrees that 'Locke is primarily concerned with our ordinary everyday knowledge', but he dissociates this knowledge from scientific knowledge: Locke, he adds, was not concerned 'with the problem of scientific inference' (*op. cit.*

---

[1] Harré points out that for the corpuscular theory in the seventeenth century, 'Primary qualities are those which are both perceived qualities and also properties of actual things' (*Matter and Method*, p. 63). Locke agreed; he sought 'to show that each primary property has a perceptual counterpart in the perceived qualities of bodies' (p. 81).

p. 13). What I have been trying to show so far is that the concern with ordinary objects *is* the concern with science as natural history. Scientific inference for Mandelbaum means inferring to insensible particles. Since Locke held that we cannot know the internal constitution of objects, he was not of course 'concerned with the problem of how we know' that constitution. While Mandelbaum sees this as a 'disparity between common knowledge and the fruits of scientific inquiry', I hope I have by now established that no such disparity exists in Locke's account of knowledge.

Mandelbaum is right in saying that according to Locke we must look to experience 'to ascertain the nature of objects' and, more importantly, 'The experience to which we must appeal is, in the first instance, our ordinary observation in daily life' (p. 40; cf. pp. 48–9, 56). But then Mandelbaum goes on to say, 'however, ordinary perceptual experience, while useful in all of the concerns of life, does not for Locke reveal the nature of material objects as they are in themselves' (p. 40). The phrase, 'the nature of things themselves', which runs throughout the *Essay*, almost never means 'the internal constitution of objects'. As we have seen, it is a phrase which Locke (and many of his contemporaries) uses constantly to urge us to observation for discovering the nature of things. It refers to the objects of observation. Ordinary observation does not reveal the internal constitution, but neither does microscopical observation. Even when the microscope reveals the minute particles making up that internal constitution, we do not know the real essence, since we do not understand cohesion. Moreover, the objects seen through the microscopes are the same in kind, though ever so small, as the gross objects of unaided perception. The metaphysic of nature with which Locke worked (in particular, the corpuscular hypothesis) located the real essence, the causal basis, of objects in the cohering particles. That metaphysic did not reduce perceptual objects to their internal constitution, nor did it identify the nature of things themselves with that constitution. That is, ordinary objects have a nature at the observational, as well as at the insensible level. The point of Locke's distinction between real and nominal essence was precisely to turn us away from the search for real essence (the limitation of knowledge excludes that), towards a careful analysis of the nominal (i.e. the observed) nature of objects. Just as Mandelbaum identifies scientific knowledge with knowledge of the insensible particles, so he tends to identify physical objects with those particles. The 'actual nature of material substances as they exist independently of us' he interprets as the group of insensible particles (p. 45). But if there are macroscopic objects (Mandelbaum calls them 'concrete entities', p. 48) which have primary qualities—as there surely are for Locke—their primary qualities are just as much perceiver-independent as are those of the particles. Moreover, I have shown how the coexistence relation yields a knowledge of the observable qualities of those gross objects. We do have *knowledge* of body. Where we lack knowledge is of the real essence, the insensible particles.[1] The difficulty in agreeing that there is a coherent concept of ordinary object in Locke's *Essay* comes from his account of secondary qualities. If those qualities are nothing in the object but the powers of particles to cause ideas in our minds, there are no qualities, only ideas. Even with the clear recognition that Locke drew a distinction between ideas and qualities, secondary qualities are not really qualities. The notion of an ordinary object (table, chair) lacking the secondary qualities is incoherent, is a violation of what we mean by such objects. Thus, Locke's account of secondary qualities would seem to force him to deny that there are tables and chairs. At the very best, he may have found his account of objects in conflict with his account of scientific activity. If the former in effect eliminates ordinary perceptual objects, the latter may be unable to make any natural histories, or it may be reduced to dealing with inferred entities as Mandelbaum suggests. The knowledge of bodies as they are in themselves could not, then, be discovered by observation. Since inference to particles does not fit any of the cognitive relations Locke cites, knowledge of body becomes impossible.

This barrier to knowledge of body is strengthened by what has always been taken as the central difficulty in Locke's theory of knowledge. Is there not a difficulty confronting any doctrine of ideas as signs or representations of things, a difficulty which is resolved neither by the existential feature of sensitive knowledge

---

[1] See p. 53 in Mandelbaum where, in denying that we have knowledge of real essence, he fails to say we do have knowledge of body, knowledge in the strong sense of certainty.

nor by repeated claims that we do observe physical objects? If the immediate objects of perception are ideas, the coexistence relation must hold between ideas, not between qualities. What justification do we have for taking the coexistence of ideas as standing for the coexistence of qualities? The so-called 'representative theory of perception' is supposed to be threatened with idealism and privacy; realism is, at best, a postulate or belief. All Locke's use of ordinary physical object and event talk to the contrary, the doctrine of knowledge via ideas seems to clash with his easy talk of observing objects. We must be cautious, however. When Locke introduces the term 'idea', he tells us that he means to use it 'to express whatever is meant by *phantasm, notion, species*' (1.1.8). These terms were part of the Aristotelian–Thomistic tradition. That tradition was firm in its insistence that being aware, in whatever form, involves mental processes and mental entities: the phantasm and species belong to the mental, not the neural, side of awareness. Nevertheless, the phantasm was the object as existing in the mind, the form of the object. That form was not altered in character by its mental existence. Physical object forms have the property of being able to exist in matter and in mind. Their locus is not a feature of their nature. The Aristotelian–Thomistic doctrine appears in Descartes as the objective existence of ideas. Locke's 'Epistle to the Reader' refers to this version: a determinate or determined idea is 'such as it is at any time objectively in the mind' (p. xxxviii). In replying to Caterus, Descartes explained that 'objective existence' means 'precisely being in the understanding in the way in which objects are normally there'. He goes on to elaborate: 'And in this case "objective existence in the understanding" will not mean merely providing the object with which my thought is concerned, but existing in the understanding in the way in which its objects normally exist there. Hence the idea of the sun will be the sun itself existing in the understanding, not indeed formally, as it exists in the mind.'[1] Kenny finds this doctrine difficult. Moreover, he thinks Descartes even contradicts himself, 'saying first that what exists in the mind in the way in which objects exist in the

---

[1] Adam and Tannery, VII, 102, or Haldane and Ross, II, 9. Quoted by Kenny in *Descartes, A Study of His Philosophy*, pp. 115–16.

mind is not the sun, but the idea of the sun, and then going on to say that the idea of the sun is the sun itself existing in the mind in the way in which objects normally exist in the mind' (p. 116). The doctrine is not without its ontological problems, the property of existing in space and in thought hardly seems to fit our ordinary concept of physical objects. I do not want to defend the doctrine. I am suggesting that there was this doctrine, that Locke's opening terminology aligns the way of ideas with this tradition, and that the doctrine was a conscious attempt to preserve perceptual realism. It would be unexpected if Locke would so consciously have used this tradition while departing from its direct realism.

It might be thought that Locke rejected this tradition in his comments against Sergeant, a stout defender of the Aristotelian–Thomistic analysis.[1] Moreover, Locke criticised Stillingfleet for following Sergeant. What Locke criticised in Sergeant was the *literal* identification of notions with objects, with holding, as Stillingfleet had commented, that 'a notion is the very thing itself existing in the understanding' (*Second Reply, Works,* IV, 390). To be persuaded by Sergeant's doctrine was, for Locke, to believe that, for example, 'as often as you think of your cathedral church, or of Des Cartes' vortices, that the very cathedral church at Worcester, or the motion of those vortices, itself exists in your understanding, when one of them never existed but in that one place at Worcester, and the other never existed any where in *rerum natura*' (*ibid.* pp. 390–1). Locke took thinking, rather than perceiving, in this exchange with Stillingfleet, but presumably he would have made the same criticism for the perception of the cathedral at Worcester. The literal reading of Sergeant's doctrine eliminates the mental component in perceiving and thinking. Sergeant did tend to present the doctrine in this way but the fact is that the way of ideas and the notional way did not differ fundamentally on this question of our knowledge of body. The latter was at pains to stress the direct realism in perception, the former wanted to stress the mental features necessary for all cognition. In stressing the mental features of knowing and perceiving, Locke did not mean to make knowledge of body impossible.

Locke frequently draws the distinction between mental con-

---

[1] See *John Locke and the Way of Ideas*, pp. 103–13.

tents or processes and physical processes. In the 'Epistle to the Reader', where he defines 'determined idea', he is careful to distinguish idea from the sound we use as a sign of it (p. xxxix). In 1.1.2 he draws a distinction between the 'physical consideration of the mind' and the non-physical consideration, although he does not have a name for the latter. He also speaks there of 'sensation by our organs' and 'ideas in our understanding'. Locke disclaimed any intention of going into the physical account of sensation. He simply accepted the current corpuscular theory. But although he is not always as precise as we would be about the physical and physiological levels of sensation, in distinction from the mental levels, he does hold to this division. 2.1.3, for instance, speaks of the senses conveying '*into the mind*' several 'distinct *perceptions* of things'. He explains that 'convey' means that 'the senses carry into the mind What produces there those *perceptions*'. Presumably what he means is that the stimulus gets to the mind via the sensory equipment of the organism. He ends 2.1.25 by speaking of the sensory impressions having ideas annexed to them, but he remarks that it is the ideas which are *perceived*, although the mind is said to *receive* the sensory impressions. In a striking passage, Locke draws a sharp distinction between the cause of a sensation and the sensation itself: 'For granting this explication of the thing to be true [the corpuscular account], yet the *idea* of the cause of *light*, if we had it never so exact, would no more give us the *idea* of *light* itself as it is such a particular perception in us than the *idea* of the figure and motion of a sharp piece of steel would give us the *idea* of that pain which it is able to cause in us' (3.4.10).

The mental content of any act of awareness or thought is called by Locke an 'idea'. There is a wide variety of mental operations and ideas cited and used in the *Essay*. Applied to vision, Locke's analysis of 'I see a desk' assumes that I have visual contents. If by a physical object we mean the insensible particles that cause seeing, we do not see physical objects. If, as he thinks is true of our ordinary talk, we mean by a physical object the gross objects in our perceptual fields, then we do see physical objects. Seeing a physical object just is (*a*) to have visual images which (*b*) are caused by particles (together with some mental operations),

(c) some of which are resemblances of (d) the qualities of objects.
To say an idea resembles a quality means for Locke both that the
quality belongs to the object non-relationally (an ontological
point) and that awareness by means of that idea reveals that
quality as it is (an epistemic point). An observed physical object is
itself caused by or sustained by the insensible particles but it is an
object which *has* primary qualities. I think Locke wanted to say
observed objects *have* secondary qualities also, though they have
them only in relation to perceivers.

The analysis of Locke's concept of object becomes complex at
this point. If we take seriously the relational/non-relational distinction which I presented in chapter 1, and recognise that the
claim that objects are what they are only in relation to other
objects applies to *observed* objects, we must now say that all
features of observed objects—primary as well as secondary
qualities—are relational. To speak of any primary quality being
relational seems to clash with the clear doctrine of 2.8, that those
are the properties objects have whether we perceive them or no.
One and the same class of qualities cannot be both relational and
non-relational. It is true, however, that my *perception* of the primary
qualities of an object is dependent upon specific conditions, e.g.
a source of light for seeing its qualities, other bodies for perceiving
its motion and size, normal sense organs fitted to receive the
stimulus. In that sense, the perceived primary qualities may be
relational. What the resemblance relation then tells us is that my
perception of the primary qualities reveals the non-relational
qualities of that object. The resemblance relation then turns out
to be as important for revealing the non-relational qualities of
gross perceptual objects as of the insensible or microscopic
particles. Correspondingly, to say my ideas of secondary qualities
do not resemble qualities of the object does not mean that the
perceived object only has primary qualities, save in the non-
relational sense of *has*, that of being perceiver-independent.

We can summarise Locke's concept of object in five propositions.

(1) Objects—both macro and micro—have primary qualities non-
relationally.

(2) Objects are observed or perceived to have both primary and
secondary qualities.

(3) What qualities they are observed to have are dependent upon other objects, both perceivers and other bodies.

(4) The primary qualities of insensible parts are the same kind as (resemble) those of the sensible parts. A corollary to this proposition would say that the same relation of resemblance holds between *ideas* of primary qualities and primary *qualities*.

(5) The causation of the perception of all qualities is the behaviour of insensible particles on our sense organs.[1]

Locke's theory of matter enabled him to say there *are* (there exist) insensible particles which have, non-relationally, primary qualities. His theory of science required there be perceptual objects which have all of the qualities that careful observation records. The primary–secondary quality distinction—which originated from the atomism of the corpuscular hypothesis and was initially applicable only to particles—Locke extended to objects as perceived. Thus, the perceptual objects cannot have, in a non-relational way, any secondary qualities. The distinction, insisted upon by Locke if not always honoured in practice, between ideas and qualities, holds just as much for secondary as for primary qualities. When I observe the yellow colour of gold, that colour is not identical with my idea. Gold is yellow, as my idea of gold informs me. But the two modes of existence now become important: the colour of gold is perceiver-dependent, while its size, degree of hardness, shape, etc., are perceiver-independent. At the same time, perceived primary and secondary qualities have something in common: as perceived, they are relational properties.

This analysis of the concept of body, which I suggest is embedded in the *Essay*, helps us to understand what it is that physical scientists were observing, on Locke's account of science. The way of ideas was his attempt to formulate perceptual realism. At least with respect to primary qualities, seeing a primary quality consists in our having visual images of extension or motion, that image being a resemblance of the quality. To see a moving train just is to have this sort of images (accompanied by various other

[1] Much more is involved in the genesis of sensory ideas than the behaviour of particles. Mental operations of an active and attentive mind are equally important causal factors. See my 'The Concept of Experience in Locke and Hume', in *Journal of the History of Philosophy*, 1 (1963). A shortened and revised version of the Locke part of this paper is in *Locke and Berkeley, A Collection of Critical Essays*, ed. Martin and Armstrong, 1968.

sorts of ideational contents), to feel that these images arise in us independent of our will, to have a conviction that there is an object apart from my awareness. Having visual images *is* seeing objects, under specific conditions. The way of ideas is Locke's method of recognising the mental features of seeing. It does not place the perceiver in some vale of ideas forever trying to break out into the world of physical objects. If we try to think of an alternate analysis, one which would not make use of mental contents, we would not be thinking of an analysis of seeing. In general it is impossible, according to Locke, to think without there being immediate objects of thought, where 'immediate' refers to some mental feature. Several times in his exchanges with Stillingfleet, Locke makes this point. 'Indeed, if what your lordship insinuates in the beginning of this passage...be true, your lordship is safer (in your way without ideas, i.e. without immediate objects of the mind in thinking, if there be any such way)... (*Works*, IV, 340). In a less sarcastic comment, Locke makes the point positively: 'For ideas are nothing but the immediate object of our minds in thinking; and your lordship, I conclude, in building your system of any part of knowledge thinks on something: and therefore you can no more build, or have any system of knowledge without ideas, than you can think without some immediate objects of thinking' (*ibid.* p. 362). Far from 'idea' being some special or technical term in a theory of thinking, these passages show that for Locke it was only the term he chose (as he said many times) to designate the immediate object of the mind in thinking, an object or feature without which there could be no thought. To think or to be aware just is to have mental contents, ideas.

The naïve realist is sometimes thought of as saying we simply see objects without the help of images, ideas, etc. But either such a view stops short of the analysis of seeing, stating only the conclusion or end-product, *or* that view is not an account of seeing. If direct perception of the desk is a perception which differs in all ways from perception as we know it, what would it be like, how are we to understand it? If the desk's real properties differ (or may differ) from those I am aware of when I perceive, what kind would they be? This last question might be answered by talking of microscopic or imperceptible properties. If direct realism is the perception of imperceptible qualities, then our perception is not (and of course cannot be) direct. If the real properties of the desk are perceptible properties but not the ones we do perceive, what can we say about properties that are perceptible but are not perceived? Sometimes when we talk of direct and indirect realism, we are lured by an implicit concept of object which gives it a perspective of its own, in which it has properties of its own different in kind from those I perceive. An object may have properties which do differ in kind from perceptual ones, but we must not be fooled into thinking this concept has the consequence of making our perceptions unauthentic, of our perceptions not disclosing the properties of objects. They do not disclose those non-perceptual properties but they do disclose the perceptual ones. The sceptic's case tends to obscure the issue by playing upon the identification of 'object' with 'non-perceptual'.

To analyse knowing in terms of our awareness of the relations of ideas does not mean that we know ideas or their relations. It is only by apprehending the relations of ideas that we can come to know anything about physical objects. The 'standing for' or representative function of ideas differs in kind from my 'standing-in for' or representing someone at a meeting, a difference which is not characterised by saying that we cannot compare idea and thing though we can compare a man and his representative. The difference must be seen as one where it does not make sense to talk of comparing idea with object. Of course, there *are* conditions in which I do compare idea with object, my idea of a man with the man when he is presented to me. But this comparing takes place within cognition, within awareness, not between awareness and some object outside awareness. The direct realist is no more able to make that sort of comparison than is the indirect realist. Whether in fact the theories of direct and indirect realism do make sense—or just what their sense is—needs some discussion. What I am suggesting is that they cannot make one kind of sense: they cannot be asserting that I either do or do not perceive the object without being aware.[1] You may resist the analysis of

[1] For an elaboration of these remarks about direct and indirect realism, see my 'Perceptual Consciousness', *Knowledge and Necessity*, vol. III of the *Royal Institute of Philosophy Lectures* (1968–9).

awareness in terms of entity-sounding terms like 'sense-data' or 'idea'; talking of such mental contents as ontological entities may encourage the dichotomy between object and idea. I see no evidence in the *Essay* that Locke thought of ideas as entities. They were, I have been suggesting, his way of characterising the fact that perceptual awareness is mental.

In the Introduction to his abridged edition of the *Essay*,[1] A. D. Woozley has also argued against the usual representative reading of Locke's account of perceptual knowledge. Starting from the fact that Locke 'talked of seeing tables, and of having ideas of tables, but never of seeing ideas of tables' (p. 28), Woozley argues that the representative or picture theory of perception is too simple-minded for Locke not to have seen through it. Woozley points out that Locke put the obvious objection to this theory in his *Examination of Malebranche* (sect. 15): 'this I cannot comprehend, for how can I know that the picture of anything is like that thing, when I never see that which it represents?' (quoted by Woozley, p. 27). I do not think this a sufficient objection to the picture theory version of a representative theory of perception, for one could hold to that theory without at the same time claiming it is *known* to be true. Woolzey is concerned with justification: 'For the picture-original thesis to have any ground at all, there would have to be some occasion of experiencing an original, and some possibility of confronting picture with original' (p. 26). I have argued that this is precisely the sense that no representative theory could make. Moreover, a *theory* of perception may find its justification in what it explains, not in its being true or known to be true. Questions of justification aside, Woozley is clearly right in stressing that Locke's way of ideas did not commit the category mistake of saying we see ideas, not tables (p. 28). Still, Woozley wants to say that Locke 'held to *some kind* of representationalism'. 'For Locke, ideas represent reality, in the sense that he is claiming, whether justifiably or not, that there can be a correspondence between what we think about the world and the way the world is' (p. 33). Ideas for Locke, Woozley insists, were not entities; they were his way of expressing what ordinary locutions like the following express: 'I have an idea that', 'I have no idea what',

---

[1] The Fontana Library (1964).

'My idea of a ... is ...', and 'What is your idea of ...?'
(p. 30).

It may not be entirely correct to say of Locke, as Woozley does,
that 'Forming ideas is identical with understanding words'
(p. 31), since Locke wants to distinguish between verbal and
wordless thought, but understanding words *is* forming ideas,
just as being aware of objects is having ideas. To talk about
objects is to use words as standing for ideas, to know the meaning
of a word just is to have an idea with which I correlate the word.
In the controversy with Stillingfleet, Locke explains that in
reading the Scriptures, he first endeavours 'to understand the
words and phrases of the language I read it in, i.e. to form ideas
they stand for' (*Works*, IV, 341). Disputes over the meaning of
some passage cannot be disputes over the nature of meaning and
understanding as requiring or not requiring something for which
words stand, since everyone must agree that meaning and understanding involve something for which words stand: 'thus we see,
that in effect men have differently understood and interpreted the
sense of these propositions; whether they used the way of ideas or
not, i.e. whether they called what any word stands for, notion, or
sense or meaning, or idea' (p. 344). The use of a word presupposes
its meaning. Most words refer to observable things and actions by
referring to the ideas by means of which I cognise things and
actions. The reference of words is not wholly to ideas, but the
ideas determine their reference to things. I can see a man run a
man through, but to recognise it as an act of murder or of stabbing
requires me to have specific ideas of murder and stabbing. In a
similar way, I compare my idea of gold with what I see, the
instance of gold in my pocket or on my watch. I may see the
colour and shape and not recognise it as or know it to be gold. The
idea of gold enables me to name the object I see in terms of that
type or class of object. In these cases of the names for physical
objects, the idea must follow nature, must be a faithful recording
of the coexistence of qualities, though the fact that that combination of qualities is called 'gold' is a function of our language. The
difference between this and the action example is that the ideas in
the action case need not be a faithful recording of the combinations
of movements, intentions, etc., that have occurred, though they

frequently are. Moreover, once formed, the action-concept does record what in fact takes place in acts of murder, of stabbing, etc.

Both of the previous examples rest upon acts of seeing or perceiving, perceiving the dagger entering the body, perceiving the colour, shape, etc., of an object. At this level of perception, it no longer makes sense to speak of comparing the idea with that which the idea stands for or represents, since to perceive an object in this sense *is* to have mental contents of specific sorts. Locke's philosophy of nature gives him an account of the nature of objects as they are apart from perception: they are groups of cohering particles. If we want to know whether the desk is *really* brown, in the primary quality sense, we must consult the general theory Locke accepts. If we want to know whether the desk in that room is brown or black in the perceptual sense, we need only take another careful look. Objects as perceived are precisely the way they appear. Their appearances enable us 'to distinguish the sorts of particular substances' and 'to discern the state' those substances are in (4.4.4). Two concepts of object are found in the *Essay*. The one concept is embedded in the corpuscular theory, it tells us what properties objects have non-relationally, both on the micro and the macro level. That concept also gives us a causal explanation of macro-objects. The second concept of object is Locke's attempt to articulate a philosophy of nature and of knowledge sufficient for the scientific activities of Boyle, Hooke, and Sydenham. This concept takes something from the tradition of the great chain of being and the notion of the interconnexion of objects and physical processes. A physical object on this concept is and does just what careful observation reveals it as doing: experimental science took as its task the delineation of objects as observed. Locke's account of thinking and perceiving, rooted in the tradition which recognised them as mental processes, linked theory of knowledge with scientific activity. The doctrine of signs sketched both the causal and the epistemic relations between ideas and things. The causal relation does not hold between perceived object and idea but only between the object under the first concept, the cohering set of particles. The epistemic relation between ideas and perceptual object is not one requiring or permitting comparisons between ideas and object. It might seem that such a comparison is possible or implied by Locke's specification that the ideas of primary qualities resemble the primary qualities, but this claim is part of the general theory Locke operates with, not a factual claim. This claim is part of the primary-secondary quality distinction; it is an answer to the question, 'Which perceived qualities are the real (i.e. non-relational) qualities of objects?'. It is not an answer to the question, 'Which perceived qualities belong to the perceived object?'. It would be wrong to draw a Berkeleian conclusion by saying objects *are* ideas, since Locke insisted upon (though did not always follow) the difference between ideas and qualities. It would be equally wrong to ask to examine or to perceive a quality apart from an idea, for that request would ask us to think or perceive without thinking or perceiving: all thought goes on in terms of and by means of ideas. Finally, it would be wrong to conclude that we can only think of or perceive ideas since most of the time we are thinking of and perceiving objects and events. As a body, we rub shoulders with physical objects, we touch objects immediately, that is, non-cognitively. As a cogniser, we experience our world in the terms appropriate to awareness. The doctrine of ideas as epistemic signs of things is Locke's way of characterising our awareness of objects.

6

ACTION AND AGENCY

Action, Locke tells us, is 'the great business of mankind, and the whole matter about which all laws are conversant' (2.22.10). Our ideas of actions are mixed modes, names of actions singled out for specific purposes by man. The actions 'are not capable of a lasting duration'; as such they stand in sharp contrast to the substances (the persons) who are the actors and agents (3.6.42; 2.27.2). It is the actor who names the actions and who acts, a fact frequently obscured by talk of willing my limbs to move or of my will being free. I can no more ascribe freedom to my will than I can say my sleep is swift or that virtue is square (2.21.14). It is customary and sometimes convenient to talk of willing and choosing as if they were properties of a faculty. Faculties are dispositions and powers of agents, not themselves real beings or agents. Locke stresses this point in a number of passages (e.g. 2.21.6, 14, 17–20).[1] The talk of a faculty, or of an ability or a power, is misleading if we take it to mean the faculty or power is the causal factor in action. Similarly, talk of faculties and powers of willing, preferring, choosing is talk of things that are able to move and persons that are able to understand and do (2.21.20). Actions are modifications of substance (72), it is the 'man that does the action' (19, 29).

What Locke is stressing by calling actions mixed modes (more properly, our ideas of actions are mixed modes) is that for anything to count as an action we must have a description, a name, for that action: 'a man holding a gun in his hand and pulling downe the triger may be either Rebellion, Parricide, Murther, Homicide, Duty, Justice, Valer, or recreation, and be thus variously diversified, when all the circumstances put together are compared to a rule, though the simple action of holding the gun and pulling

---

[1] Passmore has noted the close similarity between Locke and Cudworth in their rejection of faculty talk. See *Ralph Cudworth, An Interpretation* (Cambridge, 1951), pp. 54–5, 93–4. Cf. pp. 91–6 for Passmore's discussion of the question of Cudworth's possible influence on Locke's ethical views.

the triger may be exactly the same' (Aaron and Gibb, p. 35). We can only do what we name and under the description we as actors accept:

we find that *men speaking of mixed modes seldom* imagine *or take any other for species of them but such as are set out by name:* because they being of man's making only, in order to naming, no such *species* are taken notice of or supposed to be unless a *name* be joined to it, as the sign of man's having combined into one *idea* several loose ones (3.5.11).

For example, I could 'stab' a man in England because killing a man by the point of a sword first entering the body is in England called 'stabbing', 'it passes for a distinct *species*, when it has a distinct *name*, as in *England*' (3.5.11). If this way of killing a man is not recognised 'as a distinct species' in some other country, no one in such a country could stab another. Killing a man 'with a sword or hatchet [other than using the sword to stab] are looked on as no distinct species of action', hence those acts are not distinct ways of killing. Similarly,

though the killing of an old man be as fit in nature to be united into one complex *idea* as the killing a man's father, yet there being no name standing precisely for the one as there is the name of *parricide* to mark the other, it is not taken for a particular complex idea nor a distinct species of action from that of killing a young man, or any other man (2.22.4).

What species of actions there are in any given country depends upon the concepts and names of actions recognised by the people of that country (6), but there is no necessary connection between name and action: 'the pulling the trigger of the gun with which the murder is committed and is all the action that perhaps is visible, has no natural connexion with those *ideas* that make up the complex one named *murder*' (3.9.7). So dependent are actions upon the names we have, that we are apt to identify them with or to locate their existence in the names (2.22.8). Without the name *triumphus*, for example, the several parts of events and actions which are included in the concept of a triumph would 'no more be thought to make one thing' than any other collection or series of actions (3.5.10).

Thinking and motion cover all actions, the first of intellectual agents, the second of corporeal agents (2.22.11); but not everything signified by verbs the grammarian calls 'active' are actions: many are passions. The propositions, 'I see the moon or a star' and 'I feel the heat of the sun', employ active verbs but they do not signify 'any action in me whereby I operate on these substances'. Rather, thought or awareness is put into action by objects without me. Verbs of perception are not action verbs denoting my agency (2.21.72, 73). Other words which seem to express some action 'signify nothing of the action or *modus operandi* at all, *but* barely the *effect*' (2.22.11). For example, 'creation' and 'annihilation' give no idea of the action or production in creating or destroying: the locution 'the cold freezes water' 'signifies nothing but the effect', not the action. There are actions of the mind (e.g. consideration, assent), actions of the body (e.g. running, speaking), and actions of both mind and body (e.g. revenge or murder) (2.22.10). Any moral action belongs to the third type. All actions have 'causes, means, objects, ends, instruments, time, place and other circumstances'. Everyone, Locke assures us, 'finds in himself that his soul can think, will, and operate on his body' (2.23.20). A simple instance of mind and body involved together in action is that of bodily motion produced by thought. I can, 'by a thought directing the motion of my finger, make it move when it was at rest' (2.21.21), though I may not understand the causation involved (2.23.28). In this last passage, Locke tells us that 'we have by daily experience clear evidence of motion produced both by impulse and by thought'. Our volitions give us 'constant experience' of such mental causation, actions 'which are produced in us only by the free action or thought of our own mind', not by impulse (4.10.19). 'For example, my right hand writes whilst my left hand is still. What causes rest in one and motion in the other? Nothing but my will, a thought of my mind; my thought only changing, the right hand rests, and the left hand moves. This is matter of fact which cannot be denied' (*ibid.*). This same example of my ability to move my hand by taking thought is also found in 2.21.48 and 71.[1]

---

[1] Cf. Matthew Hale, *The Primitive Origination of Mankind* (1677), p. 22: 'When I command any Muscle or my most remote Limb to move, it doth it in an instant; in the moment I will it; and hereby I understand the motions of my Mind are no way Mechanical, though the motions of the Muscle be such; I move, ride, run or speak, because I will to do it, without any other physical impulse upon me...' Later

In these passages Locke has used the locutions of mental causation: my thought and my volition cause my actions. Besides the careful passages I have already noted, where Locke warns against letting these modes of speech mislead us into reifying faculties, there are a number of other passages in the chapter on power which show that Locke did not want to locate the causation of action in processes of willing. Section 5 of that chapter (2.21) speaks of the mind ordering or commanding. Section 7 speaks of the power of the *mind* over the actions of the *man*. 'The mind' here is proxy for 'the person', it is I who do the commanding. Nevertheless, my thoughts *are* closely linked with my doing. Agency belongs to me as a conscious, thinking person, not to me as a body, even though the body is indispensable for most of my actions.[1] Persons span both thought and body. In the sense that person-identity is located in consciousness, so agency is located there. In Locke's metaphysic of nature, action proper belongs to thought, only conscious beings can initiate action. The opening paragraph of chapter 21 in Book 2 makes it clear that power is the doing or ability to do, in a *producing* sense. *Active* power is the basic concept (cf. section 4), though it goes along with or requires a *passive* power. So fundamental is the idea of power that Locke suggests it is a simple idea, in the sense that it is 'a principal ingredient in our complex *ideas* of substances' (3). From observing bodies we get no idea, or only a very obscure idea, of active power, since bodies do not initiate motion. It is only by noting our ability to move parts of our bodies or to vary the content of our awareness that we get a clear idea of active power.

Where there is no thought, volition, or will, there can be no liberty, no action. In general, 'Wherever thought is wholly wanting or the power to act or forbear according to the direction

---

he cites some instances of bodily movement caused by will: 'I eat, I drink, I move my Eye, my hand, my Muscles, my whole Body in pursuance of this command of my Will' (p. 29). The recognition that by taking thought I can move my body is also found in Newton: 'Since each man is conscious that he can move his body at will...' (in *De Gravitatione*, quoted by McGuire in 'Force, Active Principles, and Newton's Invisible Realm', *loc. cit.* 192).

[1] Stillingfleet used the phrase, 'done in or by the body'. Locke commented that he did not see how 'by the body' comes into the discussion. The body does not act, only the person does (*Second Reply, Works*, IV, 312).

of thought, there *necessity* takes place' (13). Not only would necessity take over in the absence of thought, it would replace free action also, if I were to deny responsibility for actions I have done. In an interesting sentence in section 22 of this same chapter, Locke recognises that men are all too 'willing to shift off from' themselves 'all thought of guilt', not realising that they thereby put themselves 'in a worse state than that of fatal necessity'. Only at the peril of loss of freedom will I deny my responsibility and my agency in action. That agency is mine, not a property of my thought. In one sentence in section 21, Locke says that my preferring *is* the willing of an action, but he means, I think, to link this sentence with its immediate predecessor which speaks of preferring and being able to produce what I will or prefer. It is the agent, the person, who has that ability to actualise what he wills or prefers. Willing is not some strange process with causal powers: it is my preferring and *thereby* being able to make something happen, 'the power of directing our operative faculties to some action for some end' (40). Locke saw the absurdity in saying volitions cause actions, since, even overlooking the mistake of turning abilities into agents, powers into substances, volitions would in turn need actions to cause them, and so on *ad infinitum* (25).

In recognising the matter of fact of agent causation, Locke did not overlook the role of reasons for actions. Both the type of causation and the presence of reasons distinguish actions which are agent-caused from those actions caused by impulse. That Locke was fully aware of the difference between agents and machines, between reasons and causes, is clearly brought out by his interesting comments on the mechanical bird (2.10.10). Against the Cartesians, Locke did not think animals were automata. In this passage he says animals (including birds) have retention. He offers as evidence for this claim the fact that some birds can learn tunes. Moreover, he thinks those birds show an attempt to hit the notes right. To 'endeavour to conform their voices to notes' requires that they have ideas which serve as the patterns or tunes they are striving for, in much the way that men have ideas of actions which serve as the patterns of behaviour they are aiming for. Locke then says that sound 'may mechanically cause a certain motion of the animal spirits in the brains', this motion would be carried to the muscles of the wings and thus, by certain noises, drive the birds away. But no such mechanical account will be a *reason* why the bird learns a tune, especially since the bird can sing the notes in the absence of the tune. The need for a reason for learning a tune is even more pronounced in the phenomenon of the bird getting closer and closer to the desired pitch. For this, he must have an idea as pattern. There is 'no reason why the sound of a pipe should leave traces in their brains which not at first but by their after endeavours should produce the like sounds'.

To be a *moral* agent, a rule-following person, I have to be a free agent (1.3.14). To act and to act freely are synonymous.[1] A prerequisite for freedom and action is thought. A body, e.g. a tennis ball, is not considered to be a free agent 'because we conceive not a tennis ball to think, and consequently not to have any volitions, or preferences of motion to rest' (2.21.9). Preference is an important ingredient for Locke, but the preference must be operative and must be for actions that we can do. The terms 'ordering', 'directing', 'choosing', 'preferring' catch some aspect of the volition or freedom of the agent (15), but the best way to understand these action words, to discover what willing and choosing are, is to reflect on what each of us does when we order, will, prefer (15, 20). Willing is an action of the first sort distinguished by Locke, that of the mind, but it is closely tied to preference; so much so that 'a man must necessarily *will*' the action or its forbearance as soon as '*any action in his power is once proposed to his thought*' (23). 'This being so, it is plain that a man that is walking, to whom it is proposed to give off walking, is not at liberty whether he *will* determine himself to walk or give off walking, or no' (24). I am not free *to* will in that I am not free *in* my willing, not free *while* I will. In willing, I have already exerted my freedom (23). For any action which is in my power, and which I have considered as a possible action, I cannot avoid willing either its existence or its non-existence. One of those *must* happen. It is impossible for me to cancel my consideration

---

[1] Locke did emphasise that voluntary actions can sometimes not be free actions, as when a paralytic prefers to sit (11), or I, being carried to a room while asleep, prefer to stay there and visit with the friend I find there, even though the door is locked and I cannot leave (10). Voluntary is opposed to involuntary, not to necessity.

of those alternatives or to decide both to do and not to do the action (24).

Freedom consists in being able to do what we prefer or desire. Locke gives a varied list of situations in which a man is not free (9–13):

(1) A man falling into a river because the bridge collapsed.

(2) A man striking another man through a convulsive motion of his arm.

(3) A man carried into a room while asleep.

(4) A man is not free with respect to the circulation of the blood or the heart beat in his body.

(5) The movement of my body in *sancti viti*.

(6) The movement of my limbs afflicted with palsy.

(7) I am not free not to have some ideas if I am awake and conscious.

(8) A man on the rack cannot avoid the idea of pain.

(9) A boisterous passion sometimes usurps our attention and prevents us from thinking thoughts we would prefer to think.

Each of these events, motions of or in my body, thoughts or contents of awareness make it impossible for me to do what I prefer or desire to do. It is desire or preference which is the motive for action, once impediments have been removed. Satisfaction and uneasiness are the two fountainheads of action (29). '*Delight* or *uneasiness*, one or other of them, join themselves to almost all our *ideas* both of sensation and reflection; and there is scarce any affection of our senses from without, any retired thought of our mind within, which is not able to produce in us *pleasure* and *pain*' (2.7.2). God has annexed pleasure and pain to all our ideas so as 'to excite us to those actions of thinking and motion that we are capable of' (3). It is pleasure and pain which define for us good and evil (2.20.2; 2.21.42), but it is not the thought of a greater good which makes us act. The motive to action is some '*uneasiness* a man is at present under' (2.21.31). Knowledge of good is insufficient to bring a man to act, 'that which immediately determines the *will*, from time to time, to every voluntary action, is the *uneasiness* of *desire*, fixed on some absent good' (33). Even Locke had taken the intellectualist position on motives in the first edition of the *Essay*, but he firmly rejected it as false in later editions (33–40). Happiness and misery are the main grounds for action, pleasure and pain being indicators of each. Pleasure and pain can sometimes lead us astray, but in any case they are only the criteria of good and evil. We

should take pains to suit the relish of our minds to the true intrinsic good or ill that is in things, and not permit an allowed or supposed possible great and weighty good to slip out of our thoughts, without leaving any relish, any desire of itself there, till, by a due consideration of its true worth, we have formed appetites in our minds suitable to it and made ourselves uneasy in the want of it, or in the fear of losing it (53).

Applied to moral actions, we should form appetites for doing what reason discloses is right. Reason and judgment can aid men in doing what is right by bringing into clarity short-term and long-term pleasures attendant upon specific actions. Just as tastes in food can be learned, so preference for right actions can be acquired. 'Men may and should correct their palates and give relish to what either has, or they suppose has, none' (69). Morality 'established upon its true foundations, cannot but determine the choice in anyone that will but consider', but what determines the choice is not the knowledge of the true morality but the recognition of the rewards and punishments (i.e. infinite happiness and misery) consequent in the long run (70). Realisation of these rewards and punishments will, Locke believed, generate in us an uneasiness and a desire for moral action.

It is sometimes said that Locke was trying to combine two strands in his thinking on these matters, rationalism and hedonism, two strands which may not be compatible. The fact that chapter 21 of Book 2 gave Locke trouble and was revised frequently is cited as evidence that hedonism grew in his favour, leading to embarrassment, preventing him from carrying out the demonstrative ethics (the ideal of a rationalism in ethics) he suggested. The problem here is not clear-cut. Locke *may* be called a hedonist in his non-moral view of good, what he called 'natural good and evil' (2.28.7–10). In a similar way, he points out that ' *Morally good and evil*...is only the conformity or disagreement of our voluntary actions to some law, whereby good or evil is drawn on us from the will and power of the law maker' (5).[1] Pleasure and

---

[1] Wilkins also distinguished between *natural* and *moral* good, the former being the well-being of man as a sensitive creature, the latter relating to the 'Well-fare of man as a *Rational voluntary and free Agent*' (*Principles and Duties of Natural Religion*, p. 19).

pain can function as criteria of moral good and evil, but they can also mislead us. In no way can they be said to be for Locke the definitions of moral good and evil. The main role Locke sees for pleasure and pain is, as I have stressed, as the motives for action. Only reason or revelation can tell us what is morally good or bad, right or wrong, but reason is incapable of motivating us to do moral good. The supposed problem about Locke's hedonism disappears, I think, with the careful distinction he draws between natural and moral good. There is a clear difference for Locke also between obligation and motivation. The law of nature obligates because it is the will of a superior. The actions those laws require or enjoin against are obligations. The relation between right and obligation is that we are obliged to do what it is right for someone to require us to do. It is the recognition of this relation between right and obligation which should be the proper moral sanction leading us to meet our obligations: 'not fear of punishment, but a rational apprehension of right puts us under an obligation'.[1] But the rational apprehension of right is insufficient to motivate us to action.

It was a basic truth of human nature for Locke that 'every intelligent being really seeks happiness', happiness being 'the enjoyment of pleasure without any admixture of uneasiness' (2.21.62). It is the desire for happiness which is a basic spring of action. Locke carefully distinguished these natural springs of action, 'things that are grateful and others unwelcome' to man, 'some things they incline to and others that they fly', from innate practical principles (1.3.3). That these 'principles of action' have no moral bias, are even potential enemies of morality, Locke also firmly recognised (2.3.13). *Two Treatises* makes frequent reference to self-preservation as one of the basic rules or principles of action, 'a strong desire of self-preservation' (1, 56, 86). In calling those desires (they are more nearly drives or instincts) 'principles of action', Locke of course does not mean they are *moral* principles: they are the springs, causes, or motives for action. Laslett, in his note to this last-mentioned passage (p. 223) suggests there is an incompatibility between Locke's denial of any innate practical principles and his saying there is a principle of action toward self-preservation in all men. But 1.3.3 and 13 show that this

[1] *Essays on the Law of Nature*, p. 185.

suggestion will not do. It is true that in the First Treatise, in the passage just mentioned, Locke goes on to say that reason as the voice of God assures us that in following the inclination for self-preservation we are following the will of God, hence we have a *right* to self-preservation, but this fact is discovered by reason, it is not an innate moral principle.

Moral principles state rights and obligations, principles of action move us to act. The moral agent is precisely the person who feels uneasy when not pursuing moral good, who takes delight in right actions. The purposive universe that Locke saw as our universe helps man tune his desires to right and obligation, because God has made his creatures have a desire for self-preservation, one of the rights of man, the one in fact which is the foundation for civil society. This natural inclination is in a unique position in the springs of action, since it is an inclination for a right. For the rest, man's pleasures and pains can take him towards all sorts of non-moral and immoral actions. We have to learn to follow the moral principles discovered by reason, but we do so by learning to adjust our pleasures and pains to right and wrong. We have to learn to let moral good take precedence over natural good. Learning to be moral is not only a matter of fitting our desires to what is right, judgment and understanding play roles as well. For example, when confronted by conflicting and different desires, I have to judge which is the more pressing and more capable of being removed (2.21.40). More importantly, I am able to 'suspend the execution and satisfaction of any of' my desires, weigh and examine the different ones. This suspension of action is absolutely essential if I am to make moral judgments informed by reason. Section 47 gives what may appear to be a different definition of freedom or liberty, since Locke there says this ability to suspend action constitutes my liberty. We might better call this 'moral liberty', since Locke is anxious for man to act on educated motives and rational preferences. It is 'a perfection of our nature, to desire, will, and act according to the last result of a fair *examination*' of proposed courses of action, not to act on unexamined preferences (47). The demand to suspend action, to put aside the preferences of the moment for consideration and judgment, does not limit liberty, as it might seem: it is, in Locke's eyes, an improvement of liberty (48). The perfection of our nature is not just to be free, but to be free to attain good. The basic definition of freedom or liberty is that of 'a power in any agent to do or forbear any particular action, according to the determination or thought of the mind' (8). This definition pertains to both types of action distinguished by Locke, thinking and moving. The power to consider any idea or to move some part of my body is the will, when actualised it is willing (5). What the definition in 47 is doing is combining the power to think and to move, precisely the combination which characterises moral actions, actions in the third class, of mind and body.

Once we decide to act, once we allow some desire to move us to act (whether it be before or after informed judgment), 'What follows after that follows in a chain of consequences, linked one to another, all depending on the last determination of my judgment' (52).[1] Once a judgment is determined by a specific desire for some goal, the action follows. The agency of doing pervades my actions, but the freedom to do or not to do stops with the determination of my judgment. Locke's analysis of action is made with intentional, deliberate actions in mind. There is another class of actions which are agent-caused but which I do inadvertently, accidentally, unconsciously. The agency may be the same in this sort of actions as in moral deeds, in both I bring it about that such and such happens. The responsibility for those actions may not differ either. Given that Locke's objective is to offer an analysis of intentional action, his remarks on judgment just quoted might sound as if he cut off the agency at the point of judgment and decision; what happens after that does so with necessity, I can only act in judging, not in doing. Such an interpretation would, however, be a gross exaggeration of Locke's remark. What he is saying is that intentional, moral action follows upon deliberation and judgment, that once I have judged and decided I cannot fail to

[1] This notion of action following upon the last determination of my judgment was common in the seventeenth century. It runs throughout Hobbes's controversy with the Bishop of Derry (see Hobbes's *Works*, v, 41, 74, 315–27). Hobbes insists that the action that follows the judgment does so necessarily (p. 317). Matthew Hale, *op.cit.*, refers to the doctrine also: 'But how far forth the Will is determined by the last act of the practick Understanding, or how far such a determination is, or is not consistent with the essential or natural liberty of the Will, is not seasonable here to dispute' (p. 58).

execute the action, save by the intervention of another judgment rescinding my original decision. To act deliberately and responsibly is to make my action dependent upon my judgment. It is I who deliberate, judge, and act. The action which follows my judgment does not happen by some necessity or power outside me, it is my agency that brings it about. I act in judging *and* in doing. Judgment can be determined precipitately or deliberately, I can make wrong judgments by assessing my future goods improperly. The wrong judgment Locke had in mind was a universal one: it is not 'what one man may think of the determination of another, but what every man himself must confess to be wrong' (62). Wrong judgment, even if it occurs on a universal scale, will not excuse a man: once he has judged, his actions will be measured by the one true morality, by 'the eternal law and nature of things' (56).

The right and justness of rewards and punishments is linked not only to the actions, it is linked as well to the agent (2.27.18). Locke's analysis of the agent concerned the conditions for ascribing responsibility. He also grappled with the question of the metaphysic of persons. That metaphysic includes an account of the person as agent of action, as well as some comments on the ontology of persons *per se*. These two aspects of the metaphysic of persons are of course not unrelated. An important question to settle is to what extent the ontology of persons influenced the analysis of agency. Locke's analysis of the agent was in terms of an embodied self, a combination of what he calls the person and the man. In 2.27.6 Locke points out that the identity of a man is a function of one organised life. An organised life is attached to, or takes place in, a bit of matter, but it is not just the particles of matter. A plant partakes of the same life throughout its growth although the particles of matter change (4). The organisation of the parts of matter partakes of 'one common life', that life is, in each particular concrete individual, 'distinguished from all others'. 'Same man' is similarly analysed into an 'organisation of the life in several successively fleeting particles of matter united to it' (6).[1] To identify the man with the soul leads to difficulties

---

[1] Cf. Hobbes: 'But we must consider by what name anything is called, when we inquire concerning the *identity* of it. For it is one thing to ask concerning Socrates, whether he be the same man, and another to ask whether he be the same body; for

about saying 'an *embryo*, one of years, mad, and sober' are the same man. Nor would we be able to differentiate Socrates from Caesar Borgia, or any two temporally distinct men, from each other.[1] The problem here is not only of differentiation: it is one of *being* the same as well. To talk this way about men in terms of souls instead of in terms of organised life in matter is to give a 'very strange use of the word *man*, applied to an *idea* out of which body and shape are excluded'. The human form is part of our idea of man (8, 15), the leading characteristical mark of man (3.11.20).[2] Talk of immaterial substance is a metaphysical way of referring to the agent of action. Agency, as we have seen, belongs to the mental side of the partnership of soul and body; but the agency, at least in finite spirits, cannot act save by means of a body. I do not find I can act on bodies distant from my own. In fact, just because I can act only in conjunction with my body, Locke suggests that it makes sense to speak of the soul moving. Souls or spirits are not *in loco* but they are *ubi* (2.23.21). I can act only *from the place* where my body is. It is not my body which begins motion or which acts, since body cannot initiate motion or act. Hence, the soul or mind is required for action. A charac-

his body, when he is old, cannot be the same it was when he was an infant, by reason of the difference of magnitude; for one body has always one and the same magnitude; nevertheless, he may be the same man' (*Works*, 1, 137).

[1] Locke cites obvious non-overlapping individuals—Seth, Ismael, Socrates, Pilate, St Augustine, Caesar Borgia. In a later passage (2.27.23) he considers the supposition of 'two distinct incommunicable consciousnesses acting the same body, the one constantly by day, the other by night'. The day and the night man could, on this supposition, be temporal contemporaries, as in Locke's example in 2.1.12 of Castor and Pollux: while Castor sleeps, his soul thinks in the body of Pollux, who is sleeping also but without a soul. Cf. 2.27.18: 'if the same *Socrates* waking and sleeping do not partake of the same *consciousness*, *Socrates* waking and sleeping is not the same person'.

[2] Locke's apparently straight-faced account of a talking Brazilian parrot is offered in evidence for saying that, while we might be led to call such a bird (that discusses with men and answers questions intelligently) a rational parrot, we would never take it to be a man; a human shape is requisite for that (2.27.8). But in a later discussion of monsters and changelings, Locke says that 'were there a monkey or any other creature to be found that had the use of reason to such a degree as to be able to understand general signs and to deduce consequences about general *ideas*, he would no doubt be subject to law and, in that sense, be a *man*, how much soever he differed in shape from others of that name' (3.11.16). He has distinguished in this passage between the physical and the moral man. Just as in cases of consciousness-transfers, so in the event of our finding an animal lacking human shape but otherwise manifesting rational properties we would have to locate identity and morality with the consciousness and rationality, not with the shape.

teristic of created spirits is that they have both active and passive powers. This fact alone would show that they 'are not totally separate from matter' (28). Human agency requires a body for action, that body is a convenient, even necessary third-person criterion of identity of agent. Nevertheless, it is not the body which makes the person. Locke insisted that one cannot think or have ideas without being aware that he is thinking or having ideas. That principle was laid down early in Book 2 (2.1.19), it is repeated in 2.27.9: 'consciousness always accompanies thinking'.[1] It is consciousness 'that makes everyone to be what he calls *self*' (9). An animated body lacking consciousness we would not consider to be a self or person. If such an animated or living body is conscious during part of its life—say the first twenty-five years— but totally unconscious for the last twenty-five years (e.g. as in severe psychotic or brain-damage cases), we would be hard pressed to go on thinking of that living organism as a person or agent of action during the second half of its life. Shorten the periods of consciousness and unconsciousness and the ascription of person to the organism becomes easier, the illness less severe and debilitating. We might find it odd to say of the first example that the person ceased to exist after the first twenty-five years of that life, but our treatment and attitude towards such a case increasingly comes to view that living body as vegetative, as lacking in person. Our treatment—up to the point where we give up—consists precisely in trying to establish contact with or to revive consciousness in the person. Thus, Locke's conclusion that 'consciousness, as far as ever it can be extended...unites existences and actions' (16), 'That with which the *consciousness* of this present thinking thing can join itself makes the same person and is one *self* with it' (17).

[1] One feature of action closely allied to consciousness, which Locke does not discuss, is that of intentional knowledge, the fact, as it is sometimes characterised, that we know without observation what we are doing. A contemporary of Locke's put this point clearly: '...I do as certainly know before I write, what I am now writing, that I think or reason touching things I am writing, or that I resolve or purpose to write them, as I am certain that I have written them when I have written them..' (Matthew Hale, *op. cit.* p. 24). Locke uses the same example, notes that I can tell beforehand what new ideas the characters I am writing will cause, but the example is used to support realism, not to explore practical knowledge: 'Thus I see, whilst I write this, I can change the appearance of the paper and, by designing the letters, tell beforehand what new *idea* it shall exhibit the very next moment, barely by drawing my pen over it' (4.11.7).

Another closely related notion to person has appeared in this first formulation of person-identity, the notion of owning actions.[1] The extreme and disturbing form of this notion is that, if I find myself conscious of any of your actions, and conscious of them as mine, at that point I become the same person as you (14). It is not enough that I *think* I am you, as some mentally ill individuals identify with great men: I must have your memories.

I do not know whether there have been any actual cases of persons having the memories of others. It would be difficult to think of ways of testing such claims. But we should not let this strange claim obscure from us what I take to be an easy truth in Locke's account, namely, that we do identify and require con-sciousness—self-consciousness—for persons. Locke's locating personal identity in sameness of consciousness might be thought to show that the person of action is only contingently tied to a body. The criterion of ownership and the ownership of action is contained in consciousness of having performed those actions (2.27.17). The only escape from scepticism of consciousness (the possibility that I may have represented to myself as done by me some actions I did not in fact do) is to trust in the goodness of God (13). If, at the resurrection, bodies and consciousnesses become confused and mixed, such that my consciousness inhabits or goes along with your body, I am the person involved and the one who is accountable for my actions. I would be the same person but not the same man I was while living (15). Whether transfers of consciousness of past actions can occur is not something we can know is possible, nothing in 'the nature of things' enables us to draw conclusions either way, the nature of immaterial substance is no more intelligible to us than that of corporeal (13). Did such a transfer happen, we would have to say the person goes with the consciousness, the man with the body and the organised life. Such cases would present us with medical and psychoanalytic (perhaps also metaphysical) problems, but the legal and moral questions would have a clear answer. That is why Locke remarks that the term 'person' is a 'forensic term, appropriating actions and their merit, and so belongs only to intelligent agents, capable of a law, and happiness and misery' (26). We can ascribe praise

[1] Hobbes speaks of an author (of action) owning his actions, see *Works*, V, 214.

and blame, rights and responsibilities, only where the ownership of actions is clear. That ownership would ultimately be determined (especially if we are confronted with instances of transfer of consciousness) by consciousness, not by bodily shape. Nevertheless, 'when we say that *man is subject to law*, we mean nothing by *man* but a corporeal rational creature' (3.11.16). *That*, Locke adds, is what we mean by a *moral man*.

Locke sees himself as revealing the various possibilities of identity of self and body, as well as clarifying the concept of identity.[1] He does not purport to know whether any of the more extravagant suppositions he cites has ever happened or could happen. We know too little about the thinking substance even to know whether those suppositions are meaningful or absurd (27). Moreover, none of his suppositions involves remembering (or claiming) actions done without a body. The actions relevant for morality and the law are actions requiring a body as well as consciousness, a person as well as a man. Parts of my body can disappear or be replaced while I remain the same person. Carried further, there is no contradiction in my consciousness belonging to another body, but there is a necessity for me to have a body in order to engage in the actions we ordinarily do. It is a conceptual truth to say I cannot stab or murder without a body, even though this truth may not specify what body I must have or even that it

[1] The concept of *identity* or of *same* is, Locke insisted, a difficult and late acquisition in the development of awareness. Concerned in Book 1 to expose the naiveté of saying this concept was innate, Locke challenged anyone of any age to explicate that concept, especially in the context of the doctrine of transmigration of souls or in that of the Christian belief in immortality (1.4.4–5). One of the difficulties with the doctrine that the soul always thinks—a doctrine Locke found not only false, but absurd—is that the identity of man changes. If it is not necessary for me to be conscious when I think, it follows that in my waking state or asleep I am not the same person (2.1.12). Transmigration has the consequence of separating soul and body, making the 'soul and the man two persons' (2.1.12). Locke was interested in this ancient doctrine only as it threw light upon the concept of identity. The separation of soul and body or of soul and man which this doctrine entailed was, for Locke, a fatal error, an error shared with the doctrine Locke *was* concerned to refute, that the soul always thinks (19). N. Fairfax, *A Treatise of the Bulk and Selvedge of the World* (1674), says that we 'are body and ghost both together'. Fairfax even saw the category mistake in ascribing soul or ghost properties to body or *vice versa*: 'and lastly, whereas *Ens Physicum* or *Naturale*, is either *materiale* or *immateriale*, body and ghost or body and not body, by bewedding to body the things that belong to ghost or bringing over to ghost, or that which is not body, the things cleaving unto body' we make a mistake (pp. 10–11).

be the same body I had yesterday. Nevertheless, what this conceptual point reveals is that it is not just the person who acts, it is the man as well. In addition, Locke has made it clear that the way we ordinarily think about specific persons includes the body we observe. In 'the ordinary way of speaking, the same person and the same man stand for one and the same thing' (15). It is not just the idea 'of a thinking or rational being alone that makes the *idea* of a *man* in most people's sense, but of a body so and so shaped, joined to it' (8).

In discussing with Stillingfleet (who thought Locke's account of personal identity inconsistent with Christian principles), Locke had insisted that the word 'person' signifies nothing until the 'common use of any language has appropriated it to any idea' (*Works*, IV, 92). Locke's account of identity of persons claims to be an explication of the meaning of that term or concept in our language and thought. *We* can see in what ways his explication was guided by a metaphysical belief about active power belonging only to spirits. He also accepted the belief in the resurrection of the dead on Judgment Day. The ontology of persons implicit in this theological doctrine may have played some influencing role in his account of agency, it is certainly a feature of Locke's metaphysic of person. Stillingfleet claimed that Locke's account of personal identity ruled out the body, at least the *same* body. Hence, Stillingfleet wanted to know what body persons will have at the resurrection. Locke points out that the scriptures talk only of the resurrection of the dead, not of the body, though Locke usually assumes that there will be some bodily form on the Day of Judgment (see 2.27.15, 26; also *Works*, IV, 303).[1] The question is, if I am to suffer for the sins I did when in my body, do I have the same body as when those sins were committed? (p. 308). Locke uses various examples to point out to Stillingfleet that *the* body I have at different stages of my life is always

---

[1] Stillingfleet was not alone in thinking the *same* body would be resurrected. Matthew Hale says that 'in the Resurrection the separated Soul is supposed to reassume his own Body again' (*op. cit.* p. 321). Thomas Browne (*Religio Medici*, 4th ed. 1656) says he does not know how the dead shall rise again but he believes 'that our estranged and divided ashes shall unite againe' at the resurrection (p.102). God, Browne says, shall command our remains 'back into their proper shapes, and call them out by their single individuals' (p. 103).

my body, though not the *same* body, where 'same' means 'same particles of matter'. The implicit concept of 'my body' in these comments (as in the *Essay*) is that it is the one *I* have, hence, what *I* am is not characterised by *the* body I have, though my actions require *a* body. Whatever 'matter is vitally united to his soul, is his body, as much as is that which was united to it when he was born, or in any other part of his life' (p. 314). If the dead are given bodies at the resurrection, those bodies will belong to the persons in the same way as their bodies were theirs in this life. God does not need bodily forms to identify men, though men do. Stillingfleet had concluded from the fact that Jesus was raised with the same body he had on the cross that men would be raised with the same bodies they had before death. Locke sees no reason for this inference. There were special reasons for the nature of Jesus's resurrection: he was only recently dead (his body was not 'dissolved and dissipated') and the disciples had to recognise and identify him as Jesus. For such human recognition, same body could alone do, not same soul. The cognitive question, 'is he the same person?', can only be resolved by men by 'the discernible structure and marks' of the body, 'by the outward visible lineaments, and sensible marks' (p. 315). Just how God's identification without bodies works Locke does not explain, but we know that it was part of Locke's metaphysic that angels and God can communicate without words and that omniscient cognition grasps all knowledge in intuition. For spirits higher on the scale of being than man, bodily senses and bodily form are not needed for cognition or recognition. Man requires both for knowing and doing.

I do not normally identify actions as mine by recognising my body engaged in those actions, though remembering having done some action is a remembrance of me as embodied. Awareness of self incorporates awareness of body, our body-image is part of our concept of self. In this way, the relation of mind to body is not contingent. Whether Locke thought the notion of person being resurrected without bodily form made sense to us is not clear from the texts. It may be that it was not intelligible to him, hence his allowing some bodily form at resurrection, even though God does not require it. The location of personal identity in 'remembrance of the same' may derive some of its force for Locke from the religious doctrine of resurrection, where 'same person' may appear before God without a body and be judged for the deeds done in life. At that time, what I remember to have done will, Locke assures us, coincide with what in fact I did do. God's knowledge of self is presumably like his knowledge of bodies: it is of the real nature. Hence he knows who I am without relying upon bodily form or upon my testimony of what I am conscious of having done. Without God, the ultimate criterion appears to be consciousness of same, not same body. The supposition of consciousness-transfers is resolved by the same criterion. It is an easy step from these suppositions and from the example of resurrection and judgment to the conclusion that Locke held that in ordinary cases the criterion of same person is likewise 'consciousness of same'. If Locke did mean to appeal to the criterion of consciousness of same in ascribing praise and blame for actions, has he not denied, as Antony Flew charges, 'that there can (logically) be honest but falsidical memory claims'?[1]

Locke has not overlooked the fact of poor memories, he even raises the question of total loss of memory (2.27.20, 23). His answer to his question about total loss of memory seems to support Flew, at least in the sense that the personal identity of man for Locke *is* the man who remembers the actions he has done. That we do not always have such comprehensive memories as to include all that we have done, is a fact Locke recognised. That *we* would say it was the same man (not the same person) who corrupted the youth at Athens (assuming that Socrates did corrupt the youth but, at his trial, claimed honestly not to remember doing any of the deeds identified as corrupting the youth) and who drank the hemlock, does not mean Locke would appeal to some new kind of agency for those unremembered actions of the man, nor that Locke would think of the man as de-souled or devoid of consciousness. Something is lacking in a man who fails to remember as his actions those which others have witnessed him doing. What is lacking, certainly when this loss of memory is large or when it pertains to important events in

---

[1] 'Locke and the Problem of Personal Identity', reprinted in Martin and Armstrong, *Locke and Berkeley*, p. 163.

a man's life, is the person-identity. A man without a person—odd as this sounds—is possible; repression is a familiar phenomenon. Locke may not be talking of such abnormal occurrences (though he cites some, e.g. 14); he may have been raising ontological queries about persons and men. But the deficiency of a man lacking a person—or having only a truncated person—is matched by the deficiency of person-claims without the requisite body.

For should the soul of a prince, carrying with it the consciousness of the prince's past life, enter and inform the body of a cobbler as soon as deserted by his own soul, everyone sees he would be the same person with the prince, accountable only for the prince's actions; but who should say it was the same man? (15).

My body is defined in terms of me as a person. In replying to Stillingfleet, Locke even says that soul and body are individuals before their union (p. 439). He was using Stillingfleet's vocabulary there, but it is no great distortion to write 'person' where Locke puts 'soul' in this brief remark. The defining of person in terms of consciousness, the doctrine of resurrection which does not make even *a* body necessary for receiving one's just deserts, both seem to support the charge that Locke's metaphysic of person is a version of the Platonic–Cartesian doctrine 'that people essentially are incorporeal spirits, and that human bodies in fact are controlled by internal shadow beings' (Flew, p. 169). The sentence I have referred to from the Stillingfleet exchange surely does come out of the Platonic tradition of separately existing souls. Locke's religious beliefs must include this kind of notion: it goes with the doctrines of immortality and resurrection. I do not, however, find this notion at work in Locke's analysis of the agent of action, unless we are to draw Flew's conclusion from Locke's insistence upon active power (and hence the cause of action) belonging to spirits only. Nevertheless, even there the analysis of agency has shown that we do not act without our bodies. To say that it is consciousness which individuates and personates need not be a derivation from the doctrine of separately existing souls; it need only be an articulation of a quite ordinary fact, that we do require for our concept of a person more than an animated body. The consciousness that we require besides the live body does not work alone behind the body's scenes, it works in close union with the body. The two features of Locke's metaphysic of the person—the account of agency and action *and* the ontology of self—should be kept distinct. The conceptual difficulties of the separate soul, of the soul indifferent to bodies, pertain to the ontology of Locke's religious belief. To understand this concept we would need to have a knowledge of the real essence of souls or persons. In default of such knowledge, Locke can only explicate the concept of person in our thought and language. He has as well looked to human action and sought to fit the conceptual explication to the facts of human life.

In all cases of action, it is the embodied self who is the agent and who acts: that 'which determines the general power of directing...is nothing but the agent itself' (2.21.20). There are various ingredients at work in the production of an action, motives, reasons, uneasiness, but the action itself is agent-caused: 'the proper and only object of the *will* is but some action in our power' (40). The production here is causal. I produce the revenge or murder no less than I produce the movement of my finger on the gun. The agent puts himself into action (72). A cause, Locke says, 'is that which makes any other thing, either simple *idea*, substance, or mode, begin to be' (2.26.2). In the brief analysis of his chapter on cause Locke distinguishes types of cause in the physical world: creation, generation, making, alteration. He does not talk of causes of actions. The role of 'cause' is played by 'power' when he deals with action and the will. Doing is another species of cause, what Locke calls 'active power'. He talks, as we have seen, of producing actions, even of causing my hands to move. Active power is an idea we get only or best from reflecting upon our own abilities and doings; it is his term for 'agency'. Difficulties arise over ascribing causes to actions in the moral sense just because, as Locke recognised, the same bodily activity can be described in different moral terms. That I am the cause of the trigger being pulled, of the death of my victim raises no special problems. That I am the cause of revenge having occurred or of justice being wrought begins to cloud the concept of cause. If killing differs from murder, parricide, or homicide only in the intentions, motives and circumstances of the killing, it looks as if there is no new event to be caused, once I have caused his death. I can be the agency for a slip of paper with marks on it being put in a box but once I have done that, what additional event is there for me to cause such that I have cast a vote for the Liberal candidate? Nothing more physically has or could happen save that I put a slip of paper in a box.

When the placing of a slip of paper in a box becomes an act of casting a ballot, my physical action is related to the customs and practices of my society where names and descriptions for that physical action apply. Locke saw and stressed this important point. He recognised that a man may become a citizen or burgher by virtue of certain *instituted* relations. The man does not change as man, but he now 'has a right to certain privileges in this or that place' (2.28.3). The same holds for patient, client, constable. Some differences in physical activities may accompany instituted relations, but that a man is entitled to these rights and privileges or to act in these ways is a function of the instituted relations of the society. In a similar way, Locke saw that it is the moral relations of the society that make actions of specific sorts acts of gratitude or kindness, justice or injustice (4). The category of mixed modes is Locke's way of showing how pervasive are our linguistic and conceptual categories, how they shape our account of the world and of human doings.

7

MORAL CONCEPTS AND MORAL PRINCIPLES

Besides a knowledge of things themselves, which the natural scientists were accumulating through their careful observations and experiments, another area falling under the human understanding concerns 'that which man himself ought to do, as a rational and voluntary agent, for the attainment of any end, especially happiness' (4.21.1). Here we are in an area where the objects of consideration and attainment, actions, are under our control. Just as the probable science of bodies prospers when we apply our faculties properly, so 'the attainments of things good and useful' rests upon the 'skill of right applying our own powers and actions' (3). Locke names ethics as the main, though not the only, subject-matter coming under the science of action. Ethics is characterised as 'the seeking out those rules and measures of human actions which lead to happiness, and the means to practise them' (3). The goal in the science of action is not 'bare speculation and the knowledge of truth' but 'right and a conduct suitable to it'.

The concepts of action Locke uses or mentions are varied: hypocrisy, parricide, triumph, apotheosis, wrestling, fencing (2.22.2, 4, 8, 9); justice (3.11.17); adultery (3.6.44); obligation, drunkenness, lying, sacrilege (2.22.1); gratitude, polygamy (2.28.4); murder, incest, stabbing (3.5.5–6); procession (3.5.13). These concepts can be obtained and learned 'by experience and *observation*' of human action, but the more usual way is by having the names of actions explained to us (2.22.9). A third way of acquiring the concepts of action is 'By *invention*, or voluntary putting together' of the characteristics of such concepts (*ibid.*). The first origination of such concepts may be an attempt to name specific, witnessed actions; but, even if those attempts turn out to be incorrect characterisations of the actions witnessed, the concepts and names thus formed have meaning (see Locke's Adam example, 3.6.44). Action-names and -concepts do not wait upon instances for their meanings. They can be descriptive, but they are primarily prescriptive or definitional. Locke's way of putting this last point is to say that the ideas of actions are *notions*, a seventeenth-century word for ideas not observation-dependent; notions were not looked upon as being marks of real beings, as the ideas and names of bodies were.[1] Notions were 'scattered and independent *ideas* put together by the mind' (2.22.1). The significations of the concepts and names of actions cannot be given *precisely* and unambiguously by showing instances of them: that can only be done by definition (3.11.15).[2]

Action words (Locke was mainly interested in moral words) can be precisely defined, thereby making moral knowledge clear and certain. Falsity here is impossible, there can only be lack of instances or incorrect naming of instances (3.11.17).[3] While we cannot learn about body by an examination and analysis of our ideas (a consequence which would arise had we an understanding of the real essence of body), one learns the meaning of moral concepts just by an analysis of those concepts. There are some conceptual truths about body which we discover by an analysis of ideas. There are necessary relations between the properties of body, most of which are beyond man's discovery. The necessary connexions between moral concepts are easily discovered, since their discovery is a matter not of uncovering real essences but of conceptual analysis. For example, from a definition of 'property' as 'a right to anything' and of 'injustice' as 'the invasion or violation of that right', we can see the certainty of the proposition, 'where there is no property there is no injustice' (4.3.18). From the definition of 'government' as 'the establishment of society

---

[1] The difference between 'idea' and 'notion' is clearly drawn by Locke in replying to Stillingfleet. 'Idea' was Locke's term for any immediate object of the mind in thinking. 'Notion' was much less general in meaning: 'the term "notion" is more peculiarly appropriated to a certain sort of those objects, which I call mixed modes: and, I think, it would not sound altogether so well, to say the notion of red, and the notion of a horse, as the idea of red, and the idea of a horse' (*Works*, IV, 133).

[2] For repeated examples of action-concepts whose independence from any real instances is stressed, see 3.5.3, 5, 12; 3.9.9; and 3.10.33.

[3] There is, or course, a sense in which falsity arises in action-propositions or concepts, when my idea of justice or of frugality differs from that generally accepted in my society. Cf. 2.32.10, 17.

upon certain rules or laws which require conformity to them', and the definition of 'absolute liberty' as 'anyone doing what he pleases', we can assert as certain the proposition, 'no government allows absolute liberty' (4.11.13). From the ideas of 'man' as 'intelligent but frail and weak' and 'God' as 'eternal, omnipotent, perfectly wise and good', and 'man' as 'dependent upon God', we come to the certain proposition, 'man is to honour, fear, and obey God' (4.13.3; cf. 4.3.18). This last proposition is related to two other concepts: (1) the concept of laws and obligations requiring a law-maker (1.4.8; 1.3.12), and (2) the concept of the law-maker as having the power to punish and reward (2.28.6).

Such conceptual truths simply make explicit the meaning-relations between concepts. With the indicated meanings for those terms, it is impossible for those propositions to be false. The conceptual truths which express relations between moral concepts are as certain as mathematical truths, e.g. as certain as the proposition 'that *three, four,* and *seven* are less than *fifteen*' (4.13.3). To explicate these truths is 'as certain as any demonstration in *Euclid*' (4.3.18; 3.11.16). Could the natural history dictionary find a moral counterpart, as the definitions in Euclid constitute a geometrical one, the conceptual clarity and necessity in morals would be more apparent than it is.[1] But we 'have no sensible marks' for our moral concepts, thus we must rely upon words (4.3.19; 4.4.9). Differences of meaning between two people may obscure the conceptual necessities. The remedy for such obscurity is careful explication of the meanings of our moral concepts, as a moral-word dictionary would do. Self-esteem, riches, power and bias tend to prevent a clear explication of these concepts, but there is no reason in principle why it cannot be done. The confusions of language not only lead to linguistic and conceptual unclarity, they breed moral disorder as well (4.4.9). Once we appreciate the fact that moral concepts need not be tied to moral experience, we should be able to clarify the conceptual connexions.[2] For that clarification, it is

---

[1] Locke saw the need for such a dictionary of action words and moral concepts, a 'dictionary of the greatest part of the words made use of in divinity, ethics, law, and politics, and several other sciences' (2.22.12). The natural history dictionary was to consist of little pictures with names opposite.

[2] A standard move by Locke in dealing with controversy (on those few occasions where he does so, e.g. the polemic against innate ideas, the long analysis of Filmer)

not important for us to determine whether we are characterising the same experience as others do by the same words. Moral actions, however, with their attendant praise and blame, require the meshing of moral language with actions: the language of morals must also be the language of human action. What we describe in our concepts ordinarily finds its example in experience. Actions exemplify moral relations whether we name them or not. Clarification of moral concepts and their connexions, without tying them down to experience, may give me a precise use of the language of morality but leave me in ignorance about which particular actions, if any, my language refers to or picks out.[1]

Conceptual clarification of moral concepts does not indicate whether there are actions named by our concepts or whether such actions are good or bad, right or wrong. The rightness or wrongness, the good or evil of any action can only be determined by a reference to a rule. This important distinction between a concept and a rule or principle Locke expresses as the difference between '*the positive idea* of the action *and the reference it has to a rule*' (2.28.16; cf. also 4, 15). In terms of this distinction, Locke handles the old example of the madman and his sword: taking the sword away from a madman without his knowledge or consent is stealing—it fits the definition of the action-concept 'stealing'—but stealing is wrong only when the action is referred to 'the rule of right'. In the madman example, there is an overriding or supreme rule, the law of God. Locke does not specify this law but presumably it would be one of the laws of nature he elsewhere cites. We confuse matters when we fail to distinguish the rule of right from the content or meaning of our action-concepts. (Cf. 'Ethics in General', *loc. cit.* pp. 129–30.)

One of the confusions resulting from a failure to recognise this distinction is an obscurity about Locke's claim that '*morality is capable of demonstration,* as well as mathematics' (3.11.16; see 4.3.18). The programme Locke envisaged was twofold: it was to display the conceptual connexions of concepts, and it was to

---

is to look for conceptual connexions, to point out that the requisite necessary connexions are lacking. His treatment of Filmer on property, and his analysis of the concept of property itself, are taken as examples of this method in the next chapter.

[1] 'Ethics in General' in Peter King, *Life of John Locke*, II, 124-6.

determine the measure of right and wrong' (4.3.18).[1] Locke was clear about the difference, as his distinction between moral concepts and principles testifies, even though he does not always make the distinction. The confusion was further complicated because all demonstrations for Locke were essentially the same, the presentation of concepts so that we can grasp the necessary connexions between them. Sometimes we see the connexions just by considering the concepts involved, at others we need the help of intermediary concepts. Just as with our knowledge of body there are a few obvious and trivial conceptual truths, so in moral action connexions of concepts without reference to rules of right and wrong are easier to see and more trivial than connexions between concepts which relate to rules and lead to conclusions of what is right and wrong. The second part of Locke's demonstrative claim was to derive moral rules from some basic notion: 'from self-evident propositions, by necessary consequences as incontestable as those in mathematics, the measures of right and wrong be made out to anyone that will apply himself' (4.3.18; cf. 4.3.4).

It was this second, more exciting and more dubious part of Locke's programme for a demonstrative ethics which attracted some of Locke's friends. William Molyneux repeatedly urged Locke to write a treatise on ethics, following up his suggestion in the *Essay* (*Works*, IX, 291–310). Molyneux thought a demonstration of the principles of morality could correct the pravity of men's morals (p. 299), missing Locke's recognition that a *knowledge* of right and wrong was not a sufficient *motive* for action. Just as Locke did not conceive his analyses of body to be of any practical help to the scientists, so he did not view his analyses of actions, of moral concepts and principles, as aiding men's lives. His analysis of both body and action was primarily oriented to his doctrine of signs, the third branch of human understanding about which the *Essay* is mainly written. The first part of his demon-

---

[1] In the light of Locke's recognition of the value, for conceptual clarification, of dictionaries of words, it is interesting to find Berkeley commenting, presumably critically, that 'To demonstrate Morality it seems one need only make a Dictionary of Words and see which included which, at least. This is the greatest part and bulk of the Work' (*Philosophical Commentaries*, entry 690). For the first part of the programme, a moral-word dictionary *would* prove helpful.

strative programme for ethics clearly falls under the doctrine of signs, since it concerns the internal relations of signs, those that are necessary or contradictory. The second part of this programme relies upon the doctrine of signs to the extent that it seeks to expose necessary relations between propositions. Since a proposition is composed of signs (ideas, he most frequently calls them, 1.4.1), any demonstration of propositions is a demonstation of conceptual connexions between signs. But Locke's *Essay* is not a treatise on signs only; the analysis of signs takes place in a context of belief. Locke had firm views on the nature of body (influenced by science, theology, and philosophy). He had equally firm views about the nature of right and wrong. In fact, here his views had none of the tentative character of the corpuscular hypothesis, since in this domain Locke claimed to be working with self-evident principles as the basis for morality and the ground of other, derivative principles. The self-evidence of the derivative principles has to be demonstrated, it is not intuitively clear, we can always demand a reason for these principles (1.3.4).

Even with reasons for moral principles, there are differences of kind; some are contingent upon particular basic principles of some general attitude. For example, the reason for the rule 'men should keep their compacts', cited by a Christian, will differ from the reason cited by a Hobbist or an 'old heathen' philosopher (1.3.5). Among these reasons, Locke selects the Christian one as 'the true ground of morality' (6). He formulates that true ground of morality as 'the will and law of a god, who sees men in the dark, has in his hand rewards and punishments, and power enough to call to account the proudest offender' (6). Unless I know that some rule has been set up by God and that God will punish the breach of that rule, I can never know 'that anything is my duty' (13). The 'true and only measure of virtue when virtue is used to signify what is in its own nature right and good' is a 'rule prescribed by God' (18). It is only if 'I have the will of a supreme invisible law-maker for my rule' that I can correctly call an action right or wrong (2.28.14). Other measures may operate as well but for different ends, e.g. I may use the standards of my country to determine whether an action is a crime or no; Locke cites three common measures of right and wrong: the law of God, of politic societies, and of fashion or private censure (2.28.13, 7; cf. 2.21.60). He is unequivocal about the law of God being 'the only true touchstone of *moral rectitude*' (8). God has given us a measure of right and wrong because we are his creatures and because his goodness and wisdom directs our actions to what is best. God also has the power to enforce the laws he has laid down or any laws derivative from that basic touchstone (8). To James Lowde who had charged Locke with taking the law of fashion or reputation as the true measure of right and wrong, Locke calls attention to those sections where he clearly says the law of God is that measure, adding that those passages show his firm conviction in 'the eternal and unalterable nature of right and wrong' (2.28.11).[1] It was from the idea of God as good, wise, creator of man and from the idea of man as rational that Locke suggested we ought to be able to derive the measures of right and wrong, by going from self-evident propositions to necessary consequences (4.3.18). The precepts of natural religion are said to be 'plain and very intelligible to all mankind and seldom to be controverted' (3.9.23).

Locke's suggestions about the demonstrability of ethics intrigued not only his contemporaries; logicians have always been interested in attempts to formalise wherever possible. The very recent discussions of the practical syllogism have attempted to apply formal logical concepts to action-concepts, to injunctions about what we ought to do. It is questionable whether any of these attempts to apply formal relations to informal concepts could be successful.[2] In presenting Locke's notion of demonstration I have argued that he was replacing the formal, syllogistical order by an informal order of concepts and propositions. A number of the commentators on Locke recognise the informal logic of concepts embedded in his notion of demonstration, though these same writers go on to insist that Locke's programme of demonstrative ethics fails because it was not *formally* successful.

[1] This remark is found in the note to section 11 on p. 298 of vol. 1 of the Everyman edition.

[2] The fact that modified formal concepts have been employed by recent writers on the practical syllogism, e.g. 'contextual implication', 'being entitled to infer', suggests that action-concepts and their relations have proved recalcitrant to formalisation, suggests in fact that formal relations are out of order in this domain.

Aaron recognises the conceptual connexion feature of Locke's programme.[1] John Dunn, in a brilliant study of Locke's political thought, points out that 'follows from' for Locke is informal, 'is not used in any approbation of the rigour of the logical proceedings'.[2] The inference Locke has in mind in the early *Essays*, Dunn says, 'is, of course, very informal' (p. 24 n. 3). Dunn puts the point somewhat differently later in his book by saying that Locke's analysis of moral ideas in the *Essay* was 'concerned not with the exposition of effective obligations but with the possibility of constructing a coherent moral language' (p. 191). Even Kemp, the interpreter who most strongly reads Locke's programme as a quest for complete formalisation of ethical relations, admits that we 'may be able to derive' ethical conclusions from premises 'in a non-deductive way', though Kemp insists that such informal derivations would not be demonstrations. To demonstrate for Kemp, and he claims for Locke also, means to produce premises which, if accepted and true, entail the conclusion: the conclusion can be rejected while accepting the premises only on pain of self-contradiction.[3]

Kemp does not produce any texts in support of his interpretation of what Locke means by 'demonstration', he only asserts this to be his meaning. My earlier discussion of demonstration in Locke should cast serious doubt on taking Locke in such a formal way. We are too much influenced by the logical associations of the concept of demonstration. Locke, as we saw, took geometrical demonstration as his model, emphasising that the demonstrative force of geometrical diagrams lay in their ability to make us see the properties of the figures drawn on paper. Locke was much closer to our more recent adaptations of logical concepts to informal reasoning (e.g. Toulmin, Nowell-Smith) than he was to the syllogistic tradition of formal logicians. The conceptual truths present in moral propositions are *necessarily* true, sometimes merely trivially so from the definitions of the concepts, but more importantly only when properly related to the true measures of right and wrong. The task of demonstration is

---

[1] *John Locke*, 2nd ed. p. 261; cf. 263-4.
[2] *The Political Thought of John Locke*, p. 24.
[3] *Reason, Action and Morality*, pp. 17, 24, 25.

to disclose these truths and those relations they have to the fundamental principles of moral good and bad on which are bottomed all true moral propositions. Most of the commentators on Locke have taken his programme as claiming to demonstrate not just the truth of moral propositions, but their obligations as well. For example, Aaron says that, while Locke assumes that true moral propositions obligate men, a proper science of morals would demonstrate that obligation (p. 264). To demonstrate an obligation is, apparently, not just to show that there are duties and obligations but in some way to make that obligation a result of the demonstration. Aaron charges Locke with neglecting the basic difference between *moral obligation* and *logical validity*. Kemp argues that, even if Locke could demonstrate (in Kemp's strong logical sense) some conceptual truths, those truths cannot 'of themselves function as guides to, or rules of action' (p. 21), because from none of the truths does it follow that man is obliged to do what they say. In other words, Kemp thinks a demonstrative morality must demonstrate obligation. Similarly, von Leyden says that for Locke the 'reason why a moral rule is said to be binding is of the same sort as the reason why a geometrical demonstration is valid'(*Essays on the Law of Nature*, p. 55). I think it very doubtful that Locke was claiming that seeing the connexions between moral concepts or propositions would reveal their obligatory force, certainly not that the conceptual connexions *were* the obligatory force. If, as Locke claimed in the seventh of the early *Essays on the Law of Nature*, propositions about moral obligations would follow from the concept of man's nature, the 'following from' would not establish the obligation. The truth of 'I ought to do p' may follow from 'my nature is q'. Moreover, *that* I ought to do p would be seen from q, is linked with it. But this does not equate 'obligation' with 'follow from'. Von Leyden sees the voluntarist aspect of Locke's account of ethics as also providing a source of obligation, a view somewhat at odds, he believes, with the demonstrative ethics. The question is, how does obligation arise? The voluntarist says I am obligated to do p because God wills it. Von Leyden says that the suggestion of the demonstrative ethics is that I am obligated to do p because it follows from q. The only sense I can give to this suggestion is that a rationalist theory of obligation says that I am obligated to do *p* if *p* is rational, the test for rationality being that *p* follows deductively from a set of premises. In this way logical validity might be said to establish obligations. But I see no evidence that Locke's notion of rationality took this form. What he does say several times is that the phrase 'law of reason' is interchangeable with 'law of nature'. Thus, to be rational is to act in conformity with the laws of nature, those laws being the ones God has willed for man. The measure of rationality is, in short, identical with the measure of morality.

There can be no question about the touchstone and source of moral right and wrong for Locke. What is difficult is to discover what these precepts of natural religion are, how the ideas of God and man lead to specific rules. It seems to have been self-evident to Locke that, if man was made by God on whom he depends, and if God is wise, good, and infinite and the bestower of rewards and punishments, we have the criteria satisfied for anything to be a law, a being with right and power. It was self-evident to Locke that there are laws for man to follow. Since man is rational and since God's expectations for man are reasonable, man's reason can discover God's laws. It was just this move from God and man to rules of action which Molyneux wanted Locke to make explicit. Locke would say, I am sure, that the conclusion that God has given us rules follows from an analysis of the ideas of God and man: this step belongs to the first part of the demonstrative programme. If 'demonstration' be taken in the sense Locke most frequently used it, making clear and evident, the derivation of specific moral rules from his touchstone may have been easy, given his context of belief. Still, Locke did not produce the demonstration. He had not said in 1690 (or in the earlier versions of the *Essay*) that this way to the principles of morality was easy, though by 1695 (with *Reasonableness*) perhaps he had discovered that even after revelation it was no easy task to arrange moral principles into a demonstrative pattern. Whatever the reason was for his not writing a treatise of morals, it is clear he took a second and easier way to moral principles, those revealed in scripture, aided by his own reason as a guide to others consistent with God and man.

There are a number of possible explanations for Locke's failure to produce the claimed demonstrative morality. The possibility already discussed, that the claim rests upon an impossible identity between moral obligation and logical validity, will not stand up as an account of why the demonstration was not produced, since the claim does not make this comparison. Another possible explanation is that one of the foundations for the demonstration is the nature of man and, since the real essence of man is unknown, this element in the demonstration is lacking.[1] This explanation for the failure also will not do, since Locke had a set of beliefs about man's nature—that he is frail, made by God, dependent upon God, rational, etc.—which was quite adequate for his subsequent account of morality. The demonstrative morality was not, in other words, to be a deduction from essence, it differed markedly in this way from the potential demonstrative physics Locke said was beyond man's ability but possible for other spirits. In deducing all the properties of body from the essence of body, we would be going from a knowledge of the cohering particles to a knowledge of all the properties of macroscopic bodies, together with a knowledge of the effects of body upon us, an epistemic movement which parallels the causal process in nature. In demonstrating moral principles, we would be showing the interconnexion of moral concepts. A variety of starting points would be possible for this demonstration since, if moral concepts are linked as Locke thought they were, the demonstration ought to be able to start anywhere in the class of moral concepts. Ultimately, some principles would have to be self-evident, else the demonstration would be merely circular. Kemp thinks that Locke rendered the demonstration impossible by remarking (in 1.3.4) that the truth of moral rules—and Locke cites 'that most unshaken rule of morality and foundation of all social virtue, that *One should do as he would be done unto*'—depends upon other, antecedent principles. This dependence, Locke adds, would be impossible if these fundamental rules were innate 'or so much as self-evident'. Thus, the demonstration fails because Locke denied the condition for any demonstration, a self-

---

[1] Matthew Hale, *op. cit.*, thought it was deducible 'from the Knowledge of the Humane nature' that I should be careful not to injure my nature through sin and evil, since I am made in God's image (p. 42).

evident starting place. But this explanation for Locke's failure to produce the demonstration won't do either. Locke's point in 1.3.4 is that the truth and obligation of even the basic moral rules are not self-evident, are not self-generating. In his own case, the truth and obligatory force of the rule he cites arises from the fact that there is a God and he requires us to act in accordance with that rule (1.3.5). The justification and force of the laws of nature stem from their being the laws of God. They bind because they are rational and willed by God. Moreover, the basic condition for any principle being a law is fulfilled in their case, there is a law-maker with the power and right to enforce them.

What the demonstrative programme Locke suggested was claiming was that demonstration, in his sense of 'demonstrate', could produce a full and complete morality based solely on the laws of nature as God's laws. In *Reasonableness*, Locke said that there are only two ways in which such a true morality can be established, through revelation or through natural reason. The latter way is difficult since it 'involves long and sometimes intricate deductions of reason', having to work from 'unquestionable principles to an entire body of the law of nature' (*Works*, VII, 138–40). *All* the parts of morality must be derived from first principles (p. 142). It was this task of laying out the entire system of moral rules and concepts (the language of morals) in an interconnected way which Locke found difficult to do. It is doubtful whether there is a systematic connexion among the concepts making up those few laws of nature and moral rules which Locke cites here and there. I think it much more likely that Locke was unable to discover the truth of *this* claim—that all moral concepts are linked by necessary relations—than that he failed on the demonstration. Of course, if a set of concepts are not in fact linked together such that an understanding of any one concept will lead on to others and eventually to the entire set, a demonstration of those connexions will be impossible. Failure to reveal the connexions may be the same as failure to produce the demonstration of the entire body of moral rules. But I think it important to see the difference between the two claims, especially since most discussions of Locke's programme have concentrated upon the demonstrative failure. With attention focused upon the demonstrative claim, it has been easy to miss both Locke's informal notion of demonstration and the backbone of his claim that all moral concepts are linked together in necessary ways. There is a conceptual failure in Locke's general claim, not a logical lacuna. The demonstrative morality he had hoped to produce would not have worked magic, by producing from deductive apparatus rules of conduct with obligatory force. There was no pretence (and hence no confusion) to identify logical validity with moral obligation. At the very best, a demonstration would have been a way of leading each of us, when we followed it, to an understanding, and hence to a discovery for ourselves, of moral rules for action. But of course, not even Locke's informal demonstration can produce more than is there to start with. If the conceptual links are not there, they cannot be demonstrated.

Unable to show the systematic connexions between all moral concepts, Locke abandoned the demonstrative programme and settled for a haphazard listing of moral rules as required for illustration or for appeal to sanction some action. The nearest he ever came to a listing of moral rules is found in the *Reasonableness*, where he cites a large number of moral injunctions as interpreted by Jesus (pp. 115–22). That list is nothing more than the standard Christian morality. That such injunctions as he there cites (taken mainly from Luke vi and Matthew v, vi, vii, but elsewhere as well) gained their sanction by being the will of God was undoubtedly the attraction for Locke of the 'law of nature' doctrine. Locke could at any time have referred his readers to the scriptures for the long list of commandments and injunctions to be found there. That he had hoped to be able to offer a more systematic listing, even a listing of rules that were the basis and grounding of most moral rules, is a reasonable assumption. He never at any time wavered from the firm belief that the basic laws of nature were identical with God's laws. Nor was he at all unique in looking for such a set of basic laws ready to hand for man's instruction and use. The doctrine of innate practical principles accepted by many of Locke's contemporaries was the context of Locke's 'law of nature' doctrine. It grew out of that doctrine (as the early *Essays on the Law of Nature* show) and played the same role in the account of human action as did the doctrine of innate principles.[1] The polemic against innate knowledge in the first book of the *Essay* used to be thought to be against a straw man. But I have shown that the theory was held in various forms throughout the seventeenth century in England.[2] The naïve form of the theory used the terminology of a truth 'stampt' and its 'characters' indelibly written in the hearts of men, of 'red letters', 'heavenly beams of light'. Examples of truths said to be innate in this way are: 'there is a God', 'God is powerful', 'promises are to be kept', 'parents are to be honoured', 'we must not injure and harm any Person, but render to every Man his due'. The terminology and the examples were used by many writers in the seventeenth century, even where they were attacking the doctrine. Locke was not the first to attack the naïve form of the theory but he formulated the most extended argument against it. The modified version is that the test for innateness is the 'ready and prompt assent given to such truths once they are presented to us'. Henry More followed this version of the doctrine of innate knowledge,[3] and Culverwel expressly linked it with the law of nature. 'There are stamp't and printed upon the being of man, some clear and undelible principles, some first and Alphabetical Notions; by putting together of which it can spell out the Law of Nature.'[4] He stressed the activity and spontaneity of the soul in the generation of its ideas and in its ready and immediate assent to certain moral and speculative principles. The modified version of innateness treats truths as implicit in man, waiting to be recognised once the light of reason has been turned upon them; it advances a dispositional claim for innateness. Wherever a writer finds reasons for relinquishing the naïve form of the doctrine—and there were many in the seventeenth century who did—it is always the dispositional

---

[1] Some of the material on the following pages appeared in my article, 'Locke on the Law of Nature', *The Philosophical Review*, LVII (October, 1958).

[2] *John Locke and the Way of Ideas*, ch. 2. It is surprising to find Peter Gay, writing in 1964, saying, 'The precise target of his long polemic remains a matter of discussion' (p. 7, *John Locke on Education*). In his abridgement of the *Essay* (The Fontana Library, 1964), Woozley agrees that Locke is not attacking men of straw, but he cites only the old guesses of Descartes, Cudworth, and Herbert of Cherbury (pp. 16–17).

[3] *An Antidote against Atheisme* (1653).

[4] *An Elegant and Learned Discourse of the Light of Nature* (1654), p. 47.

formulation which replaces it. The appeal to self-evident truths, particularly moral truths, was everywhere felt to be necessary for the preservation of morality. Morality could in this way be given an objective foundation.

What Locke was doing in his polemic against the naïve form of the doctrine was to organise the various actual and possible objections in such a way that the adherents to the doctrine would be led to spell out in precise terms just what they were claiming. He argued, in effect, that either the theory (in its naïve form) asserts something which not only is odd but which can never be verified, or that the theory (in its dispositional form) states an obvious fact about man, namely, that some truths are recognised as self-evident once we have acquired the mature use of our rational faculties. Locke's polemic was not directed towards the modified version of innateness. He did not refer to the truths or the knowledge obtained by the light of reason as 'innate'. He was always ready to point out that he recognised self-evident truths and principles but he prefers to restrict innateness to the naïve claim of literal truths imprinted on the mind or heart. Locke was not unmindful that his polemic against innate knowledge might be interpreted as an attack upon the law of nature but he expressly warned against such an interpretation. 'There is a great deal of difference between an innate law and a law of nature, between something imprinted on our minds in their very original, and something that we, being ignorant of, may attain to the knowledge of, by the use and due application of our natural faculties' (1.3.13). The law of nature and the dispositional version of innateness are clearly linked together.

The closeness of Locke's discussion of the law of nature to the doctrine of innate knowledge is evidenced by the terminology, the examples, and the objections he offers to various aspects of the 'law of nature' doctrine in the *Essays*. A synonym for law of nature, he says, is right reason, 'to which everyone who considers himself a human being lays claim' (p. 113; cf. pp. 134-5, 203). The distinction in this remark between men of reason who are human beings proper and those others not yet at the age of reason (children, idiots) was a frequent one in the literature on innate principles during the seventeenth century. The dispositional test for innateness reappears in his criterion for the law of nature in a passage almost identical with statements by Culverwel:

We do not maintain that this law of nature, written as it were on tablets, lies open in the hearts, and that, as soon as some inward light comes near it (like a torch approaching a notice board hung up in darkness), it is at length read, perceived, and noted by the rays of that light. Rather, by saying that something can be known by the light of nature, we mean nothing else but that there is some sort of truth to the knowledge of which a man can attain by himself and without the help of another, if he makes proper use of the faculties he is endowed with by nature (p. 123).

Such a criterion as this can be made to include almost any truth, particularly those truths deemed necessary for morality. The law of nature for Locke plays the same role in morality as the appeal to innateness did for his contemporaries: it furnishes a firm and unalterable foundation for moral goodness. What he was arguing for in the second of these *Essays* was that the law of nature (what we might call the 'moral rule') is not known through inscription or handed down by tradition but is known by reason through sense experience. He pretends, that is, to offer an experiential (empirical) foundation for the moral rule, in radical opposition to the believers in its innate basis. But how precisely do the senses and reason work to produce the apprehension of the law of nature?

He argues first of all that, 'if man makes use properly of his reason and of the inborn faculties with which nature has equipped him, he can attain to the knowledge of this law without any teacher instructing him in his duties...' (p. 127). From the appearances of sense perception, 'reason and the power of arguing ...advance to the notion of the maker of nature' (p. 133). Just as soon as man has the idea of God 'the notion of a universal law of nature binding on all men necessarily emerges' (p. 133). Reason and sense are the sole foundations for all knowledge.

But since, as has been shown elsewhere, this light of nature is neither tradition nor some inward moral principle written in our minds by nature, there remains nothing by which it can be defined but reason and sense-perception. For only these two faculties appear to teach and educate the minds of men and to provide what is characteristic of the light of nature, namely that things otherwise wholly unknown and hidden in darkness should be able to come before the mind and be known and as it were looked into (p. 147).

There are many assumptions contained in Locke's inference from sense experience to God and from that to God as a law-maker, and thence to a law of nature. But the important point is not that his inferences rest upon unexpressed assumptions. What is important for us to notice is that he failed to see all that the appeal to reason contains. Sense and reason as faculties of the soul are by no means of equal status. The concept of reason for Locke is the discursive faculty, the ability to argue, to infer, to advance step by step from premise to conclusion. But reason as the light of nature which reveals to man the law of nature is a faculty which makes inferences on the basis of sensory material alone, with no other rational premises as the basis of the inference. The inferences to the law of nature are more like immediate than mediate inferences. The conclusions are of the utmost importance for morality and religion. Locke was seeking to justify a system of morality by grounding the moral law in something objective. The law of nature is a decree of God, not of man's reason. It is part of God's will. Locke does not tell us how reason recognises laws as being laws of nature. He simply announces specific laws as laws of nature. The announcement is not systematic or exhaustive; he cites laws when he needs them. The following list is taken from the *Essay*, the early *Essays*, and from *Two Treatises*.

(1) Love and respect and worship God (*Essay*, 1.4.7; *Essays*, p. 195).
(2) Obey your superiors (*Essays*, p. 129).
(3) Tell the truth and keep your promises (*ibid.*).
(4) Be mild and pure of character and be friendly (*ibid.*).
(5) Do not offend or injure, without cause, any person's health, life, or possessions (*ibid.* p. 163; *T* II, 6).
(6) Be candid and friendly in talking about other people (*Essays*, p. 195).
(7) Do not kill or steal (*ibid.*).
(8) Love your neighbour and your parents (*ibid.*).
(9) Console a distressed neighbour (*ibid.*).
(10) Feed the hungry (*ibid.*).

(11) 'Whoso sheddeth man's blood, by man shall his blood be shed' (*T* II, 11).

(12) That property is mine which I have acquired through my labour so long as I can use it before it spoils (*T* II, 29–30).

(13) Parents are to preserve, nourish, and educate their children (*T* II, 56; cf. *Essay*, 1.3.12).

It would seem a gross overstatement to argue that all of these concrete rules are derivable from a law of nature which is apprehended by the function of reason and sense. In fact, it is clearly impossible to derive these precepts from any single principle, whether it be innate, the light of reason, or a standard agreed upon by men. What these rules do is disclose the moral framework in terms of which Locke examined society and civil government. Some of them are the same rules which his contemporaries claimed to be innate. All of them perform the same function as the principles said to be innate: they provide the moral foundation for his views on individual and social action. Just as the line of argument for those who believed in innate ideas was that certain moral rules are correct because they are innate, so Locke's main defence for any moral rule is to say it is known to be true by the light of reason, that it is a law of nature. He nowhere formulates a general maxim which he calls 'the law of nature'. There is no such single and general law. The law of nature turns out to be a list of laws, all of which are apparent to the rational being. These laws are taken as finding their justification in God, as being God's will. All positive law must, to be justified, be a reinforcement of these natural moral laws.

The precise relation between moral and civil (positive) law is not clear in what Locke writes. Could the derivation which his demonstrative programme envisaged have been successful, the set of rules thus derived would not replace civil laws, since moral and civil govern different areas of action. There must be no inconsistency between them, but both are needed. Even where Locke offers the New Testament as a perfect rule of life and conduct—a notion which is found both late, in *Reasonableness* and early, in *Two Tracts*[1]—he is careful to note that its injunctions relate to the moral, not the civil domain. Scripture is even limited

---

[1] Edited by Philip Abrams (Cambridge University Press, 1967).

to general moral rules, it does not specify 'each particular duty of our lives and prescribe what should be done and what left undone by each of us in every circumstance' (*Two Tracts*, p. 324). This fact, that the Bible does not contain rules for all our actions, is important in Locke's thinking on civil government: 'the Scripture is very silent in particular questions, the discourses of Christ and his Apostles seldom going beyond the general doctrines of the Messiah or the duties of the moral law' (*ibid.* p. 172). The law of works of the Old Testament contains 'the law of nature, knowable by reason, as well as the law given by Moses' (*Reasonableness*, p. 13). Moses's law had two parts, the one dealing with 'the outward worship, or political constitution of the Jews'—the ceremonial and judicial law—and the second part dealing with morality and the eternal law of right (*Reasonableness*, p. 13). When St Paul says 'that the Gospel establishes the law, he means the moral part of the law of Moses' (p. 14). The civil and ritual part of the law of Moses 'obliges not Christians', only Jews, that part of Moses's law having been expressly added by God for the Jews, and it is, Locke assures us, 'a part of the law of nature, that man ought to obey every positive law of God, whenever he shall please to make any such additions to the law of his nature' (p. 15).

It was this difference between civil and moral law which interested Locke in the debate over indifferent things in *Two Tracts*.[1] While most of that debate centred around questions of whether the magistrate could lay down rules for religious dress and ceremonies, Locke typically saw a more fundamental question behind this local controversy. In his commentary, Abrams does not find such a sharp distinction as I do between civil and moral laws. He says that 'the great question of indifferent things has made the need' for principles of moral authority an urgent one (p. 6). Abrams links Locke's resolution of the question of indifferent things to the quest for a 'demonstrable knowledge of the fundamental principles of universal order', especially moral order (p. 37). Thus, he sees as fundamental in Locke's thinking the

---

[1] The debate was with Edward Bagshaw, especially with his *The Great Question* (1660). The following few pages are adapted from my review of Abrams' edition, in *The Journal of the History of Philosophy*, VI (1968), 291–4.

axiom of knowledge, 'the assumption that all the presumed means
of knowledge were equally competent and would give access to
fundamental moral truths' (p. 85). The move from the authoritaria-
nism of the *Tracts* to the liberalism of *Two Treatises* was due
largely, Abrams suggests, to Locke's inability to produce the
demonstrative morality (pp. 102, 106, 107). Abrams concedes that
'theologically he remained certain that an objective morality
existed and was available to reason' (p. 107), but he insists that
Locke grew more and more convinced of man's inability to
discover such a morality (p. 98). Abrams finds Locke recognising
and accepting—what Locke denied to Lowde—'the equal status
and partial nature of every man's subjective knowledge' of right
and wrong (p. 98). I cannot see that Locke ever retreated into such
a relativism. Nor did Locke ever relinquish, as Abrams suggests
he did in the *Reasonableness*, 'the supposition of a law of nature for
purposes of obligation' (p. 89). Abrams sees the *Reasonableness*
as playing a fundamental role in Locke's mature philosophy. I do
not see what the evidence is for giving this work any greater
prominence than the *Essay* or *Two Treatises*. The only major
change I can discover in *Reasonableness* is Locke's scepticism about
being able to produce a demonstrative morality. That work does
not show Locke ending 'where he started—with no consequential
idea of the law of nature as a distinct moral norm because such an
idea cannot be squared with the voluntarism that was from first to
last essential for his theory of obligation' (p. 89). The *Reasonableness* does not reject the law of nature, it merely argues for revelation
through Christ's mission as a clearer and more thorough statement
of that law. The law of nature is not inconsistent with a voluntarist notion of motivation: that law obligates for the same reason
that any law does. The *Reasonableness* reaffirms that 'without a
clear knowledge and acknowledgement of the law-maker, and
the great rewards and punishments for those that would or
would not obey him' we cannot *know* that we are obligated
(p. 144). Without a complete and full demonstration of the laws of
nature the range and scope of our obligation cannot be seen.
The ground and nature of our obligation arises from the constitution of man's nature; 'nor can it be taken away or dispensed
with, without changing the nature of things, overturning the

measures of right and wrong, and thereby introducing and autho-
rising irregularity, confusion, and disorder in the world' (p. 112).
Far from any kind of voluntarism determining the obligations a
man has, that obligation is rooted in the very nature of things.

What Locke said in 1695 in the *Reasonableness* was that no one
had, before Christ's coming, given mankind the law of nature in
all its parts. From the fact that no one had produced the true and
complete morality by deductions of reason, Locke does not
conclude that there was no such law. 'It is true, there is a law of
nature' (p. 142). The law of nature is God's law, Jesus Christ
has given us that law in the New Testament (p. 143), he cleared it
of false glosses (p. 50). In talking of Adam's fall, Locke identifies
the law of nature (or of reason) with God's law (pp. 11, 13, 15).
He speaks throughout of God's eternal moral law or of the
eternal law of right (pp. 112, 115, 133), of Christ confirming the
moral law (pp. 122, 125), of the light of nature revealing parts of
that law (pp. 130, 133). This law of nature can be discovered
either through reason or through revelation. *Reasonableness* opts
for revelation. What Christ revealed by way of explicit laws (cf.
especially pp. 135-44) were *moral*, not *civil* laws. Even recognising
Locke's firm conviction in moral laws as laws of nature, Abrams'
linkage between morality and civil polity needs, I think, modification. The areas are not unrelated, but Locke always seems to have
recognised that there are details necessary for civil life which
are not covered by moral laws, which society itself, through the
magistrate or the legislature, must regulate. The controls of what
can be done by civil polity are found in the goals of society, i.e.
peace, welfare, and protection of property.

8

PROPERTY: AN EXAMPLE OF
MIXED-MODE ANALYSIS

Locke's science of action ranges over most of the important
meta-ethical topics and issues. Of most interest today, perhaps the
most original then, is his analysis of agency and the person. Of no
less importance for the general position Locke accepted and
developed are his distinctions between moral concepts and moral
rules, the central place of laws of nature as the basic moral rules,
and his suggestion that all moral concepts were interlinked in
such a way that a systematic demonstration of their connexions
ought to be possible. Behind these declared distinctions and claims
stands Locke's general view on the nature of man, his rationality
and his dependence, within a purposive universe, on God.
Action and morality is the domain of mixed modes, those ideas
which, according to Locke's science of signs, are in their origin
and validity freed from the dependence upon close and careful
observation of things themselves. Universal certainty can never
be derived from observation, systematic truth is a property of
abstract concepts. Geometry and mathematics were the examples
of abstract disciplines used by Locke and his contemporaries.
But Locke was not content to extend the parallels to the science
of ethics beyond the point of demonstration and conceptual
clarification. Ethical knowledge had to be real, no less than knowledge of body. Moreover, the reality of ethical knowledge must
extend beyond its own abstract nature: being their own archetypes is an inadequate kind of reality for ethical ideas. Conven-
tionalism was clearly rejected by Locke in favour of an objective
test of moral truth. If our moral concepts are to fit human action
they must correctly describe what men do. If these same concepts
are to be true, they must fit the measure of right and wrong laid
down by God, captured by the laws of nature.

Getting clear about the meanings of our words, seeing the

relation between our ideas are important, even fundamental, functions within the science of action. Much of the analysis Locke gives of action-concepts is neutral between ethical systems, is in fact presupposed by any account of moral truths. The nature of an action, the roles of body and consciousness in action, the conditions for liberty, property, law: these constitute the major features of Locke's science of action. Those clarifications are independent of his objectivist views of moral right and wrong, they can be viewed as transcendental deductions showing how action is possible. The line between conceptual clarification and descriptive truth may sometimes be thin. Locke frequently said that his clarifications were of the action-concepts in our thought and language. For the most part, I think his claim is correct. His conceptual analysis is not designed to tell us what we ought to do —the law of nature does that—although had he been successful in his systematic demonstration of ethics, that demonstration would have enabled men to see more clearly, even more completely, the range of their obligations. Metaphysical beliefs lie at the background of Locke's science of action (those beliefs about separately existing souls, about God's nature and power), just as the science of nature arises from a metaphysic of nature. Locke makes no pretence of demonstrating or of justifying these background beliefs. Conceptual clarification goes on inside these general frameworks and is analytic not substantial.

Even in his political treatises, Locke is not always concerned to advance substantive doctrines. The transcendental, conceptual concern is always present. One very interesting instance of this concern is Locke's comments on how a society can act. The consent of those in the state of nature who agree to form a society makes that society 'one Body, with a Power to Act as one Body' (*Two Treatises*, II, 96; cf. 95). It is the consent of its members which 'acts' any community; for it to act one way, rather than be torn asunder by conflicting motives and volitions, the community must follow the greater force, i.e. the majority. The only other possible alternative to the acts of the society being identified with those of the majority of its members is to identify the acts of the society with the acts of every individual. But this alternative reduces to the state of nature where each man acts for himself. Moreover, there are practical difficulties in the way of such an individualistic notion of social action (98). Thus, 'where the *majority* cannot conclude the rest, there they cannot act as one Body' (98).[1] Locke is not advancing any personal views here, he is rather making a conceptual point about social action, about the application of the concept of action to a group.

Perhaps the most extended bit of such conceptual clarification in *Two Treaties* is over the concept of property. There were a number of claims made by Sir Robert Filmer to which Locke took strong exception. Filmer (in Locke's words) held that '*all Government is absolute Monarchy*' and that '*no Man is Born free*' (1, 2). Filmer also claimed (again in Locke's words) that 'God gave *Adam* Property, or as our *A*—calls it, *Private Dominion* over the earth, and all inferior or irrational Creatures' (1, 24).[2] The debate between Locke and Filmer on these points was, in Locke's eyes, as much conceptual as textual. The crux of the debate lies in the question whether God gave to one man private dominion or property over nature and its creatures or whether, as Locke maintained, God gave everything to all men in common (1, 24, 29, 40). It was a question of property. Most importantly, it included a question about the person as property. Locke's restatement of Filmer on this point is as follows: the right of fatherhood

is a Divine unalterable Right of Sovereignty, whereby a Father or a Prince hath an Absolute, Arbitrary, Unlimited, and Unlimitable Power, over the Lives, Liberties, and Estates of his Children and Subjects; so that he may take or alienate their Estates, sell, castrate, or use their Persons as he pleases, they being all his Slaves, and he Lord or Proprietor of every Thing, and his unbounded Will their Law (9).

Even if Filmer's claim for private dominion of land and inferior creatures was right, Locke sees no way to go from (i.e. finds no conceptual links between) property in land to power over the

---

[1] This analysis of social action is closely linked with the careful distinction between the legislative representative whose decisions *qua* representative constitute the *public will*, distinct from his own *private will* in his non-official acts or when he ceases to be the public representative (II, 151). Hobbes' account of representation —itself a careful conceptual clarification—must be in the background of Locke's remarks here.

[2] Whether Locke has correctly read Filmer on these and other points is not important for my purposes since I want to call attention to the way in which Locke's response to Filmer was one of denying the conceptual connexions he took Filmer to be asserting and of offering an analysis of his own of the concept of property.

lives of persons, a 'Soveraign Arbitrary Authority over the Persons of Men' (41).

The importance and pervasiveness in Locke's thought of his notion of mixed modes as concepts made arbitrarily by the mind 'without patterns, or reference to any real existence' is easily lost sight of when examining his polemical writings (*Essay*, 3.5.3). The first of *Two Treatises* is careful to point out where Filmer misreads the Bible; but, since the concepts of right, sovereignty, ruling, property, etc. are mixed modes, the major test of claims made that employ such concepts must be conceptual, not empirical. The names of such concepts '*lead our thoughts to the mind, and no further*' (3.5.12). From this fact about mixed modes, there follows a consequence for controversies involving them.

Where shall one find any either *controversial debate* or *familar discourse* concerning *honour, faith, grace, religion, church,* etc., wherein it is not easy to observe the different notions men have of them; which is nothing but this: that they are not agreed in the signification of those words nor have in their minds the same complex *ideas* which they make them stand for, and so all the contests that follow thereupon are only about the meaning of a sound (3.9.9).

Decisions about the meanings of sounds are decisions about what ideas the sounds refer to or stand for.[1] Locke had insisted that, while the common use of words was usually adequate for fixing the meanings of words in ordinary conversation, it was quite insufficient for determining the meanings of words in philosophical discourses (3.9.8).[2] From this stress on the arbitrariness of

---

[1] I do not mean to suggest that *Two Treatises* is in any detailed way an application of epistemic and methodological principles established in the *Essay*. Locke is not a systematic philosopher—his writings do not present a system—in that traditional sense. It is wrong to assume that because he holds to certain doctrines in the *Essay*, he will conclude thus and so in other works. Nevertheless, one of the features of Locke's work which mark him out as a philosopher—rather than a scientist, theologian, or political theorist—is his constant interest in clarity and conceptual connexions. This feature of his science of signs, the analysis of mixed-mode concepts, occurs in all his writing.

[2] Even for ordinary conversation, Locke had doubts about the effectiveness of the criterion of 'propriety': 'Besides, the rule and measure of propriety itself being nowhere established, it is often matter of dispute whether this or that way of using a word be propriety of speech or no' (3.9.8). Locke was not engaging in linguistic analysis, the clarification of concepts is not just the elucidation of the word for that concept in our language. It is precisely at the juncture of language and thought that conceptual analysis may begin to be prescriptive. But Locke

the meanings of moral words, it should follow that, barring inconsistency, any writer could claim what he wanted about the meanings of those names. But then of course he could not hope to make his case for the correctness of his meanings: he could only try to persuade. The only basis for making non-arbitrary claims about moral words would be some firm and unalterable rules of right and wrong. Controversy over moral concepts can be settled by agreeing on common meanings or by reference to moral principles. For Locke, the laws of God, nature and reason contained the principles of right and wrong by reference to which controversy over these concepts could be settled.

In the debate with Filmer, the polemic does not always have to go that far. Filmer's claims about Adam's sovereignty can usually be shown faulty because there are no necessary connexions between the concepts he uses. To advance claims in morals, one must show the necessary connexions of concepts. That is a prerequisite to discovering whether the claims made at the conceptual level are conformable to the standard of right and wrong. Filmer repeatedly failed to satisfy this prerequisite. If, as Filmer claimed, as soon as Adam was created '*he was Monarch of the World*', there should be a necessary connexion 'betwixt *Adam's Creation* and his *Right to Government*' (1, 19). If there were such a connexion, we could not without inconsistency suppose a '*Natural Freedom of Mankind*' without supposing '*the denial of the Creation of Adam*'. Locke failed to find the necessary connexion between these concepts. Similarly, the concept of 'the person as a *private* father' is inconsistent with the concept of 'a title to obedience to the *public* magistrate' (1, 66). Filmer had claimed that by a natural right of father, Adam had an 'Absolute, Unlimited Power over all his Posterity', while Adam's children 'had by the same Right Absolute Unlimited Power' over their children (1, 69). Obviously, two such absolute unlimited powers cannot exist together: 'To have one *Absolute, Unlimited,* nay *Unlimitable Power* in Subordination to another, is so manifest a Contradiction, that nothing can be more' (*ibid.*).

never meant to say mixed modes lack prescriptive content. If Locke has misread Filmer, his dispute with Filmer may come down to a difference in definitions. The point of his analysis of mixed modes is that they are not just arbitrary presentations of personal definitions.

Filmer was struggling to derive regal from paternal power, public from private right. Parental power is, by its very nature (because every parent was also a child) limited, operative within a fixed scope. Regal authority encompasses all, parents and children, who are subjects under that authority. If royal authority is derivable from parental authority, it follows that Adam's children 'even in his lifetime, had, and so all other Fathers have ...*By Right of Fatherhood Royal Authority over their Children*' (1, 70). The consequence is clear: 'there will be as many Kings as there are Fathers'. Locke gives once again a conceptual lesson to Filmer: from parental power it necessarily follows either that all fathers have royal authority—in which case a contradiction arises—or that no one has royal authority.

The lesson is repeated on a similar point a few pages on. Fatherhood (*natural* dominion) was only one of two foundations Filmer cited for his claims on monarchal power. The other was property, *private* dominion of Adam over his land and possessions. Difficulties arise, Locke points out, in seeing how the two dominions can descend to Adam's children. If, as probably would be said, Adam's private dominion passes through inheritance to his eldest son, the natural dominion of fatherhood cannot descend through inheritance, since that right 'accrews to a Man only by *begetting*' (1, 74). Thus, from Filmer's principle that '*every Man that is born, by his very Birth becomes a Subject to him that begat him,* this necessarily follows, *viz.*, That a Man by his Birth cannot become a Subject to his Brother, who did not beget him' (74). The consequence then is that 'the Sovereignty founded upon *Property*, and the sovereignty founded upon *Fatherhood*, come to be divided' (75). Thus, of the two foundations cited by Filmer, 'one of them will either signifie nothing, or if they both must stand, they can serve only to confound the Right of Princes', since there will always subsequently be doubt about which title to dominion any given ruler has or is claiming.

Filmer's argument based on fatherhood is, so Locke claims, riddled with inconsistencies and fails to establish those necessary connexions required of any argument in morals. The argument based on private property fails to show how dominion of land and possessions can encompass persons. It also ran into difficulties because Filmer had followed the standard story which gave each of Adam's children private dominion over different portions of the inheritance left by Adam. If private dominion of property is to be the basis for sovereignty, Abel's sovereignty over Cain 'is gone with this *Private Dominion*' (76). From privacy of possession, publicity of sovereignty does not follow. Locke was clear in his own mind that 'no Man could ever have a just Power over the life of another, by Right of property in Land or Possessions' (42). That truth follows from, so Locke claimed, the right all men have to self-preservation. The same right to self-preservation includes the right 'to make use of those Creatures' which God has given to all men in common (88). The original justification of property is 'from the right a Man has to use any of the Inferior Creatures, for the Subsistence and Comfort of his life' (92).

Locke places the issue on the question of rights, without in any way showing us how we can confirm that the rights he cites are in fact rights. He was not much concerned in *Two Treatises* (or anywhere else, for that matter) to establish the rights he claims. He was rather concerned to point out the conceptual failings of Filmer and, in the case of the concept of property itself, to work out some of the conceptual problems to which that concept gave rise. Locke was firmly of the belief that we are all God's property who made us, hence we are 'made to last during his, not one another's pleasure' (II, 6). Political power is the right of making laws for 'the Regulating and Preserving of Property' (II, 3), each person's property as well as God's property, i.e. each person. Assuming that Locke is correct in his scriptural interpretation, that God gave the earth to mankind in common, there is a difficulty of explaining how 'any one should ever come to have a *Property* in any thing' (II, 25; cf. I, 87). The main concern (both in bulk and in importance) of the chapter on property in the second Treatise, about which so much has been written, is with explaining how private property of individual men can arise out of the common property of all men. Moreover, Locke wants to explain how private property arises prior to and without 'any express Compact of all the Commoners' (II, 25). The working out of the answer to this problem is largely a conceptual matter for Locke, how particularisation of the common is possible.

That this was the intent of the chapter on property is further supported by a reference in the first Treatise. Speaking of Adam and the right to property, Locke said: 'But if any one had began, and made himself a Property in any particular thing, (which how he, or any one else, could do, shall be shewn in another place)...' (I, 87). Alan Ryan recognises this important point but is not concerned to develop it. Locke, he says, is 'faced with the question of how undifferentiated goods become the exclusive property of some one man'.[1] Laslett comments that 'Locke and his fellows were in some difficulty in accounting for the fact that the original communism had given way to private property',[2] but he does not stress the conceptual nature of Locke's solution. Seliger's recent extended discussion of Locke on property appears to miss this point, even to deny that Locke accepted the notion that God gave everything to man in common. Seliger says:

> It has been usually taken for granted that Locke retained the traditional idea of an originally existing community of all things. No notice has been taken that it might have been contradictory to assume on the one hand that men share all things in common and on the other that individual appropriation is the necessary condition of using anything.[3]

Locke, Seliger asserts, 'broke with the long-established idea of an original community of things' (p. 181). That long-established doctrine was an attempt (e.g. by Grotius and Pufendorf) to say that everybody as a group, as a collective, actually owned everything. As Seliger paraphrases Pufendorf, 'Nothing belongs to anybody and everything belongs to everybody, because no object belongs to one person more than to another' (p. 183). But the notion of everything belonging to everybody is incoherent unless it means that the concept of 'ownership' does not apply or that what is meant is only a *potential* ownership. It was precisely this problem of explaining how ownership can arise out of a condition of no-ownership that Locke sought to solve. Seliger states this as Locke's objective (p. 188) but what Seliger is interested in is Locke's denial that the movement is achieved by consent. Locke

---

[1] A. Ryan, 'Locke and the Dictatorship of the Bourgeoisie', *Political Studies* (1965) reprinted in *Locke and Berkeley, A Collection of Critical Essays*, ed. C. B. Martin and D. M. Armstrong, p. 245.

[2] His edition of *Two Treatises*, p. 100.

[3] M. Seliger, *The Liberal Politics of John Locke* (Allen and Unwin, 1968), p. 180.

was in fact rejecting two features of the traditional doctrine: that the original community of things was an ownership and that consent is requisite for the acquisition of property.

Since the earth was given for man's use, there must, Locke says, 'of necessity be a means *to appropriate*' the fruit, venison, etc. (II, 26, ll. 10–12). Use implies appropriation. To be useful to any *particular* man, the goods of the earth must be appropriated by that man. The example Locke uses here is appropriation and possession of food. There must be a means of appropriating the food before it can nourish me. That food becomes mine 'upon the first gathering' (28, 7–8). There is an ambiguity at 26, 12–15, an ambiguity which is not settled until 28, 7–8. In 26, 11–15, Locke speaks of the fruit or venison which nourishes the wild Indian, those food items 'must be his, and so his, i.e., a part of him, that another can no longer have any right to it before it can do him any good for the support of life'. The food will not nourish unless eaten, it is clearly mine once eaten. Therefore, we might think that the becoming a part of me that Locke has in mind here is a literal becoming part of me, that is, through eating. In this way, I make private part of what was common. In so doing, the right of another person to what was common has been abrogated to that extent, since 'no Body has any Right' to my person but myself (27, l. 2). But from what Locke goes on to say, it becomes clear that to make the fruit or venison mine, it is not necessary that I eat it, I need only pick it or kill it. The concept of person is fundamental for such rightful appropriation. The property which a master has in the slave, the property which is rightly God's, namely, my person, Locke now says is my property: 'every Man has a *Property* in his own *Person*'. The earth and all its creatures are *common*, but each of us has a *particular* in our person. Locke said in the *Essay* that we own our actions, now he says we own our persons. Locke is trying to answer the question, if *all* is common, how do we ever get to the non-common, to private property. But we begin with something not common. 'Property' means for Locke 'non-common', hence my person is my property since it is not common, it was not given to any man or men by God, save to me alone. My person is the starting point for the particular. Where all is public, there can be no property.

'Person' means more than 'body' for Locke, though the body is an integral part of our concept of the person. Bodily movement is essential for action'(other than the action of thought alone). It is bodily movement which enables me to add to the property I enter the world with (my person), certain movements are the manifestation of my person as property, they are the means of appropriation. The work I do, the expenditure of energy is mine (27, 3–4). By mixing my work, my energy, with some object, I particularise that object, its commonness is made particular. It is only if we have something particular that we can get other particulars. We have also to have a way or method of particularising the common. From the fact that the nourishment of the food I pick and eat is mine, Locke then asks when that food became mine (28, 4–5). He comments that the nourishment I receive from eating the food I have gathered is mine, it is literally mine since it is part of my body. Locke's question is not about the ownership of the nourishment, though that is closely tied to the appropriation. He wants to know, 'When did they [the food items] begin to be his?' (28, 4–5). The answer to that question is, at the first gathering. Particularisation in this way excludes the right of others to what I have made mine, but only under the condition that there is plenty left for others to particularise (27, 13–14). The right which attaches to particularisation is a right without consent (28, 11–12). Consent is not necessary, because if it were men would have starved. Eating for self-preservation cannot wait upon consent of others (28, 15). Even in those parcels of land made commons by compact, it is the actual taking part of what was common 'which *begins the Property*'. Without such taking, the common is of no use (28, 17–20). Moreover this taking does not depend upon the *express* consent of all the commoners. 'Thus the Grass my Horse has bit; the Turfs my Servant has cut; and the Ore I have digg'd in any place where I have a right to them in common with others, become my *Property*, without the assignation or consent of any body' (28, 21–24).[1] Whether the common

---

[1] This question seems to assume, as Ryan remarks (*op. cit.* p. 236) that 'Locke never doubted that one man could appropriate the labour of another and thus become the owner of it. "My" labour includes the labour of anyone I employ' and of the animals I own. Laslett concedes that 'perhaps in *Second Treatise*, 28, 20–6, Locke does imply in passing that a master could own the labour of his servant', but

be so by God's gift, as it was in the first ages of the world, or by express compact, appropriation does not require consent. It is the labour-mixing which makes anything mine, not consent. In these areas of food, drink, turf-cutting, and mining, so long as there is plenty for others, consent is (*a*) silly and pointless and (*b*) irrelevant, not what makes property.

This principle of appropriation, which states how in fact property arises out of what is common to all, is also a law of reason, an original law of nature (30, 1–6). Just as reason tells us that following our desire for self-preservation is following the will of God and hence is right, so the way in which what is common to all is in fact made private is also in accord with God's plan. In Locke's purposive universe, it is easy to go from what is to what ought to be, from fact to right. Nature in the first ages of the world has set *natural* limits to what can be appropriated, in the sense that no man is able to enjoy, consume, or use unlimited goods. Hence, the rights of others to property were protected by two features: (*a*) there was plenty to go around and (*b*) man's capacities were limited (36, 1–10). The *normative* limits are introduced by the principle of appropriation. The main scope of that principle as a law of nature is 'for the *beginning of Property*, in what was before common', primarily in the first ages of the earth (the central concern of this chapter), though holding as well for the appropriation from commons formed by compact (30, 6–7). This law of nature also tells us that we may not appropriate any more than we can use before it spoils. Here we have a normative limit to what can count as our property. The principle of appropriation by itself simply explains how in fact I can make something my own from the common. Its status as a law specifying rights comes in conjunction with this restriction. Since 'Nothing was made by God for Man to spoil or destroy' (31, l. 11), the property-making function of man's activity ought to be curbed at the point of spoilage. If my acquisition spoils, I offend against the law

Laslett's more considered opinion is that we must place this passage in the contex t of the patriarchal relationship between master and servant: in that relationship 'the servant was included in the person of the master' (review of Macpherson, in *The Historical Journal*, VII, 1964, 153). In the turf-cutting example 'the labour owne d is not the servant's alone, but the master's (the last mentioned) and his horses" (*ibid*. n. 4).

of nature, since I have, in the beginning, '*no Right, farther than*' my use (37, l. 40). What is useful and is used has value and the person who uses them a right to them. The same rules are cited for land as for the produce of land (38).

The main object of property after the first ages of the earth is land itself. Land 'takes in and carries with it' all the rest of property (32, 2–3). The same principle holds for land, it is my enclosing and cultivating a bit of land which makes it mine. Again, the assumption is that 'there was still enough, and as good left' for others (33, 3). Especially in talking of land, Locke equates 'common' with 'uncultivated' or 'unused'; 'use' requires appropriation. Appropriation requires an appropriator and a means of appropriation. With the explication of these concepts, Locke has answered the question he raised at the beginning of this chapter on property. He points out that he has answered that question, and summarises the answer, in sections 39, 44, 45, and the final section 51: 'And thus, I think, it is very easie to conceive without any difficulty, *how Labour could at first begin a title of Property* in the common things of Nature, and how the spending it upon our uses bounded it' (51, 1–4). The stress in this passage on 'conceiving' how particularisation of the common is possible is also clearly found in section 39:

And thus, without supposing any private Dominion, and property in *Adam*, over all the World, exclusive of all other Men, which can no way be proved, nor any ones Property be made out from it; but supposing the *World* given as it was to the Children of Men *in common*, we see how *labour* could make Men distinct titles to several parcels of it, for their private uses; wherein there could be no doubt of Right, no room for quarrel.

There are several other related matters raised in this chapter on property, though they presuppose the answer to his question which we have just examined. For one, Locke was anxious to explain how the value of property gets altered, potential property having value in respect to the usefulness it can have for some person. Locke speaks of this value as an intrinsic value. In cultivating land I make it useful, I increase its produce and hence increase its usefulness for men. This cultivation adds to the intrinsic value of the land (37, 11–13). Let anyone consider,

Locke urges, 'what the difference is between an Acre of Land planted with Tobacco, or Sugar, sown with Wheat or Barley; and an Acre of the same land lying in common, without any Husbandry upon it, and he will find, that improvement of *labour makes* the far greater part of *the value*' (40, 4–9). Sections 41–3 give some examples of how labour yields more use-value from the land and its natural objects than was there without man's work.

Another point Locke tried to deal with in this chapter was how the introduction of money altered the nature of property from the first ages of the earth. Barter was one way to avoid spoilage, since it enables me to exchange something I have made mine, but no longer need, for something of yours. Even if a person bartered his goods for beads or pieces of metal 'he invaded not the Right of others' since that right only specifies that he must not let his property spoil. The only way a person could exceed '*the bounds of his* just *Property*' is in having goods that perish before they are used, not in the size of his possessions (46, 28–30). The value of money differs from the intrinsic value of goods or land, since it is fancy or agreement only that puts the value on gold, silver, and diamonds, not any real use they have for the support of life (46, 5–7). Their value has a kind of use value, but the use is only indirectly useful for life (47, 3). It is important to notice that Locke relates money to the goods needed for life, since it shows that the primary task for money is to be exchangeable for those needed items, not just as a way of amassing goods.

Much has been made, e.g. by Macpherson, of Locke's allowing money as a way of increasing property. Locke also makes some point of the way in which money marks the different degrees of industry of men, giving them a chance to enlarge their possessions. Money gives men a reason and a means for increasing their land (48, 10). Commerce and the sale of produce draws money to one (48, 21–2). Wherever there is a durable item which has the use of money, there Locke says men will seek to enlarge their possessions. Macpherson sees in Locke's comments on money the views of Locke's own landed-gentry status, but I cannot see that Locke is praising the invention of money. He is describing what happens when money comes into use. In agreeing to use money, men have, Locke says, 'by tacit and voluntary consent found out a way, how a man may fairly possess more land than he himself can use the produce of' (50, 5–8). The word 'fairly' here surely relates to the consent. The right which the consent to use money gives to larger possessions (36, 39–40) is a function of the consent. Man may not, through informal agreement or by positive law, run counter to the laws of nature. The law of nature which is the rule of propriety or the principle of appropriation is not violated by anyone's amassing large quantities of durable goods, so the consent in this case is legitimate. What is more important for Locke's purposes of conceptual clarification in this chapter on property is to distinguish between the *intrinsic* value of nature's goods—the land and its produce with which all men were supplied in the first ages of the earth—and the *conventional* and *secondary* value men assign to money. In commenting that in calling the value of money 'fanciful' (46) and 'Phantastical' (184) Locke confused conventional value with no value, Ryan[1] overlooks what I take to be Locke's concern to explain that the analysis of the concept of 'value' which he has given shows that gold, silver, and diamonds do not have value in the primary sense of that concept. At best, they are valuable indirectly. They have borrowed value, not real (i.e. use) value.

A final conceptual matter Locke considered in the chapter on property is the differences there are between appropriation in its first beginnings and in civil society. In civil society, compact and consent is necessary for appropriation since what belongs to all the people in that society does so by compact. Where compact has designated common land, compact is required to move to the particular (35). This is so because the condition which prevails in the first ages of the earth—that what is left after appropriation is sufficient and as good as what was taken—does not hold under civil society. There is a restriction on the amount of land and on its quality. Hence different rules apply for appropriation: when limits to territories have been set out by consent and when positive laws have been formed, we have a changed condition. Consent must apply when land and produce are limited (38, 27–30). My labour is still what *in fact* makes what I work on mine, but under conditions of limited land the *rules of right* change. There is a

---

[1] Ryan, *op. cit.* p. 242.

suggestion that scarcity gives value to land (45, 8). In these conditions, the communities settle the bounds of their distinct territories by agreement and make laws regulating 'the properties of the private men of their society' (45, 10–11). In this way, compact and agreement '*settle the property* which labour and Industry began' (45, 12).

Quite apart from what Locke's own views on the nature of industry, money, acquisition of property may have been, what his chapter on property seeks to do is not to advance those personal views but to clarify concepts. It may be charged, as I am sure Macpherson would do, that Locke's clarifications were influenced at every turn by his own entrenched opinions. If I have succeeded in placing the chapter on property in its proper context (in particular, its intimate connexions with the rejection of Filmer's treatment of property) and if I have succeeded in isolating its main concern, we can see that chapter as an exercise in the clarification of the concepts required for dealing with the kind of issues raised by Filmer. Locke's response to Filmer in the first Treatise was largely one of exposing the lack of conceptual connexions. I would not wish to say that Locke's intentions in the second Treatise were mainly or largely conceptual clarification of the civil and moral mixed modes which make up the subject-matter of that work, though Locke frequently resorts to careful clarifications of those concepts, especially in the early sections of the second Treatise. All that I want to claim here is that the troublesome chapter on property does address itself primarily to a conceptual question: how is it possible (conceivable) to get from what is common that which is private and particular?

9

SIGNS AND SIGNIFICATION

The three sciences or disciplines which comprise all that falls within the compass of human understanding were characterised in the final section of the *Essay* as 'three great provinces of the intellectual world, wholly separate and distinct one from another' (4.21.5). Locke hinted that the doctrine of signs might lead to 'another sort of logic and critique than what we have been hitherto acquainted with' (4). The same hint had been dropped when he was presenting the outlines of his informal logic of demonstration. The account in Book 3 of word-signs and their signification, the doctrine of simple ideas and their derivation in Book 2, and the analysis of the different kinds of agreement-relations ideas exemplified in Book 4 constitute the main features of Locke's contribution to that new logic of ideas. The doctrine of signs in the *Essay* is hardly 'wholly separate and distinct' from the sciences of nature and action, but Locke did not mean to separate the three sciences so sharply as that final phrase of the *Essay* suggests. The account of how words and ideas signify does not rest upon the other two sciences, but the value of the doctrine of signs lies in its explication of '*ideas* and *words* as the great instruments of knowledge' (4). It is as instruments of knowledge that Locke is interested in signs. The business of the third division of the sciences is 'to consider the nature of signs the mind makes use of for the understanding of things, or conveying its knowledge to others' (4).

Locke is quite explicit in 4.21.4 that signs include both words and ideas. He had been equally explicit elsewhere in the *Essay*. 2.32.19 says that 'The signs we chiefly use are either *ideas* or words.' 3.3.11 couples both together as signs. 4.5.2 tells us 'there are two sorts of signs commonly made use of, viz. *ideas* and words.' 4.18.3 speaks of 'words or any other signs', without specifying other kinds; but, since he is there speaking of revelation, the other signs would presumably be events in nature which would be taken as signs of God. The *Essay* is not concerned with signs of this sort, its sign-domain is exhausted by words and ideas. These two kinds of signs are not, of course, unrelated. Words signify only by standing for ideas, their sign function is idea-dependent. Locke did not want to overlook the intimate connexion that there is between ideas and words, but he wanted to say there is some non-verbal thought, that we have some ideas without names.

The order of development is ideas, then names. Infants acquire some ideas in the womb, other ideas after birth but before language. Generally, 'the mind having got any *idea* which it thinks it may have use of either in contemplation or discourse, the first thing it does is to abstract it, and then get a name to it' (2.21.7). It is to a large extent use, interest, and the demands of communication which determine which ideas are named: 'there are great varieties of simple *ideas*, as of tastes and smells, which have no names, and of modes many more' (2.18.7). General words wait upon general ideas, the abstraction from particularity of ideas takes place without words (3.3.6, 11). Locke would prefer that 'the examining and judging of *ideas*' be done 'by themselves, their names being quite laid aside', since this is 'the surest way to clear and distinct knowledge' (4.6.1). In reading, Locke recommends that we represent to ourselves 'the author's sense by pure ideas separated from sounds' so that the 'false lights and deceitful ornaments of speech' (and, I presume, of written words) can be avoided (*Conduct*, sect. 42). But he recognises that this method of separating ideas from words is 'very seldom practised'. Mental is distinct from verbal proposition, the former being 'nothing but a bare consideration of the *ideas* as they are in our minds stripped of names' (4.5.3). That we do sometimes so consider some of our ideas is attested by introspection. 'For if we will curiously observe the way our mind takes in thinking and reasoning, we shall find, I suppose, that when we make any propositions within our own thoughts about *white* or *black*, *sweet* or *bitter*, a *triangle* or a *circle*, we can and often do frame in our minds the *ideas* themselves, without reflecting on the names' (4.5.4). He does not think such consideration is either easy or often done. In fact, 'it is unavoidable, in treating of mental propositions, to make use of words', though he thinks this is more true of complex than of simple ideas. Not being able to separate idea from word is 'evidence of the imperfection and uncertainty of our ideas' (4.5.4). In this sense, simple ideas are more clear and certain than complex ideas. Language is, however, not always a potential impediment to clarity. In fact, in some cases we need to look to words rather than to ideas in order to discover meanings. With some complex ideas the names are more 'clear, certain, and distinct' than the ideas; hence, the names more readily occur to our thoughts than the ideas. Locke cites the following ideas as instances where the name is 'more clear, certain, and distinct': man, vitriol, fortitude, glory.

There is danger in separating word from idea, a danger which Locke, in common with other partisans of the new science and the expansion of knowledge, stressed: the danger of mistaking words for things. When words are separated from ideas, we have no way of knowing to what things the words refer, since their reference to things is only conveyed by ideas. Complex ideas require

time and attention to be recollected and exactly represented to the mind, even in those men who have formerly been at the pains to do it, and is utterly impossible to be done by those who, though they have ready in their memory the greatest part of the common words of their language, yet perhaps never troubled themselves in all their lives to consider what precise *ideas* the most of them stand for (4.5.4).

The vice of most scholastic thinking for Locke lay just there: words were used without precise ideas for their meanings. Many men would have nothing to think on, the force would go out of their debates, if they were made to set aside the words they used, e.g. in talk of religion, conscience, church, faith, power, right. Even 'learned and ingenious physicians' sometimes overlook the need to define their words by pinpointing the ideas they stand for (3.9.16). In this last passage Locke reports on such a group of physicians who were debating whether 'any liquor passed through the filaments of the nerves'. The debate had waged for some time when Locke tried out on the group his suspicion that 'the greatest part of disputes were more about the signification of words than a real difference in the conception of things'. He asked this learned group what the word 'liquor' signified. To their surprise, they discovered that 'each of them made it a sign of a different complex *idea*', their dispute was accordingly seen to be not substantial but rather about the signification of that term (3.9.16).

This autobiographical example—a typical instance of a philosopher asking for the meaning of a term—was, Locke believed, symptomatic of 'the greatest part of disputes men are engaged so hotly in' (17). The *Essay* itself was an attempt to show how many of the terms used in philosophical debates were unclear or entirely lacking in clear, distinct, or determined ideas: real essence, substantial form, substance, person, freedom. In each of these cases (and many more), Locke sought to clarify the word by specifying the idea for which the term stood, or by showing that no idea could be designated for that term. Throughout Book 2, coupled with the account of the genesis of ideas, is a careful explication of terms, what is meant by words like space, solidity, extension, same place. Some of these explications are conceptual, not just defining the term as it is used in the language. To give the meaning of more ordinary words is to define those words. Defining and determining the signification of names are the same (4.8.10). To define is to cite the ideas for which the word stands. I might explain the signification of 'lead' by saying it is a metal, but to one who did not know what 'metal' signified, I could list the ideas, i.e. a body heavy, fusible, malleable (4.8.4). To list ideas in this way is of course to cite the coexisting qualities which we have taken as characterising the object. Different ideas may be linked together under one name or concept, yielding different meanings. If I say that 'man' stands for the ideas (hence also for the qualities) of body, sense, and motion, or that a 'romance knight' meant by 'palfrey' a body of a certain figure, four-legged, with sense, motion, ambling, neighing, white, used to having a woman on his back, I have in both cases cited the ideas (and therefore given the meaning) which constitute the definition of those terms in someone's usage (4.8.6).

These linguistic and conceptual clarifications were part of the science of signs, they are used by Locke in various ways throughout the *Essay*. To those who offered as innate the proposition, 'Men must repent of their sin', Locke replies than 'sin' is unclear and unspecified: 'what great principle of morality can that be to tell us we should be sorry and cease to do that which will bring mischief upon us without knowing what those particular actions are that will do so?' (1.3.19). In general, Locke thinks it doubtful that God 'should engraven principles in men's minds in words of uncertain signification, such as *virtues* and *sins*, which amongst different men stand for different things'. The appeal by the innatists to the fact that all societies have the idea of God is similarly rejected as an inadequate criterion of innateness because 'those people who agreed in the name, had, at the same time, far different apprehensions about the thing signified' (1.4.15). Variety of meanings is no proof of innateness of ideas, but at least in these cases the words do have meanings. 'Substance' was a word which, as commonly used, Locke insisted had little or no meaning. The danger here is of 'taking words for things', of assuming that because there is this word in our language it designates or names a fact about the world (2.13.18). How can 'substance' have a determined meaning when it is applied to such diverse entities as God, finite spirits, and body? If it has three different significations in these instances, the users of the term 'substance' would do well to make known those

distinct *ideas*, or at least to give three distinct names to them, to prevent in so important a notion the confusion and errors that will naturally follow from the promiscuous use of so doubtful a term; which is so far from being suspected to have three distinct, that in ordinary use it has scarce one clear distinct signification (*ibid.*).

One of the main abuses of language is the failure to use words 'constantly and steadily in the same significations' (4.8.11). '*Dubious words* and uncertain signs *often*, in discourses and arguings, when not warily attended to, *puzzle men's reason* and bring them to a *nonplus*' (4.17.13).

Locke may have been echoing Hooke in these sentiments, though the dangers of ill-defined words were becoming commonly recognised by the second half of the century. Hooke had also warned against philosophical words leading us astray: 'the Signification of many words ought to be more defin'd' ('The

Present State of Natural Philosophy', p. 10). Locke agreed entirely with the following remark of Hooke:

For Words being ill set Marks on very confused Notions, the reason of a Man is very easily impos'd on by Discourse, unless the Mind be extreamly attent, and watchful not to take any thing for granted, that is not evidently prov'd and very perspicacious in finding out the distinct Notion of the Word in every such Sentence, wherein it is used, for the Notions signified by some words being very many and very perplex, unless that Notion there meant be ...determin'd to be always signified when that word is pronounced (p. 11).

In dedicating his *Dioptrica Nova* to the Royal Society, William Molyneux remarked that men used to content themselves with words and not with the ideas that should stand behind them. Molyneux praised Locke and the Royal Society for ridding us of scholastic verbiage, for leading us to the things themselves. As another contemporary said, the intention of the Royal Society was 'not the artifice of Words, but a bare Knowledge of Things'.[1] P. Nicole remarked that we study words only to gain a knowledge of things but all that we learn from word study is that 'men have employed certain sounds to stand for certain things, without gaining thereby the least knowledge of the nature of the things themselves'.[2] The programme for knowing things themselves instead of words was, as we have seen, to make careful observations and to record those observations in a natural history. It was in the recording of the observations that another interesting feature of the seventeenth century's method for advancing knowledge arose, the construction of a language adequate for catching the properties of things. The goal of a universal natural history (first set out for the century by Bacon, picked up by Hooke's philosophical algebra, and affirmed again and again throughout the 1660s and 1670s) was matched by that of a universal language or characteristic.

Interest in language as an aid to knowing and understanding things appeared in a number of writers around 1668. It was part of the pansophic programme of Comenius and Hartlib. Comenius

---

[1] B. Kennet, preface to *The Whole Critical Works of M. Rapin* (1706).
[2] *Discourses*, trans. by Locke, p. 51.

said (in his *Vis Lucis*, 1668) that the main function of such a language is that it be an antidote to ignorance.

And it can only be that if its course is parallel with the course of things, that is, if it contains neither more nor fewer names than there are things; and joine words to words with the utmost precision as things are joined to each other, by constantly expressing the nature of the things with which it deals by the very sounds which it uses, and so presenting them to our mind (pp. 183–4, trans. by Campagnac).

Not only must the relation of words mirror things, words themselves must be 'commensurate with things' (p. 185). Comenius speaks of a 'reciprocal harmony between things and names', such that this language would 'by its very sounds' express 'the essential qualities and characteristics of things' (p. 186). At one point, he calls this language 'a Real Language' (p. 187). The best method to follow for constructing such a language is to 'follow the guidance of things themselves; since everything in our new language must be adapted to the exact and perfect representation of things' (p. 191). W. Simpson included in his *Hydrologia Chymica* (1669) a 'digression concerning a Universal Character' which, he explains, was written before Dr Wilkins's book appeared. Simpson had hoped for a character by means of which children could be trained 'not in the knowledge of letters, or words alone; but in the true *Characteristical* knowledge of things themselves, according to their most External distinguishable *Signatures*' (Preface to Reader). What Simpson had in mind was a system of notation like the number system or chemical symbols that would be intelligible in all languages. He suggests that there was an original, primitive, pre-Babel language which was universal, a rather common belief (p. 221). Simpson suggests that the most common objects (e.g. man, book, horse, stone) be put down in a book, with 'Radical Characters' standing for them.

Whether these Characters should not be so contrived, (as to their form) as that they might indicate to the mind, the things they represent; which (perhaps) might not better be done, then by making (where occasion offers) the Characters to Signaturize the thing represented, thereby becoming a short *Hieroglyphic* of the things understood (p. 224).

The universal character should be set down as 'Vocabularies or Dictionaries, with the signification thereof in every particular Language' (p. 236).

Locke's recognition of the importance of dictionaries—the natural history dictionary of pictures of things, the moral-word dictionary of action words carefully defined—was clearly part of this general recognition of the role language and signs can play in the advancement of knowledge. Bishop Wilkins's *An Essay towards a Real Character and a Philosophical Language* (1668) is the most obvious and usual book cited in this connexion. Wilkins's programme-statements are more significant than his actual tables, the latter are set up in a kind of shorthand which is so complex and prolix that it is very difficult to see how that character could be of much aid even to the memory. But the statements by Wilkins of what this character was supposed to accomplish, its rationale, are most instructive for understanding the interest in language and its relations with natural histories. The scope of Wilkins's Real Character is broad: 'the distinct expression of all things and notions that fall under discourse' (Dedication). He speaks of a 'Repository' begun by the Royal Society which he thinks may be relevant to his tables of the species of natural bodies. The task is identified by Wilkins as dictionary-making. Attempts in the past have proceeded from a dictionary of words in some particular language *without reference to* the nature of things, *and that common Notion of them, wherein Mankind agree*' (To the Reader). The real character he has in mind is to be constructed '*from the Natural notion of things*', not in isolation from things. The tables will be 'a regular *enumeration* and *description* of all those things and notions, to which marks or names ought to be assigned according to their respective natures' (p. 1). This is the 'scientifical' part of his programme, a universal philosophy. The aim of this procedure is very similar to that of Comenius' universal language, to 'reduce all things and notions unto such a frame, as may express their natural order, dependence, and relations' (p. 1). The characters used must not signify words but things and notions, i.e. ideas (p. 13). Ideally, the names and their order will be such that the natures of things can be learned from the names; names must fit the nature of things, though Wilkins no more tells us how this correspondence of word and thing is to be achieved than did Comenius (p. 21). In fact, Wilkins distinguished two ways in which characters or signs signify, naturally and by institution. Under natural signification he cites pictures of things 'or some *Symbolical* Representation of them' (p. 385). Such a representation is difficult if not impossible. Thus, Wilkins opts for instituted signification, which would seem to undermine his announced aim of finding characters which fit the nature of things.

These hopes for a universal language or character (a system of signs), which would capture the nature of things, were not realised: Wilkins's programme did not prove useful. The focus upon language as important for knowledge remained. Locke pointed out that men do feel that there is some intrinsic connexion between names and objects: 'When anyone sees a new thing of a kind that he knows not, he presently asks what it is, meaning by that inquiry nothing but the name, as if the name carried with it the knowledge of the species or the essence of it' (2.32.7). Naming and knowing are linked but the connexion is conventional, not natural. Understanding how words signify will help us in our clearer knowledge of things, just because it will show us that the supposed intrinsic relation of name and object does not exist. Locke aligned himself on the side of the conventionalists in meaning. Henry Rose, publishing anonymously in 1675 (*A Philosophical Essay for the Reunion of the Languages, or the Art of Knowing All by the Mastery of One*) formulated the concept of word-signs accepted by Locke. 'Words being in the opinion of all men but significant sounds, they may be taken either as they are *Natural Sounds,* or *Arbitrary Signs,* I would say, either as they are the proper effect of the motion of our organs, or as the lively representation of the thoughts of our minds' (pp. 44-5). Rose insists also that ideas, not words, are the proper cognitive signs. 'I suppose that words being the expressions of our thoughts, and our thoughts the representations of objects, the different significations that are given to words' depend upon the different conceptions men have of the objects (p. 51). Locke thought that words as articulate sounds were by nature well adapted to stand as signs of ideas, mainly because there is a great variety of sounds which men can make and with ease (3.2.1). Locke probably had in mind as well that these sounds first appear at the time that the child is acquiring its first ideas. Sound and idea can be easily associated.

Thus we may conceive how *words*, which were by nature so well adapted to that purpose, came to be made use of by men as *the signs of* their *ideas*: not by any natural connexion that there is between particular articulate sounds and certain *ideas*, for then there would be but one language amongst all men; but by a voluntary imposition whereby such a word is made arbitrarily the mark of such an idea.[1]

Long and familiar use associates words and ideas so habitually together that men 'are apt to suppose a natural connexion between them', but the signification of words is done '*by a perfectly arbitrary imposition*' (3.2.8).

Locke insisted too that words are the marks of 'the *ideas* of the speaker', they cannot be signs of (certainly not immediately or primarily) ideas in other men's minds (3.2.2). Nor can words be signs of the qualities in things. Immediately and properly my words are only signs of the ideas I have, but Locke admits that we give words a 'secret reference' to other men's ideas and also to things. He explains the first secret reference by saying that unless we *assume* that our words stand for similar ideas in each other's minds, we would not put any faith in communication. If in fact the sounds I applied to one idea 'were such as by the hearer were applied to another', we would be speaking two different languages (3.2.4). Using a word as it is used in the 'common acceptation of that language', we suppose that the referent of the word is the same in all users' minds. The other secret reference of words is to the reality of things, we suppose our words for substances stand for bodies (3.2.5). This supposition is made because we take our talk to be about the world, not just about our 'own imagination'. With his strong interest in the science of nature and with his recognition of the importance of language, Locke needed a doctrine of signs which could do more than stand for our ideas. The conditions for communication and the conditions for the

---

[1] This suggestion, that if the connexion was natural between word and idea there would be only one language, should be paired with Locke's remark that if our knowledge 'were altogether necessary', as it would be did we know real essences, 'all men's knowledge would not only be alike, but every man would know all that is knowable' (4.13.1).

reality of our talk make necessary these referential suppositions about words standing for other than our own ideas. The reference to things has another function. In his discussion of confused ideas, Locke remarks that in ranking things as to kinds, according to nominal essences, we suppose that different names stand for different things (2.29.6). Marking different types of objects with different names enables us to talk about those objects 'upon any occasion'. If the 'difference which keeps the things...distinct, and makes some of them belong rather to the one and some of them to the other of those names' is left out or ignored, the relevant ideas under which we think of these objects as different may, Locke suggests, lose their distinctness and difference. In this way, '*names*, as supposed steady signs of things' become 'the *occasion of denominating* ideas *distinct or confused*, by a secret and unobserved reference the mind makes of its *ideas* to such names' (10). The point Locke is trying to make in these passages is not entirely clear, but he seems to be saying that it is because we take our words to stand for objects as well as for ideas that we are able to differentiate between clear and confused ideas of things. Words and language, as it were, capture the distinctions of our ideas, such that should we lose some of the clarity of our ideas (through faulty memories, for example), language may help us regain that clarity. Locke has in mind only those ideas taken from things themselves and the words we have used to name those ideas. Careful observation discovers what qualities coexist. Words record those coexistences in tables or propositions. If subsequent thought becomes unclear about the properties that coexist and define for us the classes of things, we can check our verbal record against the objects. In so doing, we are of course making further observations and thereby clarifying our idea of the object again. We cannot check our words against things without acquiring ideas but in making that check we may discover that our verbal record is in fact more correct that our recollected ideas.

In identifying the proper and immediate signification of word-signs as the ideas of the speaker, Locke no more wanted to say we can only talk about our ideas than he meant his account of perception to restrict knowledge to ideas. There would always be an indirect way to the reality of our talk of bodies, through the ideas of bodies which are real. But Locke recognised that we do apply names to things (3.3.2), our names of substances are 'not put barely for our *ideas*' but are 'made use of ultimately to represent things' (3.11.24). We want a verbal record of our discoveries, not just an ideational one. Hence, the signification of our names of bodies must 'agree with the truth of things as well as man's *ideas*' (*ibid.*). Definitions of substance words are a good way for explicating those words as standing for ideas; but the additional check of going to the things themselves must be made if we are to be sure that our substance words are accurate. To define those names correctly, '*natural history is to be inquired into*' (3.11.24). It is by this double check of substance words against ideas and things that the mistake of taking words for things can be avoided. We teach children words before they have clear notions of the things to which they apply. This habit is apt to carry over into adult life, words being learnt before clear ideas of things are acquired.

By this means it comes to pass that men speaking the proper language of their country, i.e. according to grammar-rules of that language, do yet speak very improperly of things themselves and, by their arguing one with another, make but small progress in the discoveries of useful truths and the knowledge of things as they are to be found in themselves, and not in our imaginations (3.11.24).

It was precisely this fault that Locke (and many others) found with the language of the Schools. It was grammatical, even deductive, but was unreal and useless. 'Hence it comes to pass that one may often meet with very clear and coherent discourses that amount yet to nothing' (4.8.9). Names can be joined, propositions made, deductions derived, demonstrations and undoubted propositions made in words 'and yet thereby advance not one jot in the knowledge of the truth of things' (*ibid.*).

The only escape from nominal or verbal truth in our talk of things is to make this check upon the accuracy of our ideas of things (4.5.8). The quest for natural histories of phenomena joins forces with the goal of a clear and accurate language for recording and talking about those phenomena. The reality of knowledge must be matched by the reality of language. What criteria are there which tell us our language is real, is about things? Is it not the case that Locke's account of idea-signs as the medium for cognition has a parallel in his account of word-signs? The epistemic difficulty of getting from ideas to things (which I have claimed is not a genuine difficulty) appears to have its analogue in language. 'How can we *know* body?' has its correlate in 'how can we *talk* about body?'. If words immediately and properly stand only for ideas, not things (the reference of words to things being only secret and a supposition) Locke's demand that we make a reality check on our language may not be possible.

Professor Norman Kretzmann[1] has recently offered a solution to this problem about the reality of language. His analysis is illuminating but does raise some difficulties. Kretzmann wants to free Locke from the charge that words can only refer to ideas. The standing-for relation between words and ideas is not a referential one, it is a meaning or signifying relation: ideas are the meanings of words. 'What Locke does mean by speaking of one's *applying a word to something* is one's *giving the word a meaning*' (p. 186). Kretzmann distinguishes two arguments in the *Essay* which yield the conclusion that words stand for ideas. The one argument is from the uses of words. This argument is mainly based upon the use of words for communication, but Locke also speaks of words used to record ideas to assist my memory, and to signify my own ideas in thinking. In all three uses of words, Locke is saying that words immediately stand for ideas. Kretzmann thinks it important to note the word 'immediately', since this would seem to leave the way open for non-immediate standing-for by words of non-ideas, where the 'standing-for' relation would then be reference, not meaning. Immediate signifying is meaning, mediate signifying is reference.

It is important to note and to stress, as Kretzmann does, that Locke did distinguish between the use, the meaning, and the reference of words. The second argument Kretzmann distinguishes for the conclusion that words stand for (i.e. mean) ideas, not things, is what he calls 'the argument from the doctrine of representative ideas'. There are a number of misleading claims in this part of Kretzmann's analysis. The first difficulty is that the

---

[1] 'The Main Thesis of Locke's Semantic Theory', *The Philosophical Review*, LXXVII (1968), 175–96.

passage he cites as an instance for this argument does not rest
upon any notion of representative ideas. Kretzmann cites 3.2.2,
where Locke is commenting that to apply words as marks for
'anything else but the *ideas* that he himself hath' would be 'to
make them signs of his own conceptions and yet apply them to
other *ideas*, which would be to make them signs and not signs of
his *ideas* at the same time, and so in effect to have no signification
at all'. Kretzmann is correct in seeing in this statement a *reductio
ad absurdum*, for Locke is saying that, before I can use words
meaningfully, I must have ideas as their meanings. 'A man
cannot make his words the signs either of qualities in things or of
conceptions in the mind of another, whereof he has none in his
own' (3.2.2). As Kretzmann remarks: 'Therefore, if X is something other than an idea of mine, to suppose that I can apply a
word to signify X *immediately* is to suppose that I can apply a word
to signify X while I have no idea of X, which is impossible'
(p. 187). But there is no representative theory lurking in the
background here, the *reductio* does not depend upon that theory,
but rather upon a theory about meaning, the same theory present
explicitly in the argument from the uses of words. My words can
primarily and immediately signify only my ideas, not because I
can know things only by ideas, but because knowing, understanding, and meaning require ideas. Whether or not the idea–
thing relation is representative is a quite separate question from
'can my words signify things?'. Kretzmann is, I think, right in
saying that Locke has mainly in mind those words and ideas which
we use to talk about and cognise body. His suggestion for the
non-immediate signification of things by words is that that
signification comes by ideas of things. 'Once it becomes clear that
it is only *immediately* that words signify *nothing but* the user's ideas,
it is clear also that where the ideas immediately signified are
themselves signs—that is, are representative ideas—their originals
may be *mediately* signified by those words' (p. 188).

The second difficulty with Kretzmann's reading of a supposed
second argument, one from the doctrine of representative perception, is that he confuses the question of 'can I know the real
essence of body?' with the question 'can I know body?'. If I
imagine that the word 'gold' signifies the bit of matter in the

ring on my finger, Kretzmann says that 'In Locke's view this would be to imagine that the name "gold" was applied (*per impossibile*) to signify that substance *immediately*' (p. 188). Where 'signify' means 'mean', Locke's account of word-signs makes the 'immediate' (that is, the meaning) relation hold between word and idea. Words cannot be used referringly if they have no meaning, if there are no ideas that constitute their meaning. This distinction between meaning and reference is, as we have seen, a fundamental feature of Locke's account of signs. But Kretzmann cites a passage about real essence to support the claim that words cannot *mean* (immediately signify) things. He cites 3.10.19 in support of this remark:

by this tacit reference to the real essence of that species of bodies, the word *gold* (which, by standing for a more or less perfect collection of simple ideas, serves to design that sort of body well enough in civil discourse) comes to have no signification at all, being put for somewhat whereof we have no *idea* at all, and so can signify nothing at all when the body itself is away.

In this passage, Locke has clearly indicated where the referential relation stands, between my substance words and a collection of simple ideas (i.e. qualities) which in *civil* discourses is quite adequate for designating the sort of bodies we observe. In addition to this reference to observed bodies, the passage raises the question of whether my names for substances might have a secret reference to the real essence or real species of those substances or bodies. When substances are taken as the objects I observe in my environment, the question of reference to things is quite different; in that case, the case most important for the science of nature, ideas play a mediating role in the same way that they do for cognition of things as coexisting qualities. If names or words cannot refer to things, of course they cannot refer to real essences either. The reason that words cannot refer (either immediately or in any other way) to the real essence or real species is that we have and can have no idea of real essences.

Kretzmann goes on to offer a doctrine of word-signs which he thinks is consistent with Locke's account of signs and significations, which he thinks Locke is very close to on several occasions, and which would make the science of signs more unified with the way of ideas than Kretzmann finds it in Locke's explicit remarks. Just why the doctrine of signs must be unified with the way of ideas is not clear, but it turns out that what lies behind this remark by Kretzmann is a notion that Locke's epistemology forces him to interpret everything, words as well as things, in terms of ideas. Kretzmann's construction of the account of word-signs which he thinks Locke was close to is interesting and suggestive but, I think, wrong, certainly misleading. That construction is that for Locke words *are* ideas (p. 190). It should be clear from the analysis of 'seeing' which I have given in an earlier chapter that Kretzmann is correct in saying that to see a lump of metal just is, for Locke, perceiving 'a particular complex idea of sensation in my mind' (p. 192). To hold this view is not, as I hope to have shown, to be committed to saying we do not really see the lump of metal, since to see just is to have ideas. But one might miss this point, especially under the steady influence of those who find an object-denying representative theory of perception in Locke; one might then come to the conclusion that what Kretzmann's suggestion about words being ideas has done is to match the reduction of things to ideas with the reduction of words to ideas. The doctrine of ideas is being pushed to its literal limits: if all that is ever present to the mind are ideas, then all that there is are ideas.

Taking the passage in 2.21.5 where Locke distinguishes three kinds of perception—(1) perception of ideas in our minds, (2) perception of the signification of signs, and (3) the perception of the connexion or repugnancy between ideas—Kretzmann gives the following interpretation of my being told that a particular lump of metal is gold:

I see and feel the lump of metal: that is, I perceive a particular complex idea of sensation in my mind—an instance of Perception 1. Next, I hear the sound 'gold': that is, I perceive a particular simple idea of sensation in my mind—a second instance of Perception 1. Next, I perceive an abstract complex idea in my mind (yellow–heavy–malleable–fusible–fixed–etc.)—a third instance of Perception 1. Next, I perceive that the sound 'gold' is in my mind associated with, or 'annexed to', that abstract complex idea: that is, I perceive a connection between two of my ideas—an instance of Perception 3. Finally, I perceive a connection between my abstract complex idea of gold and my particular complex idea of the lump of metal—a second instance of Perception 3—or else I fail to perceive such a connection, that is, either I think my interlocutor is right or I am (at best) uncertain about it (p. 192).

Locke frequently distinguishes between *words as sounds* and *words as signifying*. 1.2.23 says that words are only empty (that is, meaningless or non-meaning or non-signifying) sounds save as they are signs of ideas (cf. 3.2.2). In considering the proposition 'virtue is the best worship of God', Locke distinguishes the *sense* from the *sound* of that proposition. 3.1.1–2 stresses that articulate (that is, spoken) sounds are not sufficient for forming a language; for that, we need to make sounds signs of our conceptions, of our ideas. 3.4.11 says that words as sounds *produce* sound-ideas and are capable of *exciting* other ideas which stand in the relation of signified to those sounds. (4.18.3 repeats this same point.) In discussing maxims in 4.7.14, Locke comments that, if we have the names without the ideas, the force of those maxims will reach 'only to the sounds and not the signification of the words'. 4.8.5 says it is only playing with sounds when we affirm *that* 'of the name *gold* which is comprehended in its received signification'; 4.8.7 tells us that if a man does not understand the terms he uses, he talks like a parrot, only making an unintelligible noise; and 4.8.13 draws the general conclusion to his discussion of trifling propositions: 'wherever the distinct *idea* any word stands for is not known and considered, and something not contained in the *idea* is not affirmed or denied of it, there our thoughts stick wholly in sounds' (cf. 3.10.26, 31; 3.11.5, 6).[1]

If our thoughts 'stick wholly in sounds', we can think and perceive but we cannot speak. Woozley points out that Locke's definition of a word in 3.1.1 is that it is an 'articulate sound', what 'modern linguists call a *phone*'.[2] A parrot can be taught to use words, to talk in that sense but, Woozley points out, 'it is incapable of language'. To turn a string of sounds into language, we must, in Locke's terminology, have ideas for them to signify. In drawing the distinctions I have noted—between empty sounds and meaningful sounds, between the sense and sound of words, between the ideas words as sounds produce and the ideas

---

[1] In the preface to his edition of the works of Rapin, B. Kennet remarks: '*and tho' we should grant* that Sound without Sense *might* persuade, *yet then the Persuasion dies with the Sounds*'.   [2] *Op. cit.* p. 30.

those words excite as their meanings—Locke has drawn the same distinctions that a linguist might now draw between a *phone* as having meaning (i.e. a phoneme) and that same sound in isolation and without meaning. It is words as sounds (or as visual patterns, hence visual ideas) which, when they are meaningful, excite other ideas in my mind. The perceived relation between the sound-ideas and the other ideas, established by convention as their meanings, is the relation of signification. Even if Kretzmann's analysis, which takes all words to be ideas, were correct—and there is much in it that is right—it is still important to note that Locke is not much interested in words as bare sounds. It is only the sounds as full, as having a sense, as exciting ideas that give rise to the linguistic sign-relation. The human use of words takes them as having sense, not as sounds or sights alone, though of course the physical fact of sounds and sights is necessary for linguistic use. In this sense, the sense of what a word is for a language-user, a word is not a physical sound or a physical label pinned on or pointing to objects: words are not just sounds or marks on paper, but *meaningful* sounds and marks.

To say words are ideas is to make an ontological claim: whether we accept this suggestion of Kretzmann's depends upon what ontology we ascribe to Locke. If we say that secondary qualities have no real status save as powers in objects or as ideas in awareness, then words, being sounds when spoken, must be ideas. But written words have shape and size, and those are primary qualities, so written words must have some status in reality as physical. Kretzmann might turn every perceived object or quality into an idea, though I do not think he wants to read the representative theory in that way. He leaves open the analysis of idea-signs and hence does not provide us with any reading of the theory to which he appeals, the representative theory of ideas. I think his analysis of word-signs cannot rest without an explicit analysis of the science of idea-signs in Locke. I hope to have established that what it is to see an object for Locke is to have ideas, but in an ontological way there *are* ideas *and* objects. Even in the case of sounds or colours, the colour and the sound are not just my ideas: my ring *is* yellow and I have an idea of yellow when I perceive it. In this way, words as marks or as sounds are features of the physical world. They are external sensible signs, as Locke calls them and as he insisted they must be if we are to get beyond the privacy of ideas: in order to communicate our thoughts 'it was necessary that man should find out some external sensible signs whereby those invisible *ideas*, which his thoughts are made up of, might be made known to others' (3.2.1).

This last point alone would seem to establish that words are not ideas; they cannot be if they are to be external sensible signs. Nor are words just any sounds, though I am conjecturing in suggesting that Locke must have had in mind the babbling of infants and the way we adapt or turn *those* sounds into words. In this sense, sounds are more basic as words than written or tactile or other sensible marks. Kretzmann's analysis of seeing a lump of metal and hearing the sound 'gold' is correct as an analysis of perception, from the point of view of the hearer and perceiver. But unless the sound (and the metal, too) is also external and sensible, it cannot play a communicative role. Moreover, if it were not external, it is hard to see how the metal could be either. Locke's world would—as many, who find that object-denying representative theory, claim—fast collapse into the privacy of ideas. To let this happen is to fail to distinguish between my *perception* of the metal and the sound and the *metal* and the *sound*. To perceive a sound or a shape is to have ideas in my awareness, but the sound and the shape are there to be perceived. The sound or shape as part of the physical environment is distinguished from the sound as perceived. Even if we say that the sound or shape does not exist apart from perception, if we say one or both are perceiver-dependent, we can still distinguish between the qualities and the ideas. The situation is no different for the sounds and shapes that become words than it is for the sounds and shapes which, in coexisting groups, constitute our class concepts (our nominal essences) of bodies. Whether it be the reality of ideas and knowledge or of language, that reality 'depends upon collection and observation' (4.7.16).

The question, then, of the criterion of the reality of language is no different from the question of the criterion for the reality of knowledge. There is no *criterion* that body exists, save the real-existence relation. Language is not real or unreal at that level, since there is nothing for language to describe and characterise in the real-existence relation. Inside the real-existence relation, words and ideas can be real or unreal, depending upon whether they are or are not accurate recorders of observable objects. The check for reality of knowledge or language is simply careful observation. The importance of Locke's account of word-signs (especially in conjunction with his view of the science of nature) lies in his recognition that they signify both ideas and things, though he did not have a distinct term for the signification of things by words. The talk of a 'secret reference' turns out to be his way of expressing the non-immediate relation of words to things. In the same way that ideas are the *immediate* objects of the mind in thinking, so words *immediately* signify ideas. To understand or be aware is to have ideas as the contents of that awareness. An idea-less awareness would be non-awareness. Similarly, to speak intelligibly or meaningfully is to have ideas as the contents of that speech. A speech that lacks ideas is parrot-like, is mere sound without sense. There being ideas is the intelligibility-condition for awareness and for speech and language. But neither awareness nor speech need stop with intelligibility. To be useful, both must be *about* things.

Being *instructive* is to be about things. Locke's discussion of trifling and instructive propositions is not directed towards the logical problem of analytic and synthetic propositions, though there are a few points made in those chapters in the *Essay* which bear upon this issue. The chapters on maxims and on trifling propositions (4.7 and 4.8) come just before the chapters on existence (4.9–4.12) and just after the chapters on truth and universal propositions (4.5 and 4.6). These last two succeed the chapter on the reality of knowledge (4.4). Locke has been making the point that no universal, certain knowledge of body is possible, any certain knowledge we have of body is particular. The universal propositions cited by the traditional Aristotelians and Schoolmen were even worse off: not only were they not about things, they were useless and trifling. The maxims most often cited—'what is, is', 'It is impossible for the same thing to be and not to be'— 'cannot discover or prove to us the least knowledge of the nature of substances, as they are found and exist without us' (4.7.15).

Real knowledge is not aided by these maxims (4.8.1.2). The chapter on trifling propositions purports to distinguish the question of real knowledge from that of the increase of knowledge, that chapter dealing with the latter. But throughout, Locke couples 'uninstructive' with 'unreal'. Section 3 remarks that an ignorant person may 'make a million of propositions of whose truths he may be infallibly certain, and yet not know one thing in the world thereby'. Later in the same section he remarks about identical propositions (examples being 'body is body', 'a centaur is a centaur') that: 'And upon this account it was that I formerly did and do still think the offering and inculcating such propositions, in order to give the understanding any new light or inlet into the knowledge of things, no better than trifling.'

Section 4 of 4.8 begins the discussion of 'Another sort of trifling propositions', those where '*a part of the complex* idea *is predicated of the name of the whole*'. To say 'lead is a metal' or 'all gold is fusible' are instances of this sort of proposition. They simply cite part of the definition or complex idea of that sort. In these cases, we are only affirming the already received definition or signification of the word 'gold' or 'lead' (5). The proposition 'Every man is an animal or living body', is 'as certain a proposition as can be; but no more conducing to the knowledge of things than to say *A palfrey is an ambling horse*, or a neighing, ambling *animal*: both being only about the signification of words' (6). Being about the signification of words does, of course, depend upon what the significations of our words have been established as being. If 'fusible' has not been established as part of the meaning of 'gold', then to say 'gold is fusible' would be to record an addition to our knowledge of gold. Locke explicitly links the signification of words to a time and place, to what a romance knight meant by 'palfrey' or what a '*Roman* signified by the word "*homo*"' (6). If we suppose that a Roman included in his idea of 'homo', as united in one subject, the following: *corporietas, sensibilitas, potentia se movendi, rationalitas, risibilitas*, no increase of knowledge will be achieved by his affirming one or more of these properties of the notion of 'homo'. If to the ideas already accepted as constituting the meaning of 'man', someone now tells me, or I discover for myself, that 'in whatever thing *sense, motion, reason,* and *laughter* were united, that thing had actually a notion of GOD or would be cast into a sleep by *opium*' (6), then I have added to my knowledge of man.

When Locke concludes his chapter on trifling propositions, he lists two kinds of verbal proposition, the first being those 'wherein two abstract terms are affirmed one of another' (4.8.12). Identical propositions are not mentioned at all in this summary conclusion. The second type of verbal proposition cited in his summary is the type we have just been examining, those where '*a part of the complex* idea which any term stands for *is predicated of that term*' (13). This type is important since it shows us how our knowledge of things can be improved, where propositions become instructive, namely, when they assert more about the object than is contained in our definition of that object. The first type of barely verbal proposition cited in this passage (for the first and only time)—affirming one abstract term of another—deals with mixed modes. Locke seems to be saying that propositions involving mixed modes (he uses the term 'abstract idea') cannot be instructive. Examples offered are, 'Parsimony is frugality', 'Gratitude is justice', and 'this or that action is or is not temperance' (12). Propositions using any of the action-concepts Locke employs could be cited as other examples of non-instructive propositions. This sort of proposition is 'barely about the signification of sounds', that is, it defines action-concepts. Locke does not mean to deny that *my* knowledge might be extended by the moral-word dictionary. I have to acquire the action-concepts of my society. That dictionary gives me the names of the actions and links some with others; it tells me 'about the signification of words' and 'the use and application of these signs' (13).

There are two ways in which moral knowledge can be more than verbal. The one way is in demonstrations: 'he that would enlarge his own or another's mind to truths he does not yet know must find out intermediate *ideas,* and then lay them in such order one by another that the understanding may see the agreement or disagreement of those in question' (3). The second way to increase moral knowledge is to find out what is right and wrong, and the measures of right and wrong. Clearly, this second way, in which moral propositions can record new information and be instructive, more nearly fits the way our knowledge of body goes beyond the verbal and trifling. In both cases, I am acquiring knowledge about non-linguistic and non-idea features of the world. Demonstrative instruction may be closer to dictionary definition, disclosing to me relations between words or ideas known by me. But if Locke did not identify demonstration with deduction, demonstration would in that case escape being trifling or as we would say, analytic, in that it would not be just a complex way of disclosing logical relations. Hence, demonstration would be instructive just in the sense of disclosing to me more than deductive relations. It would relate for me features of concepts linked by content rather than form. Nevertheless, demonstrative instruction is dangerously near to predicating one abstract term of another, as Locke even recognises in instances of substance words. If, Locke remarks in Section 10 of this chapter, a man makes the signification of substance words 'at a venture', and not 'from an examination or inquiry into the nature of things themselves', he 'may with little trouble demonstrate them one of another, according to those several respects and mutual relations he has given them one to another wherein, however things agree or disagree in their own nature, he needs mind nothing but his own notions, with the names he hath bestowed upon them'.

If 'instructive' means, as I think it does for Locke, disclosing some new fact about the world—not just enlarging my own stock of knowledge—then the only way in which moral and action knowledge can be instructive is when it is about the fixed and eternal measures of right and wrong. Being instructive in this way is not a property of mixed-mode signs. Our definitions of moral words cannot be entirely private and arbitrary, the terms in the laws of nature must have sense for us. Locke does not confront the question of how man will understand the laws of nature. In what language will those laws be revealed to us? The particular words used to designate some action approved or condemned by a law of nature are not of importance, are quite arbitrary and conventional, but we must know what characteristics of social behaviour the laws refer to before we can understand those laws.

It may be that Locke's notion of the way language arises is at variance with his firm acceptance of laws of nature laid down by God. Stillingfleet (as others also) objected to what he took to be new terms and new meanings to old words in Locke's *Essay*: he objected to Locke's 'private mint of words'. Locke quite properly pointed out to Stillingfleet that words were not like money.

The case in short is this: money, by virtue of the stamp received in the public mint, which vouches its intrinsic worth, has authority to pass. This use of the public stamp would be lost, if private men were suffered to offer money stamped by themselves. On the contrary, words are offered to the public by every man, coined in his private mint, as he pleases; but it is the receiving of them by others, their very passing, that gives them their authority and currency, and not the mint they come out of (*Works*, IV, 279).

There can be no counterfeit words though they can be useless (if not taken up by others), inadequate, and unclear.

A prerequisite for the receiving of my words by others is that I be clear and explicit about the meanings of my words. The proper use of moral words requires a clear and distinct understanding of the various ideas included in the complex moral words comprising the language of action (e.g. 'justice', 3.11.9). Using words as others do, with the same ideas as their meaning, is a prerequisite for understanding and communicating to others. 'Propriety of speech is that which gives our thought entrance into other men's minds with the greater ease and advantage' (3.11.11). The moral-word dictionary would codify and clarify the moral words in our language or, if its authors found reasons for coining new terms, it would carefully define and explain them. But the private minting of words and the public acceptance of them must have some relation to the ideas in the laws of nature. Locke may have simply assumed that man's discovery of those laws would be made in the terms of his thought and language, but such an easy assumption would not enable us to pick out the 'correct' meanings of our moral terms.

Locke subscribed to the view that language arises by accident and the common use of people (*Education*, sect. 168). He did not have any clear or detailed theory about the origin of language, though he spent several sections in the *Essay* suggesting how

Adam, by himself, named actions and objects (3.6.44–51). Locke's account of signs and their significations is made from within a language, just as his account of the origin of ideas is much more conceptual than temporal, an account of how ideas arise for the individual within a society already possessed of systems of thought. Just as the recording of coexisting qualities in the science of nature presupposes a concept of object and of kinds, so the science of signs offered by Locke depends upon and assumes thought- and language-users. Neither idea-signs nor word-signs can escape the linguistic and conceptual structures of the social and cognitive world in which we are born and develop. The grammatical and syntactical structure of our language can be uncovered, but only after we have learned to speak and to use that language: 'if Grammar ought to be taught at any time, it must be to one that can speak the Language already; how else can he be taught the Grammar of it' (*Education*, sect. 168). Similarly, the conceptual and epistemic structure of our ideas can be discovered, but again only after we have acquired ideas. The grammar of our thought can be learned only by one who has acquired concepts and learned to use them. The way of ideas was Locke's attempt at uncovering at least part of the epistemic structure of thought, especially of our thought about the physical world. The epistemology of thought is like the grammar of language in that both reveal the structures implicit in the use of words and ideas. Recognition of the social context of knowing and speaking does not entail the sort of scepticism Locke has frequently been charged with, nor does it mean there are no criteria for the correctness of language and thought. The criteria for moral words must, as I have suggested, lie in the laws of nature, even though Locke was far from clear about the way our discovery of those laws can function to establish the reality or falsity of our moral vocabulary. The criteria for object words is much clearer and more firmly delineated, though we must always guard against the temptation to take the things themselves which are the archetypes for object words as lying beyond or outside our thought and language.

In several interesting passages, Locke raises the question of whether the inadequacy of substance words in their reference to real essence is not a fault of understanding rather than of language.

His answer is that naming and knowing are so closely intermixed that we cannot separate them. 'At least they [words] interpose themselves so much between our understandings and the truth which it would contemplate and apprehend that, like the *medium* through which visible objects pass, their obscurity and disorder does not seldom cast a mist before our eyes and impose upon our understandings' (3.9.21). Language can mislead by our mistaking words for things, as the example of those notional speculators showed. But the linguistic difficulties embedded in the scholastic distinctions and artifices—about which Locke and his contemporaries wrote—were not the only ones Locke had in mind. Those difficulties could be corrected. There is another, more fundamental feature of language which makes it impossible for us to divorce our thought of things from our human classifications.

For to talk of a *man*, and to lay by at the same time the ordinary signification of the name man, which is our complex *idea* usually annexed to it, and bid the reader consider *man* as he is in himself and as he is really distinguished from others in his internal constitution or real essence, that is, by something he knows not what, looks like trifling; and yet thus one must do who would speak of the supposed real essences and *species* of things as thought to be made by nature, if it be but only to make it understood that there is no such thing signified by the general names which substances are called by (3.6.43).

The linguistic difficulty here is not unlike Berkeley's manifest contradiction in the idea of a thing as something existing unperceived. Locke does not want to say there is a contradiction in asserting that there is an internal, insensible, particulate structure to matter, though this is not something we can know to be true if we accept the grammar of thought Locke offers. What Locke is suggesting is that any attempt to characterise that real essence for any specific kind of thing is doomed to failure, since our ideas and words for objects are derived from observation, governed by the concept of kinds of things present in our thought and language. We can rectify our ideas of the nominal essence of objects, never our ideas of real essence. The theory of real essence is meaningful and useful for articulating what the support or subject of qualities is or might be, but for man object talk cannot penetrate beyond the qualities discovered or discoverable in experience. The scepticism of Locke's way of ideas is not a doubting of the reality of body, is not even close to redefining body in terms of ideas. The sense in which Locke's doctrine of signs may be said to embody scepticism is simply that that doctrine shows the impossibility of our knowledge of body being different from what it is, being based upon real essence from which all properties of body are then deduced. Locke's metaphysic of nature clothes the traditional substance doctrine in the fashion of the corpuscular theory, adding as well the notion of a deductive or *a priori* science of nature which would be possible for one who could uncover and understand the nature and efficacy of the internal constitution of insensible parts. The faculties of man may have not been designed by God for such *a priori* knowledge. To say we cannot or do not have a knowledge of real essence has, as its obverse, saying we have an observational knowledge of body. An observational knowledge of body is still *knowledge*, though it is not the kind of knowledge God and his angels may have. Our observational knowledge reveals some non-relational qualities of body, along with relational ones. The kinds of objects that there are—we should perhaps be more cautious and say, the kinds of objects that we can *say* there are—are a function of the class concepts in our thought and language.

It is in the same way that the actions which I can do are also a function of the action ideas and words current in my society. Substance words and mixed-mode words have something in common: the species of things for the former and the species of actions for the latter which are possible for man are determined by man himself. Locke does not mean to say there is anything capricious or gratuitous about actions and things. We do not, despite his Adam fantasy, sit round and decide what objects there are, what actions there shall be. Locke did not detail or emphasise as he should the dependence each of us has upon our society for the action- and object-concepts which come to define and characterise our lived world. But I think it is clear that he was fully aware of this important fact. Recognising that fact, he stressed, as much as he could, the ways in which knowledge and talk of body could be made instructive and real, could be *about* body. The stress on the reality of the language of morals may be less striking, but it is present in his doctrine of laws of nature, God's eternal rules of right and wrong. In explicating the grammar of our thought and language, in showing how ideas and words function as signs of things and actions, Locke's account of the science of signs illuminates both the science of nature and the science of action.

BIBLIOGRAPHY

Without wanting to make too much of the fact, I have indicated by an asterisk those items in the following list which were in Locke's library, as recorded and reproduced in the John Harrison and Peter Laslett catalogue, *The Library of John Locke* (Oxford Bibliographical Society Publications, new series, vol. XIII, 1965).

Aaron, R. I. *John Locke*. 2nd edition. Oxford, Clarendon Press, 1955.

Anderson, F. A. 'The Influence of Contemporary Science on Locke's Methods and Results', *University of Toronto Studies in Philosophy*, II (1923).

Axtell, James L. 'Locke, Newton, and the Elements of Natural Philosophy', *Paedagogica Europaea*, I (1965), 235–45.

 'Locke, Newton, and the Two Cultures', in *John Locke: Problems and Perspectives*, ed. by J. W. Yolton, pp. 165–82.

 'Locke's Review of the *Principia*', *Notes and Records of the Royal Society of London* (1965), 152–61.

Boas, Marie. 'The Establishment of the Mechanical Philosophy', *Osiris*, X (1952), 412–541.

 Robert Boyle and Seventeenth-Century Chemistry. Cambridge, University Press, 1958.

 See also under Hall, Marie B.

*Boyle, Robert. About the Excellency and Grounds of the Mechanical Hypothesis (half-title: Of the Excellency and Grounds of the Corpuscular or Mechanical Philosophy) in *The Excellency of Theology Compared with Philosophy* (London, 1674). Reprinted in M. B. Hall's *Robert Boyle on Natural Philosophy* with title: The Excellency and Grounds of the Corpuscular or Mechanical Philosophy.

 Of the Mechanical Origine of Heat and Cold. Oxford, 1675. [Wing 4012.] Also reissued intact as the first of several tracts in Boyle's *Experiments, Notes, &c. about the Mechanical Origine or Production of divers particular Qualities*. Oxford, 1676. [Wing 3977.]

* *The Origine of Forms and Qualities, according to the Corpuscular Philosophy*. 2nd ed., Oxford, 1667. [Locke had the first edition of 1666.]

* *The Sceptical Chymist*. London, 1661.

* *Some Considerations Touching the Usefulnesse of Experimentall Naturall Philosophy*. Oxford, 1663.

 Tracts Written by the Honourable Robert Boyle. Oxford, 1671. Contains

(1) An Introduction to the History of Particular Qualities (verso of half-title dated 1669); (2) Of the Systematicall or Cosmicall Qualities of Things (1669).

*Browne, Sir Thomas. *Religio Medici.* 4th ed. London, 1656.

*Cimento, Accademia del. *Essayes of Natural Experiments Made in the Accademia del Cimento.* Englished by Richard Waller. London, 1684. [Locke had the Italian edition of 1667.]

Cohen, I. Bernard. *Franklin and Newton.* Cambridge, Mass., Harvard University Press for the American Philosophical Society, 1966.

Crombie, A. C. *Augustine to Galileo.* 2nd, rev. ed. Harmondsworth, Penguin Books, 1969 (© 1959), 2 vols.
'Newton's Conception of Scientific Method', *Bulletin of the Institute of Physics* (November 1957), pp. 350–62.
'Some Aspects of Descartes' Attitude to Hypothesis and Experiments', *Collection des Travaux de l'Académie Internationale d'Histoire des Sciences,* XI (1960), 192–201.
See also *History of Science.*

Dunn, John. *The Political Thought of John Locke.* Cambridge, University Press, 1969.

Euclid. *The 13 Books of Euclid's Elements,* translated and edited by T. L. Heath. Cambridge, University Press, 1956.

*Fairfax, N., M. D. *A Treatise of the Bulk and Selvedge of the World; Wherein the Greatness, Littleness and Lastingness of Bodies areFreely Handled.* London, 1674.

Galileo Galilei. *Dialogues concerning Two New Sciences.* Translated by Henry Crew and A. de Salvio. New York, Macmillan, 1914. (Reprinted by Dover Publications, 1954.)

Gay, Peter. Introduction to his edition: *John Locke on Education.* New York, Teachers College, Columbia University, 1964. (Classics in education, no. 20.)

Gibson, James. *Locke's Theory of Knowledge and Its Historical Relations.* Cambridge, University Press, 1931.
'Locke's Theory of Mathematical Knowledge and of a Possible Science of Ethics', *Mind,* V (1896).

Givner, David H. 'Scientific Preconceptions in Locke's Philosophy of Language', *Journal of the History of Ideas,* XXIII (1962), 340–54.

Glanvill, Joseph. *Plus Ultra: or, The Progress and Advancement of Knowledge.* London, 1668.

*Goddard, Jonathan. *A Discourse Setting forth the Unhappy Condition of the Practice of Physick in London*. London, 1670.

Hale, Sir Matthew. *The Primitive Origination of Mankind*. London, 1677.
Hall, A. R. *The Scientific Revolution, 1500–1800*. Boston, The Beacon Press, 1957.
Hall, Marie B. *Robert Boyle on Natural Philosophy*. Bloomington, Indiana University Press, 1965.
See also under Boas, Marie.
Harré, R. *Matter and Method*. London, Macmillian, 1964.
Hesse, Mary B. 'Hooke's Philosophical Algebra', *Isis*, LVII (1966), 67–83.
History of Science. Edited by A. C. Crombie and M. A. Hoskin. Cambridge, Heffer, VI, 1967.
Hobbes, T. *The English Works*, ed. by Sir William Molesworth. London, Longman, 1845.
Hooke, Robert. *The Diary of Robert Hooke, 1672–1680*, ed. by H. W. Robinson and W. Adams. London, Taylor & Francis, 1935.
The Diary of Robert Hooke, 1688–1693, in *Early Science in Oxford*, edited by R. T. Gunther. Oxford, 1935, vol. x.
Micrographia; or, Some Physiological Descriptions of Minute Bodies Made by Magnifying Glasses. London, 1665. (Reprinted by Dover Publications, 1961.)
The Present State of Natural Philosophy (*ca*. 1666) in his *Posthumous Works*. London, R. Waller, 1705.

Jackson, Reginald. 'Locke's Distinction between Primary and Secondary Qualities', *Mind*, XXXVIII (1929). (Reprinted in Martin and Armstrong.)
Jones, H. W. 'Mid-Seventeenth Century Science: Some Polemics', *Osiris*, IX (1950), 254–74.
Jones, R. F. *Ancients and Moderns: A Study of the Rise of the Scientific Movement in Seventeenth Century England*. 2nd. ed. St Louis, Washington University Press, 1961. (Reprinted by the University of California Press, 1965.)

Kemp, J. *Reason, Action and Morality*. London, Routledge & Kegan Paul, 1964.
Kennet, T. Preface to *The Whole Critical Works of M. Rapin*. [Trans. by T. Kennet and others.] London, 1706.
Kenny, A. J. P. *Descartes, A Study of His Philosophy*. New York, Random House, 1968. (Studies in Philosophy, 15.)
Koyré, Alexandre. *Newtonian Studies*. London, Chapman and Hall, 1965.

Kretzmann, Norman. 'The Main Thesis of Locke's Semantic Theory', *Philosophical Review*, LXXVII (1968), 175–96.

Laslett, Peter. Review of C. B. Macpherson's *The Political Theory of Possessive Individualism, Hobbes to Locke*, in *The Historical Journal* VII (1964), 150–4.

Laudan, Laurens. 'The Nature and Sources of Locke's Views on Hypotheses', *Journal of the History of Ideas*, XXVIII (1967), 211–23.
'The Clock Metaphor and Probabilism; The Impact of Descartes on English Methodological Thought, 1650–65', *Annals of Science*, XXII (1966), 73–104.

Leeuwen, Henry G. van. *The Problem of Certainty in English Thought, 1630–1690.* The Hague, Nijhoff, 1963.

Locke, John. *Works.* London, T. Tegg, 1823. 10 vols.
The Educational Writings. Edited by James L. Axtell. Cambridge, University Press, 1968.
An Essay concerning Human Understanding. Edited by J. W. Yolton. Rev. ed. London, Dent, 1965. 2 vols. (Everyman's Library.)
Essays on the Law of Nature. Edited by W. von Leyden. Oxford, Clarendon Press, 1954.
Two Tracts on Government. Edited by Philip Abrams. Cambridge, University Press, 1967.
Two Treatises of Government. Edited by Peter Laslett. Cambridge, University Press, 1960.

Lovejoy, A. O. *The Great Chain of Being.* Cambridge, Mass., Harvard University Press, 1936. (Reprinted as Harper Torchbook, 1960.)

McGuire, J. E. 'Body and Void and Newton's De Mundi Systemate: Some New Sources', *Archive for History of Exact Sciences*, III (1966), 206–48.
'Force, Active Principles, and Newton's Invisible Realm', *Ambix*, XV (1968), 154–208.
'The Origin of Newton's Doctrine of Essential Qualities', *Centaurus*, XII (1968), 233–60.
'Transmutation and Immutability: Newton's Doctrine of Physical Qualities', *Ambix*, XIV (1967), 69–95.

McGuire, J. E. and Rattansi, P. M. 'Newton and the "Pipes of Pan"', *Notes and Records of the Royal Society of London*, XXI (1966), 108–43.

Madden, W. H. *Theories of Scientific Method, The Renaissance through the Nineteenth Century.* Seattle, 1960.

Mandelbaum, Maurice. *Philosophy, Science and Sense Perception: Historical and Critical Studies.* Baltimore, Johns Hopkins Press, 1964. (Reprinted, 1966.)

15-2

Martin, C. B. and Armstrong, D. M., editors. *Locke and Berkeley, A Collection of Critical Essays.* New York, Doubleday, 1968. (Anchor Books.)

*Maynwaring, E. *Praxis Medicorum Antiqua et Nova: The Ancient and Moderne Practice of Physick Examined, Stated and Compared.* London, 1671.

Millington, E. C. 'Studies in Cohesion from Democritus to Laplace', *Lychnos* (annual of the Swedish history of science society), 1940–5, pp. 55–78.

*Molyneux, William. *Dioptrica Nova.* London, 1692.
  Sciothericum Telescopicum. Dublin, 1686.

Nicole, P. *Discourses.* Translated from Nicole's Essays by John Locke. Edited by Thomas Hancock. London, 1828. [Locke had various editions of the *Essais de Morale.*]

Passmore, John. *Ralph Cudworth, An Interpretation.* Cambridge, University Press, 1951.

Perry, David L. 'Locke on Mixed Modes, Relations and Knowledge', *Journal of the History of Philosophy,* v (1967), 219–35.

Petty, Sir William. *The Petty Papers.* Edited by the Marquis of Lansdowne. London, Constable, 1927. 2 vols.

Pointer, John. *Miscellanea in Usum Juventutis Academicae.* Oxford, 1718.

*Power, Henry. *Experimental Philosophy.* London, 1664.

Purver, Margery. *The Royal Society: Concept and Creation.* London, Routledge & Kegan Paul, 1967.

Rose, Henry. *A Philosophicall Essay for the Reunion of the Languages: or, The Art of Knowing All by the Mastery of One.* Oxford, 1675.

Seliger, M. *The Liberal Politics of John Locke.* London, Allen and Unwin, 1968.

*Simpson, W. *Hydrologia Chymica.* London, 1669.
  Philosophical Dialogues concerning the Principles of Natural Bodies. London, 1677.

*Sprat, Thomas. *The History of the Royal Society.* London, 1667. (Facsim. reprint with introduction and notes by J. I. Cope and H. W. Jones, published by Routledge & Kegan Paul, London, 1959.)

*Swammerdam, Jan. *Histoire Générale des Insectes.* Utrecht, 1682.
  et al. *The Natural History of Insects,* compiled from Swammerdam, Brookes, Goldsmith, etc. Perth, 1792.

Sydenham, T. *Works.* Edited by John Swan. London, 1842.

*Tenison, Thomas. *The Creed of Mr. Hobbes Examined.* London, 1670.

von Leyden, W. *Seventeenth Century Metaphysics, An Examination of Some Main Concepts and Theories.* London, Duckworth, 1968.

Webster, C. 'Henry Power's Experimental Philosophy', *Ambix*, XIV (1967), 150–78.
    Review of Margery Purver's *The Royal Society*, in *History of Science*, VI (1967), 106–28.
Wilkins, John. *An Essay towards a Real Character and a Philosophical Language.* London, 1668.
    Of the Principles and Duties of Natural Religion. London, 1675.
Wilson, Margaret. 'Leibniz and Locke on "First Truths"', *Journal of the History of Ideas*, XXVIII (1967).
Woozley, A. D. Introduction to his abridged edition of Locke's *Essay.* London, Collins, 1964. (Fontana Library.)
Wren, Christopher [son of Sir Christopher Wren]. *Parentalia; or, Memoirs of the Family of the Wrens.* London, 1750.

Yolton, John W. *John Locke and the Way of Ideas.* Oxford, Clarendon Press, 1956. (Reprinted, 1968.)
    editor. *John Locke: Problems and Perspectives; A Collection of New Essays.* Cambridge, University Press, 1969.
Yost, R. M., jr. 'Locke's Rejection of Hypotheses about Sub-Microscopic Events', *Journal of the History of Ideas*, XII (1951), 111–30.
    'Sydenham's Philosophy of Science', *Osiris*, IX (1950), 84–105.

INDEX

Dewhurst, Kenneth 75 n. 1
dictionary, moral word 162, 164 n., 203, 217
natural history 73, 74, 162, 203
Dublin Society 54
Dunn, John 167

essence 23 n., 27–35, 42, 51, 52, 67, 68, 79, 80–6, 89, 107, 114, 125, 126 n., 158, 161, 170, 199, 205 n., 209, 210, 214, 221
ethics 1, 2, 160–1, 163 n., 165, 168, 181, 182
Euclid 101–2, 162
experience 1, 2, 13, 23, 43, 45, 50, 53 n. 4, 57, 58, 59 n., 68, 74, 75, 93, 113, 125, 163, 222
experiment 3, 4, 7, 8, 9, 10, 41, 44, 53, 54, 56, 57, 61 n., 64, 69 n., 74, 77, 84, 85, 94, 113, 120, 136, 160
experimental method 6–8, 9, 63 n. 3, 112

faculties 138, 142, 160, 176
Fairfax, N. 17 n. 1, 153 n. 1
Filmer, Sir Robert 162 n. 1, 183–7, 195
Flew, Anthony 156–7
Franklin, B. 46 n. 1, 53 n. 4, 71
freedom (liberty) 143–4, 147–9, 162

Galileo 13 n. 1, 44 n. 1, 50 n. 1, 76, 86
Gay, Peter 173 n. 2
geometry 101–2, 162, 167, 181
Gibb, Jocelyn 100, 139
Gibson, James Boyce 64 n. 2, 101
Gilbert, William 44 n. 1
Givner, D. A. 55
Glanvill, Joseph 4, 46 n. 1, 54, 55, 56 n. 1, 78, 89, 90, 115 n. 1
Glauber, J. R. 21 n. 3
God 16, 17, 29, 34, 50 n., 80, 103, 110, 144, 152, 155, 156, 165, 166, 169, 170, 171, 172, 175–7, 178, 180, 181, 182, 183, 185, 187, 189, 191, 197, 200, 217, 222, 223
Goddard, Jonathan 9
gravitation 20 n. 2, 24 n., 68–9, 71, 72, 78, 79, 88, 89
Grotius, H. 188
Gunther, R. T. 56 n. 1

Hale, Sir Matthew 3, 9–10, 17 n. 1, 96 n. 1, 115 n. 1, 140 n. 1, 148 n. 1, 151 n. 1, 154 n. 1, 171 n. 1

Hall, A. R. 55 n. 1
Hall, H. (publisher) 55 n. 4
Hall, Marie Boas 21 nn. 2–3, 41 n. 2, 50 n. 1
happiness 1, 144–7, 160
Harré, R. x, 5 n. 2, 23 n. 1 (on p. 24), 47 n. 1, 85 n. 1, 101, 124 n. 1
Harrison, John 35 n. 2, 44 n. 1
Hartlib, S. 201
Harvey, W. 44 n. 1
Heath, T. L. 102
hedonism 145–6
Herbert, Edward, first Baron of Cherbury 173 n. 2
Hesse, Mary B. 8 n. 1, 58 n. 1, 61 n. 1, 69 n. 1
Hobbes, T. 3, 96 n. 1, 101–2, 148 n. 1, 152 n. 1, 183 n. 1
Hobbist 165
Hooke, Robert 4, 5, 8–9, 19 n. 2, 26 n. 1, 46 n. 1, 49 n. 1, 50 n. 1, 53, 55–7, 58 n. 1, 60–1, 62, 66 n. 1, 73 n. 1, 75, 77, 78, 79, 90, 94 n. 1, 114, 136, 200–1
Hooker, Richard 100
Hoskin, M. A. 53 n. 1
Huygens, Christiaan 44 n. 1, 50 n. 1 (on p. 51), 53 n. 4
Hume, David 131 n. 1
hypotheses 7, 16, 45, 56–72, 75, 76–9, 83, 86, 89, 90

identity, 91 n., 106, 108, 109, 149–56
induction 55 n. 2, 77
innate ideas (principles) 2, 170, 173–5, 177, 199

Jackson, Reginald 38–41, 122
Jones, R. F. 1, 7–8, 57 n. 1
Jowett Society x

Keat, Russell 50 n. 1 (on p. 51)
Kemp, J. 167–8, 170
Kennet, Basil 5, 201, 212 n. 1
Kenny, A. J. P. 127–8
Kepler, Johann 44 n. 1, 76
King, Peter 163 n. 1
Kneale, William 102 n. 1
knowledge 1, 4, 5, 10, 12, 14, 16, 41, 45, 52, 53, 58, 59, 62, 63, 65–8, 70–5, 80, 84, 88, 90, 94, 95, chs. 4 and 5, 144, 156, 160, 164, 175, 179, 198, 201, 215–16, 222

qualities, cosmical 19
observable (coexisting) 20, 22, 25,
28, 31, 33, 35, 36 n., 40, 58, 59,
64, 70–1, 73, 76, 79, 81, 82, 134,
199, 210, 220
of bodies 19, 22, 27
primary and secondary (*see also* property) 5 n. 2, 12, 20, 21, 23, 25–7,
35, 36, 38–41, 47, 48, 85, 107, 122–
4, 126, 130–1, 137

Rapin, M. 5 n. 1
realism 11, 127–8, 131–3, 151 n.
relations 1, 2, 16, 18–20, 21, 25, 27, 32,
47, 73 n., 78, 87, 89, 97, 100, 103,
ch. 4, 118, 130, 136, 159, 165, 171,
196, 208, 215
resemblance 34, 47–9, 130, 131
resurrection 154–6, 157
revelation 146, 171, 180
Rose, Henry 204
Royal Society 4, 5, 6, 8, 10, 30, 53–5,
56, 57 n. 1, 58 n. 1, 60, 62, 63 n. 3,
69 n. 1, 73 n. 1, 76, 77, 78, 201, 203
Ryan, Alan 188, 190 n. 1, 194

scepticism (sceptic) 12, 41, 52 n., 119,
133, 152, 179, 222
science, classifications of 1, 3, 4, 15
deductive (*a priori*) 33, 52, 70, 84–5,
115, 222
physical 2, 4–7, 24, 44
Seliger, M. 188
Sergeant, John 90, 128
signs 10, 13, 14, 18 n., 119, 120, 129,
136, 147, 150 n., 164–5, 181, 184 n.,
ch. 9
Simpson, W. 9, 54, 71 n. 2 (on p. 72),
80 n. 1 (on p. 81), 202
Socrates 150, 156
soul 8, 56, 57, 60, 140, 150, 153 n.,
154 n., 155, 157, 158, 176, 182

species 27–33, 42 n., 73 n., 124, 139,
210
spirits 16, 17–18, 26, 27, 50, 66, 80 n.,
83, 85 n., 143, 151, 157, 200
Sprat, Thomas 4, 53–4, 62–3, 69 n. 1,
89, 90
Stillingfleet, Edward (Bishop of Worcester) 24 n. 1, 27, 50 n. 1, 95, 97,
111–12, 121 n. 2, 128, 132, 135,
141 n. 1, 154–5, 157, 161 n. 1, 219
substance 27, 28, 30, 32, 33, 43, 44–5, 52,
74, 75, 80 n., 84, 107, 108 n., 113,
122, 124, 126, 136, 140, 142, 152,
153, 199, 200, 207, 210, 215,
220–1
substantial forms 28–30, 42 n., 43, 75
superposition, method of 101–2
Swammerdam, J. 10, 17 n. 1
Sydenham, Thomas 5, 16, 59, 63 n. 3,
75, 89, 114, 136
syllogism 3, 87, 88, 92, 94, 95, 96–100,
166

telescopes 11, 124
Tenison, Thomas 96 n. 1
Toulmin, S. 3, 167
transdiction 11, 65
transmigration 153 n.

Vives, Juan Luis 88 n. 1
voluntarism 168, 179, 180

Wallis, J. 101
Webster, C. 53 n. 1 and n. 3, 55 n. 2
Wilkins, John (Bishop) 17 n. 1, 96 n. 1,
115 n. 1, 145 n. 1, 202–4
Wilson, Margaret 91–2
Woolhouse, R. x
Woozley, A. D. 134–5, 173 n. 2, 212

Yost, R. M. 5 n. 2 (on p. 6), 59 n. 1,
64–5